HOCKEY *Chronicles*

HOCKEY

An Insider History of National Hockey League Teams

Foreword by Jack Batten

Chronicles

Eric Duhatschek

Trent Frayne

Lance Hornby

Gord Miller

Al Strachan

KEY PORTER BOOKS

Canadian Cataloguing in Publication Data

Hockey chronicles: an insider history of National Hockey League teams

ISBN: 1-55263-177-X

1. National Hockey League. 2. Hockey teams - Canada. 3. Hockey teams - United States. I. Duhatschek, Eric, 1956-

GV847.8.N3H58 2000   796.962'64   C00-931978-6

The publisher gratefully acknowledges the support of the Canada Council for the Arts and the Ontario Arts Council for its publishing program.

We acknowledge the financial support of the Government of Canada through the Book Publishing Industry Development Program (BPIDP) for our publishing activities.

Key Porter Books Limited
70 The Esplanade
Toronto, Ontario
Canada M5E 1R2

www.keyporter.com

Photo credits: All photographs courtesy of Bruce Bennett Studios except for the picture of Red Kelly (page 215) courtesy of Brian McFarlane.

Electronic formatting: Jean Peters

Printed and bound in Spain

00 01 02 03 04 05 6 5 4 3 2 1

Contents

Foreword

The first NHL player I ever shook hands with played for a team that no longer exists. The player was Charlie Conacher, and the team was the New York Americans. The handshake, a huge event in my young life, took place at Maple Leaf Gardens on a Saturday night in the season of 1940-41. Before the game that night, my father had led me from our seats down to the boards around the ice and waved over Conacher, who was a friend of a friend of my father's. Once the mighty right winger for the Maple Leafs, Conacher had been traded away in the fading days of his career.

"Meet the great Charlie Conacher, Jackie," my father said to me. I stuck out my small hand and watched it vanish into Conacher's massive hockey glove.

The New York Americans joined the NHL in 1925, were renamed the Brooklyn Americans briefly in 1941-42, and folded the next season—leaving the league with the half-dozen teams that came to be known as the Original Six. As a team, the Americans never had much to boast about—no first place finishes, no serious challenges for the Stanley Cup. But, in my memory, they became forever fixed as the wonderful team that Charlie Conacher played for on the night he shook my hand.

That's the way it is in hockey: identify with a member of the team—player, coach, even executive—and you tap into that team's tradition. Even with the Americans long gone, and the NHL expanded to an amazing thirty teams, nothing has changed. It still remains true that the path to each team's history is discovered through a love of the men who create hockey's glory and grace on the ice. First the man, then the team, then the game. The game above all.

JACK BATTEN

The Mighty Ducks Of Anaheim

Founded 1993

Arenas
Arrowhead Pond

Stanley Cup Wins
0

Award Winners

Lady Byng Trophy
Paul Kariya, 1996–97, 1995–96

Maurice "Rocket" Richard Trophy
Teemu Selanne 1998–99

Anaheim superstar Paul Kariya tries to put a backhand past fellow All-Star John Vanbiesbrouck.

Profile
Paul Kariya won the Hobie Baker Trophy as NCAA hockey's most valuable player while at the University of Maine and brought that tradition of excellence with him to the NHL. Possessing blazing speed and a deadly shot, Kariya is perennially among the league's scoring leaders.

Face to Face:
At the dawn of the 1990s, few people had heard of Paul Kariya and even less believed a team called the Mighty Ducks of Anaheim would ever exist in the NHL.

Paul Kariya

Fast forward to the 2000 All-Star game in Toronto. A touching "passing of the torch" video features Wayne Gretzky, Gordie Howe, and Mario Lemieux on a frozen pond, flipping the puck to four members of hockey's next generation. Standing proudly with Jaromir Jagr, Eric Lindros, and Pavel Bure is Kariya, wearing Anaheim's now familiar purple, jade, silver, and white sweaters with the duckbill logo. He's not out of place at all.

"I don't think anyone makes fun of us or our name anymore," Kariya said. "All you have to do is look around and see how many people are wearing our sweaters around the league. I think we broke some records in sales.

"By the end of my first year [the franchise's second] I felt pretty comfortable. We were playing better and making it hard on other teams."

Kariya had made a name for himself well before Anaheim chose him fourth overall in the 1993 draft. He'd shot the lights out in his native British Columbia Junior Hockey League with 244 points in 94 games with Penticton. He was the first freshman winner of the Hobey Baker Award as top U.S. collegian, with 75 assists in 39 games at Maine, followed by a stint with the globe-trotting Canadian national team.

But if playing on both North American coasts and around Europe wasn't disorienting, certainly his first days in Anaheim were.

"I can't forget that first day when I landed at the airport," he said. "I was picked up in this big Cadillac sedan, driving past all these palm trees in the beautiful sunshine and I couldn't believe this was where I was going to play hockey. The arena [Arrowhead Pond, a

Team Highlights

- April 29, 1997: The Mighty Ducks win their first playoff series 4 games to 3 over the Phoenix Coyotes.

- 1996–1997: Teemu Selanne sets a team record for points in the season with 109.

- October 8, 1993: The Ducks play their first home game as an NHL team.

marble and glass gem regarded as one of the most picturesque in the league] was quite a sight. It was a long way from college."

Kariya, who was drafted after Alexandre Daigle, Chris Pronger, and Chris Gratton, made the most of the lockout-shortened 1994–95 season. His 39 points made him a Calder trophy finalist, a stepping stone to three first-team All-Star left wing berths and a pile of club scoring records.

His world changed dramatically on February 7, 1996, when the Ducks swung a deal for the "Finnish Flash," Teemu Selanne, a right winger who had 76 goals as a rookie in Winnipeg. From the moment they were paired in Selanne's first game, heads were spinning on the ice and in the crowd. Selanne scored in his Ducks' debut and had points in his first 15 games.

"What a huge acquisition," Kariya said, the excitement still in his voice four years after the deal. "Teemu and I had a good rapport going from the very first day. He just seemed to know where I'd be and where the puck was.

"We utilize similar tools to create offense such as speed. It's not the way it works with other big lines, where I'm the passer and he's the shooter. We do a lot of both. We take whatever the other team's defense gives us."

Which turned out to be an awful lot. Kariya had 50 goals at the end of 1995–96 and came within a whisker of another 100 points the following season when Anaheim made its playoff debut. New Duck Selanne launched the first of two 50-goal years and won the inaugural Maurice "Rocket" Richard Trophy with a league-high 47 goals in 1998–99.

Kariya's 429 shots in 1998–99 were the second-most in NHL history, the same year Sellane and he were 2–3 in league scoring with more than 100 points, then came 4–5 the following year with Kariya on top.

The Ducks became a thorn in everyone's side in the Western Conference, finishing second in the Pacific Division in 1996–97.

"We beat Phoenix that year in the playoffs and though we lost four straight to Detroit the next round, three of those games were in overtime," said Kariya who has 17 points in 14 playoff games.

"I think we've laid a good foundation. There's Teemu and myself. Guy Hebert [a Day One Duck] will be here for a few more years and Steve Rucchin [his centre] is a guy who never gets credit as a two-way player. We've got Oleg Tverdovsky back [an original component of the Selanne trade].

Paul Kariya (left) and Oleg Tverdosky (right) awaiting a face-off.

"Missing the playoffs (in 1999–2000) was a disappointment, but I think we're on the right track."

Kariya likes living around Anaheim, which he says has a more small-town feel than its noisy Los Angeles neighbor.

"It's like night and day from L.A. and life slows down a lot," Kariya said. "You can go out for dinner and the people are really nice."

Kariya, who signed a new three-year deal in the summer of 1999, found the growing pains of the Ducks have often mirrored his ongoing development. A controversial cross-check to his head by Gary Suter, the fourth concussion he has suffered, held him to 22 games in the 1997–98 season. His career hung in the balance for months, but he eventually returned in 1998–99.

The retirement of Gretzky and Lemieux, Lindros's own head injuries, and the strong European influence in the NHL left him as one of the few explosive Canadian-born stars in the league. The two-time winner of the Lady Byng Trophy also became a hit with novice hockey fans in Japan, the land of his father's people.

"I'm very proud to be Canadian and I'll never forget my

Team Lowlights

- February 1, 1998: Paul Kariya suffers a concussion after being cross-checked in the face by Chicago's Gary Suter. The aftereffects of this injury force Kariya to miss the 1998 Nagano Olympics.

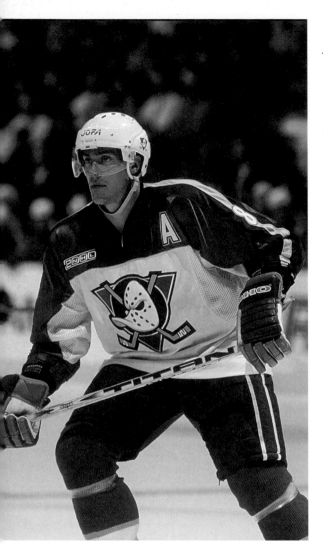

Teemu Selanne, "The Finnish Flash," was acquired in a trade with the Winnipeg Jets during the 1995–96 season. Selanne has a well-documented passion for speed both on and off the ice, racing rally cars in the off season.

roots," he said. "I'm also aware I've had some impact among Japanese hockey fans [just the rumor he would play in the historic Ducks-Canucks 1997 series in Tokyo touched off a frenzy in Asia]."

But where Kariya is looked upon as a savior is right in Anaheim, where the West Coast and indeed all of the U.S. franchises, are trying to fill the marquee hole left by Gretzky. The Ducks' captain, once ill at ease with all the attention, is being shoved more and more into the spotlight. He once said his job on the ice was a cinch compared to facing the glare of cameras afterwards.

"I'm very comfortable with it now," Kariya insisted. "I hope to get better at it and improve my relationship with the media."

Being included in the All-Star game video was a highlight for Kariya, even though below-zero conditions made it a long day of shooting.

"At the end, the seven of us all posed for a picture and signed it," Kariya said. "It was an awesome experience and the picture is on the wall, one of my most treasured things.

"It means a lot to me. There's a lot of good young talent out there in the NHL and we've got to do our share to help sell the game."

The Franchise The Mighty Ducks of Anaheim had everything a new hockey franchise could have wanted.

A dynamic owner in Michael Eisner. A sparkling new building in a populated California market. A natural rivalry with Los Angeles. And, the same year a franchise was awarded, the release of the 1992 Mighty Ducks movie, starring Emilio Estevez, one of three pictures in a series.

With all that in their favor, the Ducks were an overnight success even before they played a game. Thanks in part to Wayne Gretzky turning around the Kings up the highway, Disney chairman Eisner found it easy to get quick approval for an expansion team to join the Florida Panthers for entry in the 1993–94 season. Part of Anaheim's expansion fees went to the Kings for territorial infringement, but the two have co-existed successfully.

The Ducks' first management team included general manager Jack Ferreira and assistant Pierre Gauthier, both respected NHL scouts. Their first pick in both the expansion draft and the entry draft were sharp ones. Goaltender Guy Hebert, claimed from the Blues, remains with the team to this day and 1993 Hobey Baker

Award winner Paul Kariya, after taking off for a year to finish school and play in the Olympics, became one of the league's young superstars.

Anaheim's first-year team, stocked mostly with big and rugged journeymen, broke the 70-point barrier and won 19 road games, still a franchise record. At home in the Arrowhead Pond of Anaheim, the Ducks drew steady crowds of home-grown fans and visiting hockey fans to southern California.

Kariya arrived in the lockout-short-ened 1995 season and blossomed into a 108-point left winger in 1995–96. That was the same season the Ducks pulled a major trade with Winnipeg and secured Finnish Flash Teemu Selanne to play opposite Kariya with Steve Rucchin evolving into their regular centerman.

In 1996–97, their first playoff season with 85 points, Selanne and Kariya fin-ished 2–3 in NHL scoring behind Mario Lemieux, and the Ducks took out the Phoenix Coyotes in the first round before losing to the eventual Cup champions, Detroit. After a hiccup of just 26 wins the following season, the team brought Gauthier back as general manager, after he'd put the Ottawa Senators back on the map.

Once more, the core of Kariya, Selanne, and Hebert got rolling, allowing just 206 goals and achieving 83 points. Oleg Tverdovsky was reacquired in the summer of 1999, improving Anaheim's defense.

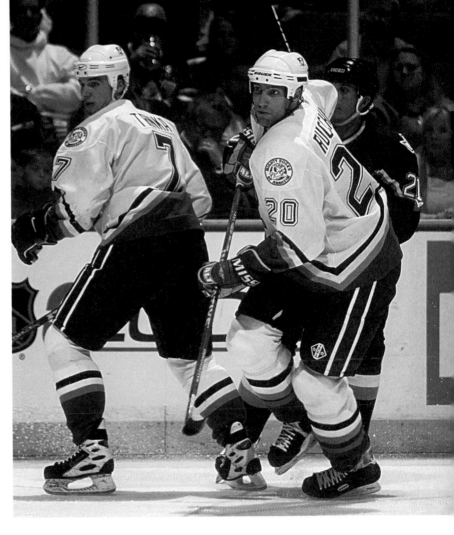

Steve Rucchin found himself in an enviable position in Anaheim, playing center between Kariya and Selanne, two of the game's most dynamic offensive forces.

TEAM RECORDS

	Career	Season
Goals	Paul Kariya, 210	Teemu Selanne, 52 (1997–98)
Assists	Paul Kariya, 254	Paul Kariya, 62 (1998–99)
Points	Paul Kariya, 464	Teemu Selanne, 109 (1996–97)
Goals-Against Average	Guy Hebert, 2.71	Guy Hebert, 2.62 (1998–99)
Games Played	Guy Hebert, 400	

Atlanta Thrashers

Founded 1999

Arenas

Philips Arena

The Thrashers hope that Hnat Domenichelli will use his quickness, and the offensive flair that he showed as a junior player, to help lead their offense in the years to come.

Profile

Vice president, general manager, and alternate governor of the NHL's 28th team, Don Waddell brings 20 years of front-office experience to the Thrashers. After an accomplished minor league career building International Hockey League franchises in San Diego and Orlando, he was assistant general manager of the two-time Stanley Cup-winning Detroit Red Wings in 1997–98.

Atlanta's Vice President and General Manager Don Waddell.

Face to Face

In some ways, selling hockey in Atlanta is like preaching to the converted.

"In the first couple of games, we could see all the Boston, Pittsburgh, New York, and Buffalo sweaters in the crowd," Don Waddell said. "When the Flames played here [from 1972 to 1980], the population of Atlanta was 1.2 million. Now it's 3.2 million and obviously a lot of those transplants came from the north and northeast and had a hockey background.

"When we checked our season's ticket sales, we found that 1,200 also had tickets when the Flames were here. That was a good head start for us. There is still an active Flames alumni in town. Players such as Eric Vail and Tim Ecclestone still live around here. Ask half a dozen people in the street and they might still remember that Dan Bouchard played goal here."

But the first general manager of the Thrashers knows his team will have to cause as big a stir as General Sherman's army did to get noticed in such a competitive sports town. Waddell has a few original ideas—and a few borrowed ones.

"We can't dispute that two of the biggest sports in this area are college football and NASCAR. Well, what is hockey known for? Lots of contact at a high rate of speed. So we try and play off of that.

"What we're trying to do is get new hockey fans to come in here and see us once. They might not come back right away, but you've planted the seed. When they do come back, maybe they'll bring three or four people with them."

Waddell won't "insult" the intelligence of patrons by relaying rules over the public address system such as icings and offsides. Some new teams have flooded the streets with free tickets, but

Andrew Brunette, one of the Thrashers' most promising young players, celebrates a goal against the Montreal Canadiens.

Waddell has kept them to a minimum in order to discourage a core of fan free-loaders.

Waddell knows a few things about introducing hockey to new markets in the southern United States. The 42-year-old from Detroit built the San Diego Gulls into one of the International Hockey League's top independent teams in the early 1990s.

When he joined RDV Sports in 1995 as vice president, he was given special operations duties with the NBA Orlando Magic and the IHL Orlando Solar Bears. His two years running the Solar Bears preceded a return to Motown to complete his executive training as assistant GM of the Red Wings, just as they peaked with their second Stanley Cup win.

His timing wasn't always that great, however. As an NCAA defenseman at Northern Michigan, he was picked for the American squad that would go into history as the "miracle on ice." Unfortunately, a pre-tournament injury kept him out of the Lake Placid Games. He was drafted by the Kings and played one NHL game.

After being mentioned for several GM openings around the league, Waddell landed in Atlanta, where the powerful Turner broadcasting empire and the new $213-million Philips Arena gave the Thrashers a much more stable base than the Flames had ever had.

"That's one of the things that will allow us to build this franchise the right way," Waddell said. "This franchise isn't going to move. We've chosen the patient approach.

"We really studied all the expansion teams in the 1990s. Where Ottawa is now is where we want to be in a few years."

Knowing that 50-goal scorers would be in short supply on expansion draft day, the Thrashers opted for a lot of smaller-skill forwards, then when free agent season opened up, they kept the purse strings tied tight.

"First of all, I'm going to believe what the NHL says about [opening the game up]. That's the way it's going and we've got to be a speed formula team."

As their first year progressed, Waddell tweaked the roster

Signed as a free agent in 1999, NHL veteran Ray Ferraro proved to be a very valuable player for the Thrashers, accumulating 44 points and 88 penalty minutes during the 1999–2000 season.

Team Highlights

- June 25, 1999: In their first entry draft in 1999, the Thrashers make a bold move in a trade with the Vancouver Canucks that allows them to move up in the draft order. This enables them to use their pick to select Patrick Stefan first overall. A coup for the team management, this sends a clear signal to the rest of the league that the Thrashers intend to compete for the playoffs soon.

with Donald Audette, Hnat Domenichelli, Frantisek Kaberle, and Steve Guolla.

"We could've easily taken a free agent when they were available. Would we be higher in the standings? Yes. But it would be a short window. Look at the Atlanta Braves. All that pitching and talent and payroll and yet they rarely look outside their organization.

"In a few years, if we have our guy who is looking for a big contract, then chances are we give it to him. It's easier to pay for a player like that."

The Thrashers were bothered by a slew of injuries, including a long absence by goaltending backbone Damian Rhodes.

"You don't measure everything in points," Waddell said of the 39 his team earned in that season. "By the time we play our 82nd game, we'll be better than when we played our first."

The Franchise
This isn't the first time peaches and pucks have crossed paths in Georgia.

The NHL pioneers were the Flames, the 1972 expansion club with the hot-stuff "A" logo that whetted appetites of fans between 1972 and 1980. Although the club moved on to Calgary, it wasn't lack of fan interest that caused their demise.

The Flames played their games in the Omni, one of the last arenas to be built without an abundance of private boxes. There was also no major television contract for the Flames to generate income. Without that bread and butter, the team was destined for economic hardship, despite a very entertaining offensive team.

Minor league hockey filled the bill until the summer of 1997. Broadcasting mogul Ted Turner and the powerful Time Warner company joined the expansion bid, which was approved on June

25, 1997. Philips Arena, located next door to Turner's CNN headquarters, was completed by 1998.

The logo, based on the state bird, the Brown Thrasher, was "cyber-launched" on the World Wide Web in April 1998, an NHL first. Its colors are capitol copper, Georgia bronze, and peachtree gold.

General manager Don Waddell, formerly with minor league teams in San Diego and Orlando, was well versed in the nuances of selling hockey in the south. He drafted a team with strong goaltending, solid leadership credentials, and as much dash on offense as could be achieved by an expansion team. The Thrashers chose Patrik Stefan first overall in the 1999 entry draft.

Despite a number of injuries, Atlanta managed 39 points its first year and drew lots of interest. Left winger Andrew Brunette was a strong contributor with 50 points, and he, Ray Ferraro, Yannick Tremblay, Dean Sylvester, and Mike Stapleton, all had 10 or more goals.

Yannick Tremblay is a capable offensive defenseman who is coming into his own in Atlanta after failing to stick with the Toronto Maple Leafs.

Team Lowlights

- June 18, 1999: The Thrashers acquire Ottawa goaltender Damian Rhodes in a trade to the 1999 expansion draft. Touted as the cornerstone of the young team, the trade proves disapointing when Rhodes becomes plagued by injuries and sub-par performances.

Team Records

	Season
Goals	Andrew Brunette, 23 (1999–2000)
Assists	Andrew Brunette, 27 (1999–2000)
Points	Andrew Brunette, 50 (1999–2000)
Goals-Against Average	Scott Fankhouser 3.20
Games Played	Andrew Brunette, 81
	Ray Ferraro, 81

Boston Bruins

Founded 1924

Arenas
Fleet Center 1995–present
Boston Garden 1928–1995
Boston Arena 1924–1928

Stanley Cup Wins
1971–1972 1969–1970,
1940–1941, 1938–1939,
1928–29,

Award Winners

see page 252

Drafted first overall by
the Bruins in 1997,
Joe Thornton had
enormous pressure
placed upon him.
Although his
development has been
gradual he has
emerged as one of the
future superstars of
the NHL.

20

Profile

Gerry Cheevers was only the fourth goaltender in NHL history to become a head coach. He led the Boston Bruins for almost five seasons following his retirement as a player on July 7, 1980. He spent all or parts of 12 seasons in the Bruin cage and was a key figure in Boston's Stanley Cup springs of 1970 and 1972. He jumped to the Cleveland Crusaders of the World Hockey Association in 1972 and returned to the Bruins three and a half years later. He was inducted into the Hockey Hall of Fame in 1985.

Gerry Cheevers

Face to Face

Cheevers was an acrobatic and colorful man in the cage, a money goaltender who was at his best in the tense moments and bored in the laughers. He was a self-effacing fellow, too. Once, observing a pack of youngsters looking for player autographs, he overheard a conversation that he later reported as follows:

"Who's that guy there?" one kid said.

"Cheevers," replied his pal.

"Oh, well," said the first kid. "Get him anyway."

When Cheevers first joined the Bruins they were terrible. It was in the mid-1960s. But in the early 1970s he changed his tune and expressed a blanket forgiveness for the lumps, bumps, and bruises he'd absorbed in the gruesome seasons before Bobby Orr and Phil Esposito began to deliver the Bruins from purgatory.

In an eight-year stretch in the 1960s the Bruins set a grisly pace: They were last in the standings six times and second-last twice. Even in 1967, after Cheevers had earned his big-league credentials and Orr was a glowing rookie, Boston finished out of the playoffs for the eighth straight spring, in the cellar and winners of only 17 of 70 league games.

So when they showed up in the Stanley Cup finals in 1970 and 1972 and twice won the old shaving mug, Cheevers dismissed all past indignities.

"One of the nice things about playing goal for the Bruins," he said, smiling past a gap of six missing front teeth, "is playing goal for the Bruins."

Before then and since, the goaltending task in Boston was rarely a heartwarming experience. Through three-quarters of a century only three of the breed won the Vezina Trophy, Cecil (Tiny) Thompson, Frank Brimsek, and Pete Peeters, the most recent Boston winner in 1983.

Accordingly, playing goal for the Bruins has rarely been a Boston tea party. Even the immortal Terry Sawchuk grew so harried and run down in two seasons there that after 34 games in 1957 he left the team and went home. A medical specialist said he was on the brink of a nervous breakdown. He was suffering the debilitating illness mononucleosis.

But later, once Bobby Orr showed up in front of him, Cheevers began to feel it was more enjoyable to play goal in Boston even in an era before face masks than to complain about the traffic surrounding him or his six lost teeth (a backhand shot by the scrawny sniper Red Berenson caught him by surprise just below the nose, knocking out three uppers and three lowers, and causing a mouth cut requiring 35 stitches).

Goaltenders were slow to accept the idea of covering their faces with masks, even after Jacques Plante refused to leave home without one. Cheevers maintained this lunacy was beyond vanity, although admitting there was some vanity, too.

"Goaltending is a very lonely and difficult task so we tend to be very proud bastards," he once explained, expanding on this theme. "Everybody says we're a different breed and I guess they're right. But sooner or later, when you start adding up the scars, you realize if you don't start wearing a mask, you may not survive."

Cheevers wore the wildest mask of the early users—he had painted on it the stitches that would have been in his face if he hadn't switched. After 250 stitches, the mask became so crowded with chicken tracks that he stowed the paint.

Still, it was hard work. Once, in the dressing room in the old Boston Garden, Gerry was naked, about to change into his work clothes, when Phil Esposito walked by.

"Jeez, Cheese, you're a mess," said Espo, "bruise city."

Gerry counted the welts and bruises. Six. "The one on my hip looked like a large bunch of grapes with streaks of red," he recalled later. "There was another almost as large in the groin, high up and on the inside of the right thigh. Also a couple of purple ones on the other thigh. There's no way to protect the upper legs without sacrificing mobility, so we all suffer."

Does a goaltender feel every puck?

"Yeah, all of 'em. Except the ones you miss, and it's too late for them."

Much of the lore of the Bruins was familiar to Cheevers when he arrived from the farm team in Oklahoma City for seven games in the dismal nights of the 1965–66 season. He absorbed more lumps for 22 games a season later, then back to Oklahoma. Enter an intense young farm-club executive named Harry Sinden, settling into the Boston Garden as Bruin coach and becoming the beneficiary of one of the great trades in Boston history.

This one was engineered by Milt Schmidt, the great star of

Bobby Orr Arguably the greatest to ever play the game, Bobby Orr revolutionized the way defense is played. He was the first defenseman to win the Art Ross Trophy for most points scored in a season and, when teamed with Phil Esposito, he lead the Bruins to Stanley Cup victories in 1970 and 1972.

On January 19, 2000,
Ray Bourque, reached
a career milestone,
joining Gordie Howe,
Alex Delvecchio, John
Bucyk, and Larry
Murphy as the only
players in NHL history
to have appeared in
1,500 games.

an earlier era, who became Boston's general manager in 1967 and almost immediately scored a coup. While everybody was sleeping in Chicago, Milt slipped in. He deprived the Blackhawks of Phil Esposito, Ken Hodge, and Fred Stanfield in exchange for three hardly distinguished Hawks, goaler Jack Norris, Pit Martin, and Gilles Marotte. The difference this threesome made to Cheevers, in particular, was that they kept the puck at the other end of the rink for vastly longer periods than he'd been used to.

With Espo and Bobby Orr, the Bruins thundered through much of the early 1970s, Phil winning five scoring championships, a relentless prowling presence in the enemy goalmouth, where he became known as "the Garbage Collector," converting rebounds into goals. Also—who can forget?—he was the generator in Canada's nod in Moscow in 1972.

But Cheevers grew annoyed following Boston's second Stanley Cup triumph. He was offered a $5,000 raise, which he thought inadequate, so was wide open for an offer from the Cleveland Crusaders in the newly created WHA. He was romanced by a salary five times greater than his Boston income, with a five-year contract. So he jumped.

But the WHA, which also lured Derek Sanderson and Teddy Green from the Bruins, and the super-shooter Bobby Hull from Chicago, had an appetite too large for its plate. When the Crusaders began losing large amounts of money, Cheevers reduced his own salary so they could meet the payroll. Early in his fourth season and with nearly two years left on his contract, Gerry told the owners he'd release their obligation if they would pay him two months' back salary. When they agreed, he called Harry Sinden in Boston and returned to the Bruins.

He shared the goaltending job for four more seasons, then became the man behind the bench in the fall of 1980. There, he inherited a budding superstar, Raymond Bourque, who had won the Calder Trophy that spring (1980) and became a perennial resident of All-Star teams. Raymond kept the Boston defense together for 20 years, then Sinden shipped him off to the Colorado Avalanche, an old lad nudging 40.

As coach, Cheevers survived almost five seasons, his teams contenders but never there when the Stanley Cup was being presented. So Sinden ousted him and turned to Butch Goring in 1985 as the next victim.

That move sent Cheevers to the television booth, analyzing the

Team Highlights

- 1970–71: Phil Esposito sets a league record for goals with 76 for the season.

- May 10, 1970: Bobby Orr scores an overtime goal to defeat the St. Louis Blues and wins Boston its first Stanley Cup in 29 years.

- 1924–25: The Bruins become the first American NHL team.

Hartford Whalers. Just before the Whalers moved to Carolina, he rejoined the Bruins as a scout, holding no grudge that he'd been fired as coach. Indeed, he was the same philosophical fellow who had said that a nice thing about playing goal for the Bruins was playing goal for the Bruins.

"When a coach can't win in four years back there," he said of life behind the bench, "a coach doesn't belong back there."

The Franchise

The fire-wagon style of the old Montreal Canadiens helped make Boston the first American city in the NHL. In 1924 a wealthy sports fan with a mild interest in the game was persuaded to travel to Montreal to see some real hockey, the Stanley Cup final.

He was Charles W. Adams, who began life as a poor lad in Newport, Vermont, and wound up as chairman of First National Stores, a major grocery chain, and as owner of the Bruins, baseball's Boston Braves, and the thoroughbred race course Suffolk Downs.

In Montreal's Mount Royal Arena in the early spring of 1924, Adams saw the flashing Habitants of Howie Morenz, Aurel Joliat, and Billy Boucher handle the Pacific Coast champion Vancouver Maroons by 3–2, and was sufficiently entranced that he put up $15,000 to acquire an NHL franchise for Boston.

Also in Montreal, Adams heard of the organizing skill of a 38-year-old former defenseman, Art Ross, who had been a strong-willed player for both the old  Montreal Wanderers and the Kenora Thistles when each won the Stanley Cup, the Thistles in 1907 and the Wanderers a year later.

By 1922 Ross was coaching the NHL's Hamilton Tigers when Adams offered to make him coach and general manager of the new team in Boston. Ross accepted and was there a year later

Anson Carter has the speed and hard shot necessary to become a scorer in the NHL. Carter's 1999–2000 season was cut short by surgery on his wrist.

The first defenseman to dominate the game offensively, Bobby Orr revolutionized the position by leading his team with end-to-end rushes.

when his former Hamilton team moved lock, stock, and liniment bottle to New York. There, they became the fabled New York Americans.

Ross was an innovator. The NHL nets were named Art Ross nets to honor the man who redesigned them from a stiff, crude

early model. He also designed the current deckle-edged pucks and was the first NHL coach to remove a goaltender to put on a sixth skater. He pulled Tiny Thompson in a playoff game in Boston on March 26, 1931. The Bruins lost anyway (to the Canadiens: 1–0).

The bright star of the early years was Eddie Shore, the fearless basher from the western plains, who had driven hard-thinking newshounds out there to such frenzy that they had anointed him "the Edmonton Express." Eddie was a balding, hemstitched bull.

Hemstitched? Once Shore, who conducted his violent business in Boston from 1926 to 1940, had his ear mangled badly enough in a collision that the club doctor didn't think he could save it. Still in uniform, Shore is said to have stomped from the rink into a swirling snowstorm searching for doctors' shingles. He entered two offices but left when physicians affirmed the opinion of the club doctor. Then a third said he'd give it a try and, eyeing the mashed ear, began preparing an anaesthetic.

"Put that stuff away, doc," Shore told him. "Just give me a mirror. I want to be sure you sew it on right."

But strong wills were nothing new to Art Ross, a tough-minded man himself and Bruins general manager from 1924 to 1954. Ross hired and fired six coaches in that span, and between coaches he went behind the bench himself. Two of his coaches had been Boston heroes and players—Ralph (Cooney) Weiland, who won the scoring championship in the 1929–30 season and Aubrey (Dit) Clapper, a 20-year Bruin who reached All-Star status as both a right winger and a defenseman. Schmidt played center between Bobby Bauer and Woody Dumart, a powerhouse trio rudely interrupted by World War II when the three of them enlisted as a unit in the RCAF.

The "Krauts," close friends, insisted that each be paid the same salary. Once, after they had finished one, two, three in NHL scoring, they visited Ross en masse to ask for a $500 raise each. He said no.

An admired player who never got the nod from Ross to coach was Bill Cowley, a smooth-skating, deft-passing center, who won the scoring championship in 1941 and made first-team All-Star four times from 1938 to 1944.

The Bruins didn't often win championships—five in their long history—but obviously they produced memorable players. One was Johnny Bucyk, who spent 23 seasons in the NHL, 21

Terry Sawchuk played less than two full seasons in Boston and battled illness during his second season. The Bruins traded the legendary goaltender back to his original team, the Detroit Red Wings, on June 10, 1957.

of them wearing No. 9 for Boston, where his number was retired in 1980.

Also there was Mel Hill, an otherwise undistinguished right winger who became known forever as Sudden-Death Hill. In a Stanley Cup spring of 1939, he nailed down victories over the New York Rangers with overtime goals in three games. The Bruins needed every one of Sudden-Death's deliveries: the series went seven games.

The Bruins were high on sobriquets that year, Frankie Brimsek's rookie season. Succeeding the revered Tiny Thompson in Boston's net, Brimsek scored six shutouts in his first ten games and, not unexpectedly, Hub scribes named him "Mister Zero." The name remained long after Brimsek went into the Hall of Fame in 1966.

That was the year Bobby Orr was elevated from the junior Oshawa Generals at age 18 to undertake the journey that made him a Boston legend. There's no telling how long Orr might have remained the NHL's premier defenseman had knee injuries not derailed his career. He underwent five knee operations between 1968 and 1975 before going to the Chicago Blackhawks as a free agent in 1976. He played 26 games, had more knee surgery, and retired in November 1978.

By then, major reshuffling had rudely altered the Bruins upper echelon. A shadowy Buffalo figure, Jeremy Jacobs, who headed a food concessions corporation that serviced hockey rinks and racetracks, had purchased the Bruins. Harry Sinden was the team's general manager and Don (Grapes) Cherry, the coach.

The Bruins went to the Stanley Cup finals in 1977 before being shaded by the Canadiens, and the same finish marked the spring of 1978. The ebullient Cherry, a lifetime minor league defenseman, was heralded for his job as Bruin leader—heralded by everyone except a man named Sinden. Harry and Don didn't get along, and since Harry owned the hammer, Don turned to terrifying television viewers on "Hockey Night in Canada" right into the new millennium.

Meantime, Sinden and the Bruins never won the Stanley Cup again from that day forward, although they did make it to the finals in 1988 and again in 1990, crushed each time by the Edmonton Oilers by a combined eight games to one.

Team Records

	Career	Season
Goals	Johnny Bucyk, 545	Phil Esposito, 76 (1970–71)
Assists	Ray Bourque, 1,111	Bobby Orr, 102, (1970–71)
Points	Ray Bourque, 1,506	Phil Esposito, 152 (1970–71)
Goals-Against Average	Tiny Thompson, 1.99	Tiny Thompson, 1.15 (1928–29)
Games Played	Ray Bourque, 1,518	

Buffalo Sabres

Founded 1970

Arenas
*The Marine Midland Arena
1996–present
The War Memorial
Auditorium 1970–96*

Stanley Cup Wins
0

Award Winners

Jack Adams Award
Ted Nolan, 1996–97

Lady Byng Trophy
Gilbert Perreault, 1972–73

Calder Trophy
*Tom Barrasso, 1983–84
Gilbert Perreault, 1970–71*

King Clancy Trophy
Rob Ray, 1998–99

Hart Trophy
*Dominik Hasek, 1998–99,
1997–98, 1996–97*

Jennings Trophy
*Dominik Hasek and Grant
Fuhr, 1993–94
Tom Barrasso and Bob
Sauve, 1984–85*

Bill Masterton Trophy
*Pat LaFontaine, 1994–95
Don Luce, 1974–75*

Frank J. Selke Trophy
*Michael Peca, 1996–97
Craig Ramsay, 1984–85*

Vezina Trophy
*Dominik Hasek, 1997–98,
1996–97, 1994–95,
1993–94
Tom Barrasso, 1983–84
Bob Sauve and Don
Edwards, 1979–80*

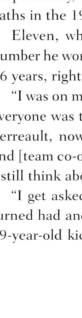

Profile
One of the most graceful players to watch in NHL history, Gilbert Perreault was Buffalo's first choice in the 1970 expansion draft. He played 1,191 games, all in Buffalo, with 1,326 points. He won the Calder and Lady Byng trophies and was center of one of the greatest lines in history, the French Connection.

He played in six All-Star games and retired in 1986 holding every major Sabres offensive record.

Face to Face
Luck certainly wore blue and gold on June 11, 1970.

All eyes were on a wheel of fortune that day in Montreal's Queen Elizabeth Hotel, as NHL commissioner Clarence Campbell spun to determine the first pick overall between the expansion Buffalo Sabres and Vancouver Canucks. The wheel was numbered 1 to 20. Vancouver had everything lower than 11, Buffalo 11 to 20.

When the pointer stopped, Campbell thought it was aiming at No. 1 and quickly congratulated the Canucks delegation. But as usual, Punch Imlach's attention to detail was better than anyone's. Imlach, the Sabres general manager, told Campbell to check again. Sure enough, the number was actually 11.

Imlach's correction, sending the Vancouver table from joy to despondency, helped send the two teams on wildly divergent paths in the 1970s.

Eleven, which was Perreault's number in junior, was the number he wore on the Sabres uniform and that he kept through 16 years, right into the Hall of Fame.

"I was on my way downtown to the hotel, and when I arrived, everyone was talking about the mistake with the number," said Perreault, now a Sabres community relations liaison. "Punch and [team co-owner] Seymour Knox were there to greet me, and I still think about it as such an exciting day in my life.

"I get asked all the time how differently things might have turned had another number come up. But the truth is, I was a 19-year-old kid who wanted to prove myself, somewhere, any-

Gilbert Perreault

After an injury plagued 1999–2000 season Dominik Hasek, one of the most dominant goalies of the modern era, announced that he would delay his retirement by one year and play in the 2000–01 season.

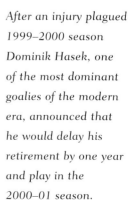

- 1998–99: Buffalo defeats the Toronto Maple Leafs to make it to the Stanley Cup finals for the second time in franchise history versus the Dallas Stars.

- 1996–97: Goalie Dominik Hasek becomes the first European to win the Hart Trophy as the league's most valuable player. He repeats the feat the following season.

- 1974–1975: The Sabres make it to the Cup finals for the first time before losing to the Philadelphia Flyers.

where in the NHL. I knew right through my last year of junior that there were two new teams coming into the league and I was ready to go to either one."

The flashy 50-goal center from the Montreal Junior Canadiens won the 1971 Calder Trophy on the strength of a rookie record 72 points. Within five years, Perreault and his French Connection Line were leading the way to a Sabres push for the Stanley Cup.

Vancouver, meanwhile, used its first pick on Dale Tallon, an excellent defenseman from the Toronto Marlboros, but a player who would spend just three seasons on the west coast before finishing a 10-year career in Chicago and Pittsburgh.

"Punch took me aside that first day," Perreault said. "He said, 'I don't want to put a lot of pressure on you, but we're going to use you a lot.' He told me I was going there to score goals."

Perreault was a baby on a mixed-bag expansion roster that included twilight NHL stars such as Phil Goyette, Reg Fleming, Jean-Guy Talbot, and Eddie Shack. The temptation in the early days of expansion was for new teams to trade top picks for veterans, as California did to its chagrin when they finished last and handed No. 1 pick Guy Lafleur to Montreal.

But Perreault was everything Imlach imagined, a combination of speed, grace, and stickhandling. He had only started playing ice hockey as an eight-year-old, emulating the great Jean Beliveau's puck control by watching the Habs on TV.

Perreault fulfilled his mandate to score and score often for the Sabres, especially after the formation of the French Connection. Left winger Rick Martin, another member of the Junior Canadiens, was picked fifth overall in 1971 and the following year, Imlach sent Shack to Pittsburgh for Rene Robert to complete the trio.

"I think Rene's was the last trade made at the deadline that

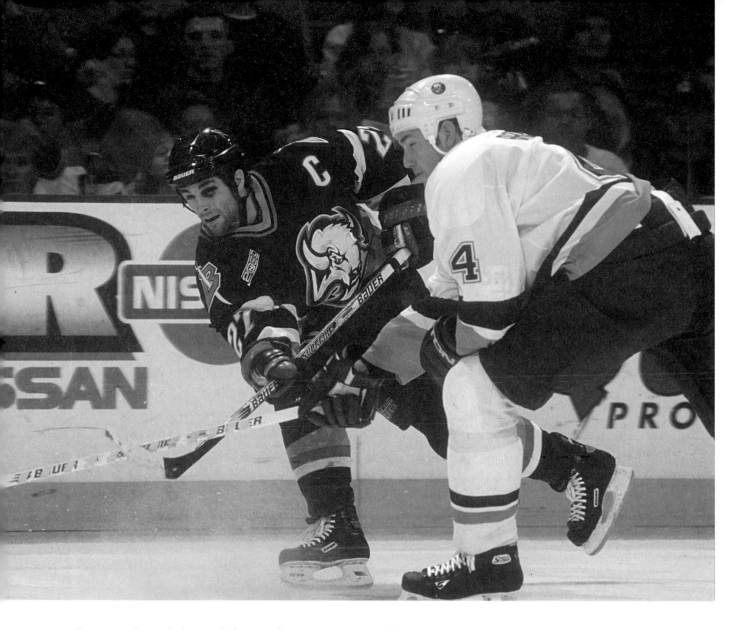

year," Perreault said. "Punch knew that getting the right blend of three French-Canadian guys would click.

"Rick was a great scorer and shooter, Rene had a great feel for the game. We were criss-crossing, there were a lot of European influences and it was a great time."

They all finished in the top 10 scorers of 1974–75 and Perreault's 113 points were third overall in 1975–76. But Perreault knew the burgeoning Sabres were much more than a one-line team.

"Punch had a good draft record and he also made some great trades. If you look at what he did in just a few years, we had Martin, Robert, Don Luce, Jim Lorentz, Jerry Korab, Josh Guevremont, Craig Ramsay, Danny Gare, Jim Schoenfeld. Every year, it seemed we were adding someone to the picture.

Small by NHL standards, Buffalo captain Mike Peca, is still one of the most feared bodycheckers in the league. A gritty player and strong leader, Peca is among the NHL's best defensive forwards.

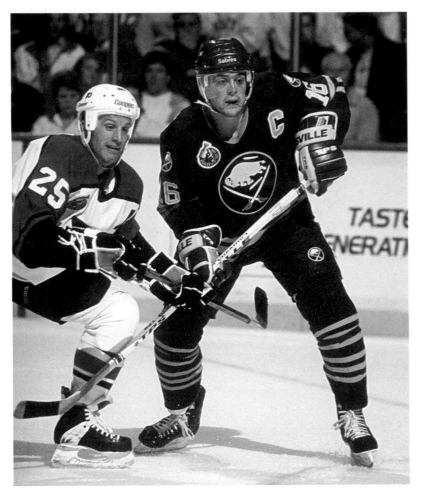

Former Sabres captain Pat LaFontaine holds the Buffalo team records for both points and assists in a season. LaFontaine's career was cut short when he was forced to retire after suffering several serious concussions.

"We were a young team of 20- to 25-year-olds, something like the Edmonton Oilers in the 1980s. We thought we had a team ready to go all the way."

There was a natural attraction to such a team in blue-collar Buffalo and across the border in southern Ontario, where there was growing disenchantment with Imlach's old team, the Maple Leafs. Within a few years, the Sabres were packing Memorial Auditorium and in 1972, they began a 10-year streak of consecutive sellouts. Broadcasting legends Ted Darling and Rick Jeanneret made even poorly played games sound exciting.

A furious rivalry with the Leafs developed, stoked by Perreault's brilliance, Imlach's barbs, and the Buffalo media's love affair with the team. Perreault even received more votes than Bills superstar O.J. Simpson in a poll of most popular athlete in the city.

"Victoriaville, Quebec, where I came from, was also a small town," Perreault, the son of a railroad engineer, said. "You got that same feeling in Buffalo. It wasn't a big market like Toronto and New York, and we didn't have a lot of money to pay stars, but it was a close team."

Perreault and many others thought the pay-off year would be 1975. The Sabres, under coach Floyd Smith, knocked off Original Six teams Montreal and Chicago in the first two rounds and then came up against the Flyers, who were at their Broad Street Bully peak.

The Sabres were no slouches when it came to muscle, but hard-hitting Flyers meant trouble for the French Connection. Philly won in six games, but not before Robert's overtime goal in the fog-shrouded War Memorial Auditorium helped the Sabres rebound from a 2–0 deficit.

"There was no air conditioning in that building and it had to be 80–85 degrees inside," Perreault said of the mist that descended at ice level. "Every two or three minutes we had to skate around and break up the fog."

Perreault laughs at the memories of arena staff stumbling around on skates waving white sheets in a further fog-busting attempt, while Jim Lorentz used his stick to whack a bat that had swooped down into the humid proceedings.

What wasn't so humorous, of course, was a wasted chance at the Cup. It was almost 25 years before another Buffalo team returned to the finals.

"We regret that we didn't win—ever since my peewee days, I'd always played on a championship team," Perreault said. "When you only get one shot and don't win, it's too bad."

There were other honors for Perreault in the 1970s: twice a second team All-Star center, 8 points in the 1976 Canada Cup, the winning overtime goal in the 1978 All-Star game, two points in the 1979 Challenge Cup, and an All-Star team berth in the 1981 Canada Cup.

"Those first 10 years were a lot of fun," he said. "But our franchise was beginning to change. They were trying to build a different kind of team and I had become 30 years old."

Perreault stayed with the Sabres until he announced his retirement in November of 1986, having spent five years serving as team captain. He hung up his skates holding every major regular-season team scoring record.

The Franchise
Buffalo, a successful minor league hockey area since the Bisons played in 1936, was first in the running for an NHL franchise during the 1967 expansion.

After missing out, businessmen and brothers Seymour and Northrup Knox laid the groundwork to get a team, determined to succeed the next time the league spread its wings.

In December of 1969, the Knoxes were awarded a franchise along with Vancouver.

The first order of business was to find a general manager and in that regard, the Sabres' timing was impeccable.

Only a few months earlier, the Maple Leafs had cut loose

A four-time winner of the Vezina Trophy, Dominik Hasek is the most feared goaltender in the NHL. Known for his unorthodox style, Hasek will often adandon his goal stick in order to pounce on a loose puck. He led the Sabres to the Stanley Cup finals in 1998–99 where they lost to the Dallas Stars. Hasek won a gold medal at the 1998 Winter Olympics with an underdog team from the Czech Republic.

Team Records

	Career	Season
Goals	Gilbert Perreault, 512	Alexander Mogilny, 76 (1992–93)
Assists	Gilbert Perreault, 814	Pat LaFontaine, 95 (1992–93)
Points	Gilbert Perreault, 1,326	Pat LaFontaine, 148 (1992–93)
Goals-Against Average	Dominik Hasek, 2.24	Dominik Hasek, 1.87 (1998–99)
Games Played	Gilbert Perrautt, 1,1191	

Team Lowlights

- June 7, 1999: The Sabres lose the 1999–2000 Stanley Cup finals on Brett Hull's controversial goal scored with his foot in the crease.

Punch Imlach, the architect of four Stanley Cup wins in the 1960s. He joined the upstart Sabres, anxious to show he still had hockey smarts and determined to prove the Leafs wrong.

"Sabres" was chosen in a name-the-team contest. The Knoxes liked the image of a slashing cutlass and looked forward to such headlines as "Sabres Cut Down Leafs." Imlach chose colors and accents on the sweaters similar to Toronto's.

Buffalo was on the right track at the expansion draft when it won a spin of the wheel and drafted Gilbert Perreault first overall. Imlach worked more than 10 trades in the first two years of the franchise, building the French Connection around Perreault, Rene Robert, and Rick Martin, a 44-goal rookie.

In 1974–75, new coach Floyd Smith struck gold with a team that boasted firepower, a big defense, and a flock of youngsters. The Sabres had a 113-point season and a trip to the Stanley Cup, losing in six games to Philadelphia.

After that brush with the Cup, 10 seasons with 88 or more points followed as the Sabres established themselves among the league's elite. But regular-season laurels couldn't be repeated in playoffs. Imlach left in 1978, and was replaced in 1979 by another giant in the industry, Scotty Bowman.

The coach of Montreal during a string of Cup wins, Bowman hoped to make his name as general manager in Buffalo. A new breed of Sabres emerged under his watch, led by Tom Barrasso, Phil Housley, Mike Foligno, and Dave Andreychuk, but as the 1980s continued there were still no tangible post-season results.

The next few years saw plenty of changes among Buffalo's marquee players as Perreault retired; Pierre Turgeon was drafted first overall and later swapped to the Islanders for Pat LaFontaine. Alexander Mogilny heralded the Sabres' first experiment with European players.

The 1990s began with another hiring from a Cup dynasty, as John Muckler left the Oilers and became director of hockey

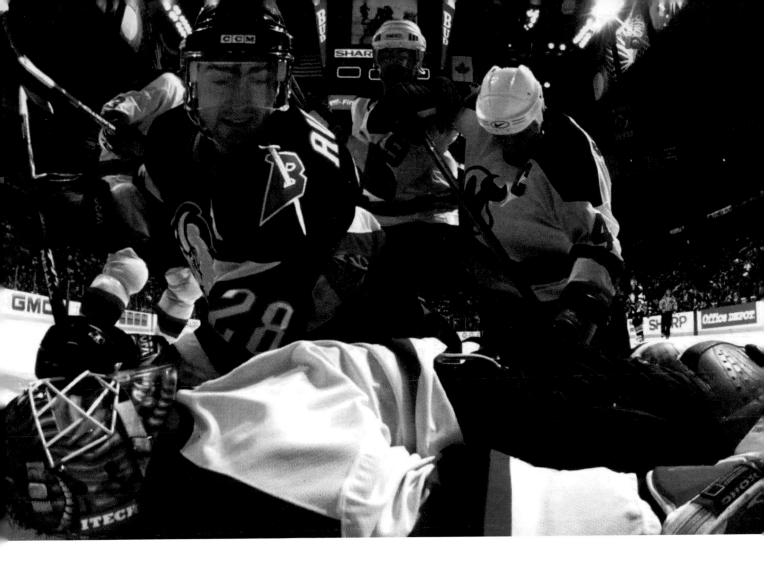

*Donald Audette crashes the New Jersey net as
Scott Stevens searches for the puck.*

operations. Buffalo advanced past the opening round for the first
time in 10 years in 1992–93, the same year they added an unher-
alded goalie from Chicago named Dominik Hasek.

A truckload of awards followed Hasek to Buffalo: Vezina, All-
Star team, and eventually, back-to-back Hart Trophies as most
valuable player. By 1996, the Sabres had moved to a new home
with completion of 18,595-seat Marine Midland Arena, later
HSBC Arena. The Sabres also changed sweaters when they went
to their new home, going to red, black, and white with a new bison
logo. New coach Ted Nolan led them to a 92-point division title.

Unfortunately, Seymour Knox didn't live to see the new-look
team, passing away in the spring of 1996.

Northrup Knox died in July of 1998, less than a year before
the Sabres were back in the Cup finals. New GM Darcy Regier
and coach Lindy Ruff won the East with a string of upsets in the
1999 playoffs and took Dallas to six games before losing.

Calgary Flames

Founded 1980

Formerly the Altanta Flames, 1972–80

Arenas
Calgary Airlines
  Saddledome 1983–
  present
 Stampede Corral 1980–83

Stanley Cup Wins
1988–89

Award Winners

Lady Byng Trophy
Joe Mullen, 1988–89,
 1986–87
Bob MacMillan, 1978–79

Calder Trophy
Sergei Makarov, 1989–90
Joe Nieuwendyk, 1987–88
Gary Suter, 1985–86
Will Plett, 1976–77
Eric Vail, 1974–75

King Clancy Trophy
Joe Nieuwendyk, 1994–95
Lanny McDonald, 1987–88

Bill Masterton Trophy
Gary Roberts, 1995–96
Lanny McDonald, 1982–83

Conn Smythe Trophy
Al MacInnis, 1988–89

Former Calgary goalie
Trevor Kidd makes a
spectacular overhead
save.

Profile Lanny McDonald was inducted into the Hockey Hall of Fame in 1992 following an illustrious 16-year NHL career that began in Toronto and ended in Calgary. McDonald holds the Flames' record for goals in a season (66) and scored 40 or more goals in a season six times. Twice an NHL All-Star, McDonald won the Bill Masterton Trophy in 1983 and the King Clancy Memorial Trophy in 1988. He currently serves as the Flames' vice president of corporate development.

Face to Face Few of Lanny McDonald's boyhood dreams revolved around the Calgary Flames, the team that he eventually became synonymous with during the second half of his distinguished NHL career. In the early 1970s, in McDonald's junior hockey days, the Flames were an NHL expansion team, based in Atlanta. The closest NHL team was situated across the Rocky Mountains in Vancouver, but Calgary? McDonald's Lethbridge Hurricanes used to play their Western Hockey League rivals, the Centennials, at the Stampede Corral.

Lanny McDonald

"Calgary was about the last place you'd ever think there'd be NHL hockey," said McDonald. "You figured, 'Junior hockey, that's the limit.' Then, all of a sudden, I remember I was in Colorado, playing for the Rockies, when I heard that the Flames were moving from Atlanta to Calgary. I thought that was pretty neat, but only because I thought, 'Great, now I can go home and play in front of family and friends for a visiting team.'

"I had no inkling whatsoever that I would get a chance to play there."

He did though.

McDonald was traded to Calgary in November 1981 in exchange for Bob MacMillan and Don Lever. McDonald remembers the circumstances as if they happened just yesterday. Playing with a bad shoulder at the time, McDonald refused to pull himself out of the Rockies' lineup but pressed doggedly

on because the team was struggling so badly. On the day before the trade, the Rockies were in Calgary and got smoked by the Flames. Afterward, McDonald bumped into the Calgary coaching staff—Al MacNeil and Pierre Page—in the parking lot following the game. McDonald was joining his parents for dinner and after exchanging pleasantries, MacNeil told him, "Hang in there, kid, it'll turn out all right."

"Not knowing what was about to come, I thought that was awfully decent of Al. The next morning, we flew to Winnipeg and as we were about to get off the plane, I saw the gate agent hand [coach] Marshall Johnston a note. He called me over and said, 'You're going back to Calgary.' My first thought was something had happened to someone in my family. Then he said, 'We traded you.' My first reaction was to say, 'You SOB.' I mean, I called him every name in the book. I couldn't believe what had happened."

McDonald grew up in an era when players viewed a trade only one way—that you were part of the problem. Accordingly, as the Rockies captain, McDonald took the news personally—and not particularly well.

"You never think someone else wants you. You think of it as a negative rather than a positive. By this time, some of the guys had come over to congratulate me, but me? I still wasn't getting it, that I was going from the worst team in the league to a team on the way up."

The Flames were a team in transition that season. General manager Cliff Fletcher added a quartet of experienced character players—McDonald, Mel Bridgman, Doug Risebrough, and Mike Eaves—in a two-year span, moves made to enhance the team's leadership. By contrast, many of the players that had followed the team to Calgary from Atlanta—and were unhappy playing in a high-pressure hockey environment—were dispatched elsewhere.

The Flames had developed a nascent rivalry with the Edmonton Oilers by then. In 1984, the Oilers started winning Stanley Cups and set a standard that the Flames were obliged to meet. The playoff format revolved around divisional rivalries, so no matter how proficient the Flames eventually became, no matter how many points they rattled off in the regular season, they were always going to meet the Oilers in either the first or second round, a monumental task in the era of Wayne Gretzky, Mark Messier, Paul Coffey, et al.

"That was an exciting time," reflected McDonald, "because

A diminutive sparkplug, Fleury is one of the most feisty players hockey has ever seen. He was the Flames' undisputed leader throughout the 1990s and his combination of speed, toughness, and natural scoring touch made him the Calgary Flames' all-time leading scorer.

Theo Fleury

we had talent and grit. We truly believed every time we went out there, we would find a way to win. Running through our minds the whole time was the question, how do we find a way to beat Edmonton? That was where [coach] Badger Bob Johnson came in. He really got us to believe we were good enough. The playoffs in 1984 was really the start of that."

In 1984, the first of Edmonton's five championships in a seven-year span, the Flames pushed the Oilers to seven games. In 1986, they derailed the Oilers' Stanley Cup dynasty by knocking them off in the second round. By 1989, after Edmonton had bounced back to win two more championships, the Flames were on the threshold of greatness themselves.

Gretzky was in Los Angeles, Coffey in Pittsburgh. The Flames boasted a team that included six forwards—McDonald, Joe Mullen, Joe Nieuwendyk, Hakan Loob, Gary Roberts, Theo Fleury—who would score 50 goals at least once in their careers, the only team in NHL history that can make that claim.

For much of the 1980s, they were the two best teams in the league.

"It was a shame that whenever we played Edmonton in the playoffs, it was always a first- or second-round playoff matchup instead of the third round of the Stanley Cup finals. For me, that was by far the most exciting time ever. The neat part about what [GM] Cliff Fletcher did was how he added one more piece to the puzzle every time out. Just try to put our [1989] team together today. Think about the money that it would cost."

By 1989, McDonald's career was starting to wind down. He entered the season needing 11 goals to reach 500 for his career and 12 points to reach 1,000, two milestones that he was anxious to reach. Even more importantly, McDonald stayed on, knowing that the Flames had a respectable chance to win the Stanley Cup. He played only 51 regular-season games that year, as coach Terry Crisp occasionally rotated McDonald out of the lineup. In the playoffs, McDonald dressed for 14 games and scored just one goal. That goal, however, will live on in his mind forever. It was the sixth game of the Stanley Cup finals against the Montreal Canadiens and McDonald, playing sparingly, took a hooking penalty against Bobby Smith in a 1–1 game. His teammates killed off the penalty, and as McDonald emerged from the penalty box, the play turned the other way. Joe Nieuwendyk threaded a pass through the skates of Chris Chelios to McDonald, who put his

head down and beat Patrick Roy with a shot under the crossbar. "Gawd, when that went in. . . ."

Pandemonium reigned. The Flames never trailed the rest of the night and became the only visiting team in NHL history to win the Stanley Cup at the venerable Montreal Forum. His goal

Valeri Bure emerged from the shadow of his superstar brother Pavel during the 1999–2000 season and excited fans as the two played on the same line at the 2000 All-Star game in Toronto.

Team Records

	Career	Season
Goals	Theoren Fleury, 364	Lanny McDonald, 66 (1982–83)
Assists	Al MacInnis, 609	Kent Nilsson, 82 (1980–81)
Points	Theoren Fleury, 830	Kent Nilsson, 131 (1980–81)
Goals-Against Average	Fred Braithwaite, 2.65	Fred Braithwaite, 2.45 (1998–99)
Games Played	Al MacInnis, 803	

of winning a championship achieved, McDonald retired that summer, one of a handful of players in the last 20 years to end their careers on the night they drank champagne from the Stanley Cup.

McDonald's departure coincided with a singular lack of success by the team on the ice. The Flames did not win a single playoff round in the 1990s, even though they went on to finish first or second in their division six times in the next seven years. McDonald moved into a front-office position—as vice president of corporate development—and now his primary objective is to keep the seats filled at the Canadian Airlines Saddledome, during a down time in the team's on-ice fortunes.

"There's frustration in doing what I do now," said McDonald, "in part because of the monetary restraints that we face as an organization. You're out there every day, selling the Flames, whether you're at the 7 Eleven or a minor hockey rink. The sad part of that is, sometimes it's such an uphill battle.

"The difference between playing and working in the front office is this: When you play the game, at the end of it, you've either won or lost. There's either the instant gratification that comes from a win or a reminder of what you need to improve on if you lost. Sometimes, on the business side, it takes a long time to know if a deal is going to come together or not. Coming from the hockey side, that was the biggest lesson. Things don't always happen overnight. It's a building process. You get people onside a little at a time. So you have to be way more patient on the business side."

The Franchise
The timing of the NHL's original flirtation with the Deep South couldn't have been any worse. It was 1972, and just as the league was going into Atlanta, the professional hockey landscape underwent a significant alteration. The World Hockey Association was about to begin, and its presence would skew the game's economics.

"When the original ownership decided they wanted a hockey team in Atlanta," said Cliff Fletcher, the Flames' original general manager, "all of their financial projections were based on how the NHL operated without the WHA. When the WHA started up the same year as Atlanta did, the economics of the league changed in a hurry."

Fletcher did an admirable job of balancing the budget and putting a competitive team on the ice. Unlike their expansion cousins, the New York Islanders, the Flames achieved respectability almost immediately. They qualified for the play-offs in their second year and finished with a winning record for the next five of six seasons. Unhappily, they didn't win a single playoff round in that time, leaving important revenue on the table. Moreover, their singular success produced a series of low first-round draft choices, and while the Islanders were busy drafting a dynasty, the Flames kept adding a series of journeymen players. In the spring of 1980, Atlanta's Tom Cousins sold the team to entrepreneur Nelson Skalbania, who brought the Flames to Calgary. Skalbania promptly sold 49 per cent of the club to a consortium of local oil men and then, as his financial empire began to crumble, eventually left the ownership group altogether.

The Flames played their first three seasons in the tiny Stampede Corral (capacity: 7,242, including standing room) until the Olympic Saddledome was completed in 1983. For the better part of the next 10 years, Flames fans were among the most devoted in the NHL, regularly filling the building to capacity. In the 1990–91 season, two years after they first won the Stanley Cup, the Flames averaged an astonishing 19,986 spectators. These were the team's glory days. They boasted a who's who of NHL stars—from up-and-comers Theo Fleury and Joe Nieuwendyk to established veterans Joe Mullen and Mike Vernon. Between 1987–88 and 1994–95, the Flames won five out of a possible eight division titles, but the curse of the original Atlanta franchise, and its playoff futility, eventually returned to plague the Calgary Flames as well. In the 1990s, despite qualifying for the playoffs six times, the Flames did not win a single playoff round.

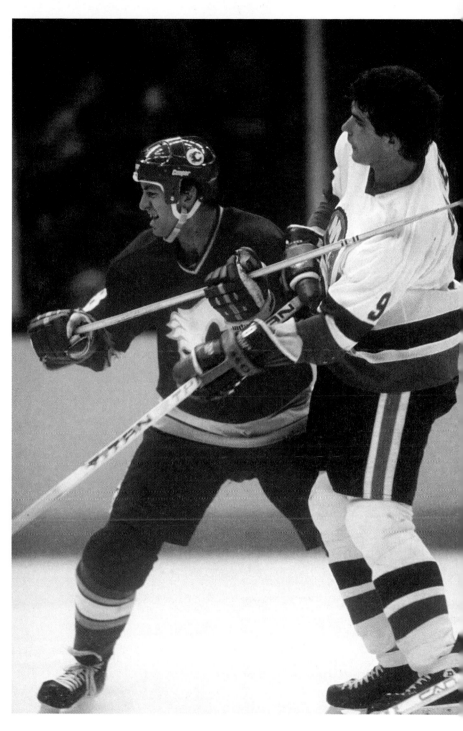

Former Flames' standout Doug Risebrough went on to a long and successful career as an executive in the Calgary organization. He was named vice-president and general manager of the expansion team the Minnesota Wild in 1999.

Carolina Hurricanes

Founded 1997

Formerly the Hartford Whalers, 1979–97

Arenas

Raleigh Entertainment and
  Sports Arena 1999–
  present
Greensboro Coliseum
  1997–99

Stanley Cup Wins
0

Award Winners

Bill Masterton Trophy
Doug Jarvis, 1986–87

Ron Francis of the
Hurricanes battles for
the puck with Petr
Nedved of the New
York Rangers.

Profile

Chosen fourth overall by the Hartford Whalers in the 1981 entry draft, Ron Francis is one of only 9 players in NHL history to score more than 1,500 points. Francis spent almost ten seasons with the Whalers before he was traded to the Pittsburgh Penguins in 1991, where he went on to help the team win the Stanley Cup twice. Signed as an unrestricted free agent by the Carolina Hurricanes after the Whalers' franchise relocated to Raleigh, North Carolina, Francis holds team records in every major statistical category, including games played, goals, assists, and points.

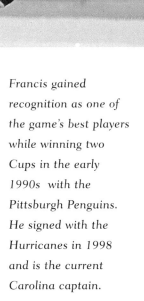

Face to Face

Once upon a time, the Hartford Whalers played all their home games in an arena plunked right in the middle of a downtown shopping mall. Share a home with Sears long enough and you learn to adapt to unusual circumstances.

So it was for the Carolina Hurricanes and their first two seasons in Raleigh-Durham. Peter Karmanos, the team owner, had determined in 1997 that he couldn't make a go of it in Hartford any longer, so he shifted the franchise to the Carolinas. Only problem was, his new home—the Raleigh Entertainment and Sports Arena—wouldn't be ready for occupancy until the start of the 1999–2000 season, or their third year in Carolina. Therefore, for their first two seasons, the newly minted Hurricanes played all their home games in neighboring Greensboro, a 90-minute commute.

Few people from Raleigh wanted to make that drive on a nightly basis and even fewer in Greensboro—knowing they had a lame-duck team—paid to watch the Hurricanes play in their temporary home. It was an unusual way of operating, effectively playing 82 road games per season.

How did that work out, Ron Francis?

"Certainly, it was a little bit of a bizarre situation," replied Francis. "I don't think you can really understand it unless you have to go through it. We all lived and practiced in Raleigh, but our home games were in Greensboro, which was 80 miles away.

Francis gained recognition as one of the game's best players while winning two Cups in the early 1990s with the Pittsburgh Penguins. He signed with the Hurricanes in 1998 and is the current Carolina captain.

49

- 1998–1999: The Hurricanes make the playoffs for the first and only time since the team moved from Hartford. In the first round, Carolina loses to the Boston Bruins in the sixth and final game. When the season ends, the team prepares to move into their new stadium in Raleigh, North Carolina.

- July 13, 1998: The team signs two-time Stanley Cup winner Ron Francis to a free agent contract.

- October 3, 1997: The 'Canes play their first home game vs. the Pittsburgh Penguins.

An intimidating physical presence and a talented scorer, Keith Primeau was the team's captain for the 1998–99 season. When he was unable to reach a contract agreement with the team's management, Primeau sat out the entire 1999–2000 season and Ron Francis took over the captain's duties. Known for his strong opinions and vocal leadership style, Primeau will help fill the leadership role in Philadelphia if Eric Lindros is forced to retire.

So every time you played a home game, you were spending basically two and a half hours on the highway.

"It was difficult to get a sense of how you wanted to work it—whether you wanted to eat and sleep at home, then get up and drive to Greensboro in the afternoon, and then get out of the car after driving an hour and a quarter; or whether you wanted to head down there in the morning and eat there and sleep in the hotel, then play the game, and end up driving home at night. It was a tough situation because technically, you didn't have a home game per se. But it was a situation everybody knew we had to face here and we really just didn't use it as a crutch. That was the way it was, so you dealt with it and went from there."

Francis became a Whaler when Hartford selected him fourth overall in the 1981 entry draft. After he started the 1981–82 season in Sault Ste. Marie (and produced 48 points in 25 games), the Whalers promoted him to the NHL. Francis made an immediate impact, producing 68 points in his first 59 NHL games. Nine years later, Francis was on his way to scoring the quietest 1,000 points in NHL history—at least, until the Whalers traded him and Ulf Samuelsson to the Pittsburgh Penguins on March 4, 1991, arguably the single biggest blunder made by an organization known for its blunders. The Whalers made the playoffs five times in Francis's first nine years, but advanced out of the first round only once. They were just kind of there, existing but without making much of an impact on league consciousness.

Anonymity, thy name was Hartford Whaler.

It was something Francis, a consummate team player, learned to tolerate, if not accept or appreciate.

"The first few years you're in the league, you're just excited to play and you're just trying to prove that you belong," said Francis. "That's the situation I was in. We were trying to build a successful team and I thought that we took strides towards that by 1986. Then, for whatever reason, there were some changes made over the next couple of years that, looking back, hurt our team more than helped it. As a result, we stumbled again. As a professional athlete, you get to this level because you're extremely competitive and you want to win all the time. When you're not able to do that, certainly, it's frustrating.

"But there's other things that evolve over your career. I started in Hartford when I was 18. I was married at 25, I had my first child at 27. Then I got traded four weeks later. I've always been of the school of thought that you're paid to do a job,

Carolina defenseman Steve Chaisson died tragically in a car accident, following the Hurricane's elimination from the playoffs in 1999.

so you go out there and try to do it as well as you can each and every night. I never really was outspoken. I was just willing to work and learn and try to make it better. We had a real good bunch of guys in the mid-80s—a lot of whom are still playing. Ray Ferraro, Ulf Samuelsson, Kevin Dineen, real quality guys and players. We were headed in the right direction. We just never got it to where we wanted to get it."

The detour to Pittsburgh enabled Francis to do what he couldn't do in Hartford—win consecutive Stanley Cup championships in 1991 and 1992, playing for a Penguins team that included Mario Lemieux, Joey Mullen, Kevin Stevens, and a young Jaromir Jagr.

"A lot of players will tell you this: Sitting in Hartford, I had a lot of success, more on the individual than on the team front. In Pittsburgh, we had a lot of success on the team front, but not so much on the individual front. To me, team success is what it's all about. If you have 20 guys playing as well as they can possibly play, accepting their roles and doing them well, then that will give you the best opportunity to win and be successful—and we had that in Pittsburgh.

"From my standpoint, that was extremely rewarding—to accomplish what I had only dreamed about up to that point."

As the Penguins crept towards bankruptcy in the summer of 1998, it became clear that they would not be able to re-sign Francis, an unrestricted free agent. Lemieux had retired by then and was preparing to make an ownership bid for the team; Jagr represented the only untouchable. So Francis cast about for a new NHL home and it turned out the best fit was Carolina, his old Whalers team. It was a homecoming of sorts, in that Francis had a chance to pad all the team records he'd continued to hold, even after a seven-and-a-half-year absence. Much had changed in the interim, however. There was a new general manager, a new coach, a new city, new players.

"Even though it is the former Whalers franchise, it's a long way from when I was a part of it in Hartford."

Now Francis plays in a non-traditional hockey market, one known for college basketball and stock-car racing. Hockey? It remains a curiosity. "It's going to take time to build up the market to where we want it to be simply because we weren't here for the first two years," said Francis.

Gary Roberts retired from hockey in 1996 after what was thought to be a career-ending net injury. After sitting out a year, he returned to the NHL and successfully rejuvenated his hockey career. The former 50 goal scorer played three seasons with the Hurricanes before signing as a free agent with the Toronto Maple Leafs in July 2000.

Team Lowlights

- May 3, 1999: Hurricanes defenseman Steve Chaisson is killed in a drunk driving accident on his way home from a team function.

"Even though we lived in Raleigh, nobody knew us or got to see us on a day-in, day-out basis. Now, with our new arena, it's made us a lot more accessible to fans. It's still in the growing stages of them learning about our sport and the players and who we are. From our standpoint, it's certainly made it easier to do our jobs every day, but we all understand, there's still some more work to be done. You have to spend time with the people, trying to educate them and interest them in becoming Hurricane fans."

It's not the sort of assignment you think about when you're a teenager, looking to break into the NHL—that apart from goals, assists, and championships, part of your job description will become sales.

"It's true," said Francis. "With the evolution of the game and reaching further and further into some southern markets where people didn't expect hockey to be 10 years ago, there is another element in the equation—answering questions, educating fans, letting them get to know you. It's an interesting new part of the game."

The Franchise Much of the cachet associated with the Hartford Whalers in their early days revolved around the presence of Hall of Famer Gordie Howe, who played for them in their inaugural NHL season, 1979–80, and posted a wholly respectable 15-goal, 41-point year—as a 51-year-old grandfather. For Howe, the attraction was a chance to play in the NHL again after an eight-year absence—two years spent in retirement, six playing in the World Hockey Association. That season, he had a chance to play with his sons Mark and Marty in Hartford. Marty, a journeyman defenseman, played only six NHL games in the 1979–80 season and spent the rest of the time in Springfield, but Mark was slowly evolving into an NHL star. Indeed, the Whalers' decision to trade Mark Howe in 1982—for Ken Linseman, Greg Adams, and a pair of draft choices—was one of many ill-advised deals that kept the franchise from the upper regions of the standings. After qualifying for the playoffs in their first NHL season, the Whalers proceeded to miss post-season action five years in a row. In 1986, they won their one and only playoff series in franchise history, defeating the division champion Quebec Nordiques. The Whalers pushed the eventual Stanley Cup champions, the Montreal Canadiens, to overtime of the seventh game, before Claude Lemieux scored the winner, eliminating Hartford. The city responded to their surge by staging a parade on behalf of the team, even though they hadn't actually won a thing. The next year, they were able to hang a banner in the Hartford Coliseum because the improving Whalers won the Adams Division regular-season title. Only problem was, the Nordiques—the team they'd upset the year before in the playoffs—returned the favor and ousted them in the opening round, the first of six consecutive opening-round defeats they would suffer. It got worse before it got better. Following the 1991–92 season, the Whalers stopped qualifying for the playoffs altogether, missing post-season play during their final five seasons in Hartford. In 1994, as the city hosted the NHL entry draft, the Whalers were sold to Detroit computer king Peter Karmanos. With crowds dwindling and the state showing little interest in helping to finance a new facility, Karmanos finally shifted the franchise to Carolina for the start of the 1997–98 season. The newly christened Hurricanes missed the playoffs in their inaugural season, but they qualified in 1998–99, only to lose in the opening round to the Boston Bruins, a perennial rival in their Hartford days. That night, upon their return home to Carolina, popular defenseman Steve Chiasson was killed in a single-vehicle accident following a post-season get-together at a teammate's house.

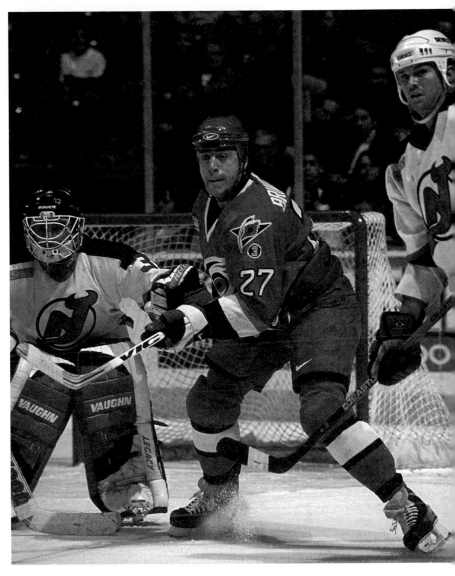

An NHL ironman known for his durability, Rod Brind'amour was acquired in a trade with the Philadelphia Flyers for holdout center, Keith Primeau.

Team Records

	Career	Season
Goals	Ron Francis, 308	Blaine Stoughton, 56 (1979–80)
Assists	Ron Francis, 638	Ron Francis, 69 (1989–90)
Points	Ron Francis, 946	Mike Rogers, 105 (1979–80 and 1980–81)
Goals-Against Average	Arturs Irbe 2.33	Trevor Kidd, 2.17 (1997–98)
Games Played	Ron Francis, 834	

Chicago Blackhawks

Founded 1926

Arenas
United Center 1995–
    present
Chicago Stadium
    1929–1994
Chicago Coliseum
    1926–1929

Stanley Cup Wins
1960–61, 1937–38,
    1933–34

Award Winners

see page 252

One of the best
defensemen of his
generation, Chris
Chelios was a stalwart
on the Chicago blue
line until 1999 when,
in an effort to rebuild
the franchise with
youth, Blackhawks
management traded
him to the Detroit Red
Wings.

Profile

Glenn Hall joined the Blackhawks in a 1957 trade with the Detroit Red Wings and played 10 starry seasons in a Chicago uniform. In an NHL career that spanned 18 years in all, he won 407 regular-season games and was a first-team all-star seven times. He won the Calder Memorial Trophy, the Conn Smythe Trophy and three Vezina Trophies. Along the way, he established a record for endurance that may never be broken, playing in 502 consecutive games between Oct. 6, 1955 and Nov. 7, 1962 when he left the 503 game against the Boston Bruins because of a back injury.

Face to Face

Of the many and varied myths that surround the career of Glenn Hall, perhaps none is as universally misunderstood—and widely mistold—as his habit of upchucking before every single Chicago Blackhawks' game.

Glenn Hall

Yes, Hall will admit, it happened—and it happened a lot more, the older he got. But in every game? On the ice? Or at the bench, during a break in the play? No. Hall could be a bundle of jangling nerves, all right, but there was a method to his madness.

"As I got older, I got to the point where I felt I played better if I really put the pressure on myself," said Hall. "So as part of my preparation, I'd work myself up and drink a glass of water and then throw it up and that would be it.

"I'd read articles that they'd stop the games so I could throw up. That didn't happen. There's more fiction than fact in some of these stories that go around. Certainly, the butterflies were there, but you wanted them there. You can't play the game if you don't put pressure on yourself. To play at a higher level, you need to scratch and claw. This is what I found out, when I was playing at a higher level, it was because I did get sick (before games)."

They called Hall The Ghoulie and it only takes one glance at his paler-than-white face to understand why. There is a ghostly cast to his complexion, even today, at 69 and it is firmly enshrined in the Hockey Hall of Fame. Hall spent 10 full seasons playing for the Blackhawks and is one of five players to have his number (1) retired by the team. He was there too for the only

Jocelyn Thibault makes a kick save in the Chicago net. Thibault was traded to Chicago on November 26, 1998 for fellow goalie Jeff Hackett.

Stanley Cup that the venerable National Hockey League team won in the second half of the 20th century, one shining moment for an otherwise star-crossed franchise. That came in the spring of 1961 when the Blackhawks ended the Montreal Canadiens' record-run of five consecutive Stanley Cup championships, with a stunning first-round upset. The Blackhawks finished in third place in the regular season, with barely more wins (29) than losses (24). That earned them a semifinal meeting with the Canadiens and after splitting the first four games, the Blackhawks swept the last two, behind Hall's spectacular, consecutive shutouts.

They followed virtually the same script in the finals against the Detroit Red Wings—the team that traded Hall and Ted Lindsay to Chicago in July of 1957—trading wins in the first four games before going to win the championship in Detroit in the sixth game. Hall's teammates lifted him up onto their shoulders and carried him off the ice. Had there been a Conn Smythe Trophy back then, Hall would have surely been its recipient. He surrendered only the 12 goals in six games during the finals.

"It was a great satisfaction, a great relief to win the Stanley Cup," said Hall. "When the season comes to an end and you've given everything you have, you take a deep breath and say, 'boy, isn't it great that you don't have to put that stinking equipment on again.' There was a lot of emotion in there. We didn't know how to act afterwards. We had Ab MacDonald there and Ab had won the Stanley Cup the year before with Montreal, so we told him, 'he was in charge of how we acted.' Consequently, we didn't act very well."

The Blackhawks won the Stanley Cup on the road in Detroit, but weather conditions grounded their plane, so they were obliged to stay overnight in the Motor City.

The fact of winning the game on the road denied the Blackhawks the chance to clinch in the always raucous Chicago Stadium, arguably the loudest building in the league for much of its existence. Playing there, feeding off the excitement of the crowd, was one of the more memorable parts of the Blackhawk playing experience for Hall.

"A woman, an acquaintance, once asked me, 'doesn't the noise in the Chicago Stadium bother you?' I said, 'no, you just blank it out.' She said: 'BS, don't tell me you can blank out the noise in Chicago Stadium.' I said, 'Well, there was always this one guy I could hear.' She said: 'Aha, I thought so. What was he saying?' He was saying: "Cold beer, get yer cold beer.'

"That was it. You certainly hear what you want to hear. I always told friends who were going to games, 'Be sure you don't get there late, you want to get the national anthem. It's something.' I remember talking to (former Blackhawks' teammate) Al MacNeil about this. One night, the crowd was really going crazy. I didn't say a word to him and he didn't say a word to me, but the hair was really standing up on the back of my neck. Finally, he gives me an elbow in the ribs and says, 'Kinda makes you want to join the army, eh?' I thought, 'That's perfect'—because it does. Or it did. If you went there and didn't feel anything during that national anthem, well, something's wrong."

Team Highlights

- 1999-2000: After several disappointing seasons the Chicago Blackhawks appear to be rebuilding. By trading veteran players, including Hawks legend Chris Chelios, and center Doug Gilmour, the team manages to collect an impressive pool of young talent to complement veteran scorers like Tony Amonte. Under General Manager Mike Smith the team takes on a more European flavor and announces the signing of former Maple Leafs assistant, Alpo Suhonen as their new head coach.

- 1969–70: Tony Esposito sets a modern-day NHL record with 15 shutouts in the season.

- March 12, 1966: Bobby Hull becomes the first player in NHL history to score more than 50 goals in a season.

Statistically, the Blackhawks put together better regular seasons in each of the next six years that led up to the 1967 NHL expansion, but they could not duplicate their Stanley Cup success. Twice they made it to the finals and lost; four other times, they exited in the first round. This was their Golden Age, a team that included Bobby Hull and Stan Mikita and Pierre Pilote and, for a time, a young Phil Esposito.

"We didn't win as many Stanley Cups as we would have liked," said Hall. "People ask why. I believe people downplay how good Toronto and Montreal were. We had Bobby Hull and Stan Mikita and Phil Esposito and some real good sound hockey players. But Montreal had Beliveau, Henri Richard, and others. Their offensive game was really good; Toronto's defensive game was really good. We were explosive, but in the playoffs, everybody else said, 'look, we've got to keep the puck out of our net.' It's common sense. If you're in one end, you try to put the puck in the net. If you're in the other end, you try to keep the puck out of the net. This stuff of trying to score goals from the other end, it doesn't work that way. Chicago, we were so good with our offensive plays, we just felt we could outgun them. It's hard to outgun teams playing good, smart hockey."

Hall was there at the forefront of one of the game's most innovative moments, the development of the curved stick. Once, in a practice, Mikita cracked the middle of his stick blade. Rather than tromp all the way back to the dressing room, Mikita kept shooting until it broke clear through. Instead of going in a straight line, Mikita discovered the puck began to dip and dive as it flew towards the net. Soon Mikita began to tinker with his blade and Hull followed suit. Sometimes, Hall was the guinea pig; sometimes, it would be the board that they draped in front of the other goal.

"That's what almost made the mask essential," said Hall. "Stan was practicing with a broken stick and he was getting good wood on it. Then everybody, all the big shooters, started doing it. They'd cut the shot and everybody started to duck."

Hull, an electrifying player, broke the single-season goal-scoring record twice during his Blackhawks' years.

"When Stan and Bobby were on top of their games in Chicago, someone asked (Blackhawks' teammate) Lou Angotti what's the difference between the two of them. Lou answered: 'Bobby will mug you in the park; Stan will pick your pocket.' They get the same results, they just go about them a little

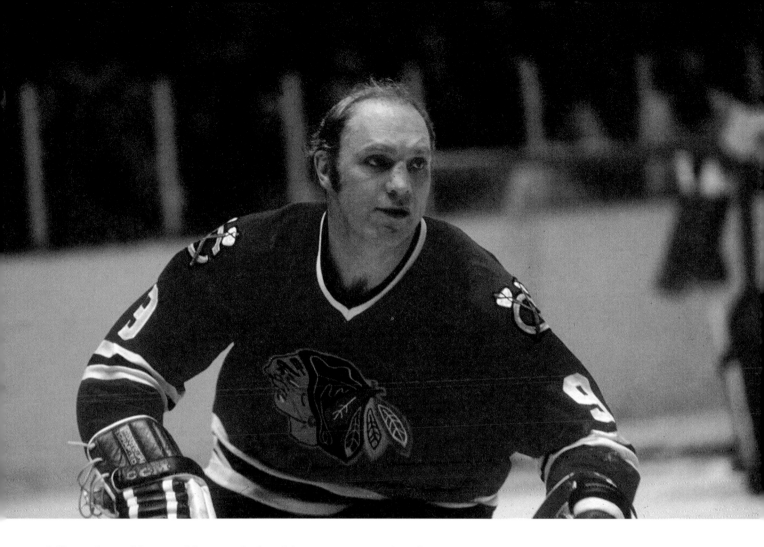

differently. Bobby would come behind his own net and gather speed. When he wound up, the whole crowd was on its feet. Just the power he had, they knew something was going to happen."

Hall left the Blackhawks following the 1966–67 season, but not before establishing an NHL record that will never be broken—playing every minute of 502 consecutive regular-season games. Add in his 49 playoff games in a row, and Hall played more than 30,000 consecutive minutes in goal for Chicago and Detroit before a back injury made it too painful for him to continue.

Hall actually intended to retire in 1966, at the age of 34, but was talked out of it by general manager Tommy Ivan. Thus began a second myth that follows Hall around even today—that he would perpetually miss training camp on the grounds that he had to paint his barn every fall. The barn yarn didn't even begin until Hall figured his career had come to a close.

"With all the retirements you see today, geez, it's such big

Nicknamed the "Golden Jet," Bobby Hull terrified goaltenders throughout the league with his incredible slap shot. One of the game's most charismatic players, Hull owns Chicago records for most total goals and most goals in a season. He is one of a handful of NHL players to ever break the 600-goal mark.

Team Lowlights

- March 23, 1999: Faced with the prospect of rebuilding after several disappointing seasons, the Hawks trade fan favorite Chris Chelios to the Detroit Red Wings.

news," said Hall, "but this is how things were back then: At the end of the 1966 season, I told Tommy: 'I think I've had enough. I'm going to retire.' He said, 'OK, OK.' I never heard from him again, except when you get the notice in the mail that training camp starts on such-and-such a day. That came, I read it, I pitched it out and never thought of it again. Then, all of a sudden, I start to get telephone calls from people, reporters, 'Why wasn't I in training camp?' I said, 'Just ask Tommy.' I had been painting the barn because I had been doing some farming, but by then, I was sitting there with a six pack. I mean, I had retired.

"Now, I didn't realize it at the time, but why they wanted me back was there an expansion year coming up. So all of a sudden, they were interested in me playing for another year. Finally, they said, 'Well, if you come back, we'll pay you.' I said, 'Holy Christ, that's a change. You're going to pay me?' It became so attractive that a guy had to play. I didn't like to go to training camp anyways. Training camp, in those days, was for conditioning purposes—and I stayed in pretty good shape. I felt there was only so many saves in the system, don't throw them away in practice.

"So, the next year, when I was in St. Louis, they were really good about me missing camp. They said, 'if you get there late, fine.' So it would always get out that I was late for camp because I was painting the barn. I really wasn't painting the barn. That was just an easy out."

The Franchise

In 1926, Major Frederic McLaughlin —a coffee baron and expert polo player—paid a $12,000 franchise fee to the National Hockey League for the rights to put a new team into Chicago. McLaughlin named his team the Blackhawks because he had served as commander of the 333rd Machine-Gun Battalion of the 85th (or Blackhawk) division of the U.S. Army during World War 1. McLaughlin's third wife— Irene Castle, a world-renowned ballroom dancer—designed the uniforms around Black Hawk, a famous 19th century Indian chief, whose likeness became the teams' popular logo. McLaughlin stocked his team by purchasing outright the Portland Rosebuds of the Western Hockey League from Frank and Lester Patrick for $200,000. The Blackhawks played a handful of seasons in the Chicago Coliseum before construction was completed on their new home the 18,000-seat Stadium. In the early 1930s, the heroics of goaltender Charlie Gardiner kept the Blackhawks' team competitive. Gardiner's

Tony Esposito dives across the crease to make a spectacular glove save.

Denis Savard played most of his career with the Blackhawks but was traded to the Montreal Canadiens for Chris Chelios in 1990. Savard would win the Stanley Cup with the Canadiens, returned to Chicago in 1995, and finished his career as a Blackhawk in 1997.

culminating moment of glory came in the 1933–34 season in which he allowed one goal or fewer in 24 of the Blackhawks' 48 games and posted an impressive 1.63 goals-against average. Gardiner was even stingier in the play-offs, surrendering only 12 goals in eight appearances, which helped the Blackhawks capture their first-ever Stanley Cup. Two months later, as he walked the streets in his hometown of Winnipeg, Gardiner collapsed and died of a brain hemorrhage. He was 29. He had played only seven NHL seasons. The Blackhawks accomplished little of consequence in the next four regular seasons, until the goaltending of Gardiner's replacement, Mike Karakas, helped them record one of the most stunning upsets in Stanley Cup history. That 1937–38 season, the Blackhawks won only 14 of 48 regular-season games, but squeezed into the playoffs anyway and then proceeded to upset the Montreal Canadiens and the New York Americans in the first two rounds, largely on the strength of Karakas' excellent play. However, in the last game of the semifinals, Karakas broke a toe, leaving the Blackhawks without a goaltender. The Toronto Maple Leafs, their opponents in the Stanley Cup finals, wouldn't agree to the Blackhawks' request to use the New York Rangers' Dave Kerr. Instead, they recommended Alfie Moore, who'd spent the year playing for Pittsburgh. Pittsburgh's season was over by then and Moore was back in Toronto for the summer. Bill Stewart, the Blackhawks' coach, dispatched a pair of his players to find Moore and get him to the arena on time. They discovered him in a local watering hole, sobered him up and put him between the pipes for the opening game, which eventually was won by Chicago. The Leafs, stung by their blunder, asked that Moore be disqualified for the second game. By then, the Blackhawks were able to get their own spare goaltender, Paul Goodman, to town for a game that Toronto won. As the series shifted to Chicago, Karakas was ready to play and the Blackhawks won two straight at home to capture the second of their Stanley Cup championships. In doing so, they upset a Maple Leafs' team that had won the Canadian division with 57 points, 20 more than the Blackhawks. That, unhappily, represented the high point of the next two decades, as the Blackhawks missed the playoffs altogether in 14 of the next 22 seasons. Following their 1961 championship, the Blackhawks stayed respectable for much of the next 35 years, aided in part by a transfer to the NHL's Western Division following the 1970 expansion. In the 1991–92 season, under coach Mike Keenan, the Blackhawks qualified for the finals again for the first time in 19 years, but were eliminated by Mario Lemieux's Pittsburgh Penguins in four consecutive games. The Blackhawks finally left the Chicago Stadium for newer, glitzier digs for the start of the 1994–95 season, transferring across the street to the United Center, where they've played ever since.

Hall of Famers Bobby Hull and Stan Mikita share a laugh in the locker room before a game. Hull is Chicago's all-time leading goalscorer and Mikita their all-time points leader.

Team Records

	Career	Season
Goals	Bobby Hull, 604	Bobby Hull, 58 (1968–69)
Assists	Stan Mikita, 926	Denis Savard, 87 (1981–82 and 1987–88)
Points	Stan Mikita, 1,467	Denis Savard, 131 (1987–88)
Goals-Against Average	Chuck Gardiner, 2.02	Chuck Gardiner, 1.63 (1933–34)
Games Played	Stan Mikita, 1,394	

Colorado Avalanche

Founded 1995

Formerly Quebec Nordiques, 1979–95

Arenas
Pepsi Center 1999–present
McNichols Arena
   1995–1999

Stanley Cup Wins 1
1995–96

Award Winners

Jack Adams Award
Marc Crawford, 1994–95

Calder Trophy
Chris Drury, 1998–99
Peter Forsberg, 1994–95
Peter Stastny, 1980–81

Conn Smythe Trophy
Joe Sakic, 1995–96

Defenseman Uwe Krupp scored the Stanley Cup winning goal for the Colorado Avalanche versus the Florida Panthers in 1996.

Profile Joe Sakic became the highest-scoring player in Quebec Nordiques/Colorado Avalanche history in the 1999–2000 season, surpassing the 1,048 points scored by Hall of Famer Peter Stastny. Winning the Conn Smythe Trophy as the playoffs' most valuable player in the Avalanche's 1996 Stanley Cup victory, Sakic also became the 56th player in NHL history to score 1,000 points in the 1999–2000 season.

Face to Face True story: For reasons even he is hard pressed to explain sometimes, Joe Sakic grew up in Burnaby, British Columbia as a fan of . . . the Quebec Nordiques?

"Maybe it was because I liked their home uniforms," said Sakic, with a smile. "Or maybe it was because I hated Montreal so much. They played each other a lot in the playoffs and I always cheered for Quebec—because I didn't want the Canadiens to win."

Ultimately, Sakic would receive a chance to get up close and personal with those cool, home uniforms—white, with blue and red trim and a series of fleurs-de-lis below the crests and numbers—after the Nordiques made him their first choice, 15th overall, in the 1987 entry draft. Sakic is 5-foot-11, 185 pounds, and in an era when size mattered, 14 shortsighted teams gave him a pass because of concerns over his stature. Too bad, because Sakic eventually evolved into one of the highest-scoring player from his draft class, the only one to win the Conn Smythe Trophy as the playoff's most valuable player.

They say good things come to those who wait—and Sakic waited a long time for his dreams to come true. The year before he was eligible for the draft, Sakic was involved in one of the greatest tragedies in Canadian hockey history, when a bus carrying members of the Swift Current Broncos junior team crashed on an icy Saskatchewan highway, killing four of his teammates.

Sakic, a first-year player on the team, took control of the

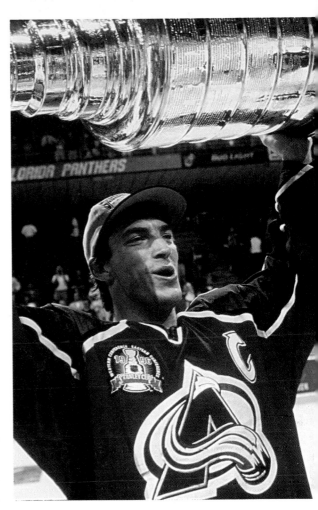

Colorado captain Joe Sakic celebrates Colorado's 1996 Stanley Cup victory.

Peter Forsberg is one of the NHL's most dominant players combining strength, toughness, and outstanding offensive skills. He has also been a key member of the Swedish National Team.

team in the aftermath of the accident and led them into the playoffs. More challenges followed upon his arrival in Quebec in the final stages of the Peter Stastny-Michel Goulet era. The Nordiques were one of the NHL's most pleasing offensive teams from 1981 to 1986, a threat to record an upset every time they qualified for the NHL playoffs.

Unhappily, Sakic didn't arrive in Quebec until the start of the 1988–89 season, when the team's talent base had already started to erode. Sakic had a wholly respectable 62 points in 70 games

in his first NHL season, but by the end of year two, the Nordiques had already decided changes were in order. Stastny was traded to the New Jersey Devils, Goulet to the Chicago Blackhawks. That year, Sakic's second full NHL season, the Nordiques won a grand total of only 12 games. Their 31 points represented one of the most futile seasons in NHL history. In all, the Nordiques missed the playoffs for five consecutive seasons. Sakic quietly went about the business of scoring more than a point a game in the last three of those years, but without an effective supporting cast, his contributions did little other than to keep the games closer than they otherwise might have been.

The Nordiques' struggles eventually paid off in a series of high draft choices and the cycle began to reverse itself. Thanks in part to the yield of players and draft choices harvested by general manager Pierre Page when he traded Eric Lindros's playing rights to the Philadelphia Flyers, the Nordiques were magically revived in a single, stirring season. They went from a 52-point also-ran to a 104-point contender, and that 1992–93 season, says Sakic, stands out as the highlight of his seven years in Nordiques colors.

"Everybody talked about what a good hockey town Quebec was and they supported us real well when we were terrible," began Sakic, "but we never really realized how good a hockey town it was until my fifth year, after we made the Eric trade. We had a great year and it was unbelievable how that city responded, the pride they showed. There was a sense of 'Here's our team, we're coming now.'"

Unhappily, they were going soon afterwards.

The Nordiques' last two years in Quebec featured a series of controversies over the aging Colisée, a building that neither ownership nor the provincial government was prepared to upgrade. Faced with dwindling attendance in an era of ever-escalating costs, the Nordiques were sold to the COMSAT Entertainment Group and shifted to Denver, Colorado.

A previous NHL foray into Denver had failed 13 years previously when the Colorado Rockies were shifted to New Jersey. In that time, the city had grown significantly and the perception was that Denver would support a team this time around, provided it was competitive and entertaining. The 1995–96 Colorado Avalanche were all that and more.

By then, center Peter Forsberg, the principal player acquired in the Lindros deal, had evolved into an NHL star in his own right. Patrick Roy, goalie twice for Stanley Cup champions, had

Patrick Roy demonstrates perfect butterfly-style goaltending as he blocks the Colorado net.

been acquired in a trade with the Canadiens to solidify the goal-tending. Other astute trades produced more quality talent: Sandis Ozolinsh, Claude Lemieux, Sylvain Lefebvre.

In one astonishing leap forward, the team that had lost so badly in the opening round of the 1995 playoffs to the New York Rangers ended up winning it all the next year, their first in Colorado. Sakic produced sensational numbers that season too—120 regular-season points, plus a league-leading 34 in the playoffs, good enough to win the Conn Smythe award.

"That was the greatest thrill in my career," said Sakic. "You go to a new city and everybody's new, everything's different. In the beginning, you're learning about everything, just trying to find your way around. On the ice, you're winning games and you end up winning the Stanley Cup. For us players, it was pretty exciting to see how the city supported a first-year team right from the first day. It was probably just some hard-core hockey fans that came out at first, but as every playoff round went by, the whole city and the whole state started to embrace us. All they talked about was hockey. Then the parade, that was incredible, all these people lined up downtown, cheering for us. We weren't expecting that. It was pretty incredible."

The Avalanche continued to roll along, winning their Division championship every year in its first four seasons in Colorado. From a player's perspective, the biggest change was in venue. The Avs played in McNichols Arena for their first four seasons, during construction of the Pepsi Center. McNichols was home to the Colorado Rockies in the late 1970s and early 1980s, but it was already showing signs of its age when the Avalanche first arrived. The Pepsi Center debuted for the start of the 1999–2000 season and Sakic will tell you, "It's a lot more fun playing there than McNichols, a lot more fun going to the rink. I mean, in the old rink, you'd park and walk by a dumpster and it just reeked. So we don't have that. As for everything else, the hockey hasn't changed. It's a great building. I would rate it for hockey second behind Toronto. You're not going to beat Toronto because it still has that Maple Leaf Gardens mystique about it—that they brought over. Everything about it is pretty cool."

By the end of the 1999–2000 season, Sakic had become the team's all-time leading scorer, overtaking Peter Stastny, his former teammate in the Quebec days.

"Peter got traded my second year right around the trading

Team Highlights

- **June 10, 1996:** The Avalanche defeat the Florida Panthers in the Stanley Cup finals to win the Cup in their first year in Denver.

- **December 6, 1995:** Colorado acquires legendary goaltender Patrick Roy from the Montreal Canadiens.

- **October 6, 1995:** The Avalanche play their first game in Colorado, defeating the Detroit Red Wings 3–2.

The final piece in the Avalanche's Stanley Cup puzzle, Patrick Roy backstopped Colorado to Stanley Cup victory in 1996. One of the most intense competitors the game has ever seen, Roy was poised during the 2000–01 season to break Terry Sawchuk's record for wins by a goaltender, during the 2000–01 season.

Team Lowlights

- May 29, 1996: During the playoffs, Colorado's Claude Lemieux checks Detroit's Kris Draper into the boards, breaking several bones in his face. This incident leads to an ugly brawl and a bitter rivalry between the two teams that lasts for years.

deadline. He was a real complete player and a classy guy. He was in the same mold as Bryan Trottier. If he wanted to be physical, he was a bull out there. You couldn't move him around. He was definitely a complete package.

"Playing in Quebec, it wasn't a problem not being able to speak French. Hockey-wise, you're on the road a lot anyway. When you're there and you go out, you get by. I had high-school French, but not very good high-school French, because I didn't do very well in it—but I remembered some of the stuff I did learn. You had to work at it a little bit, but you learn enough to get by. I didn't find it to be too much of a problem."

The Franchise
The Quebec Nordiques entered the NHL as part of the WHA merger in 1979 and made an immediate splash in the summer of 1980 by orchestrating the defection of Czech hockey stars Peter and Anton Stastny. More than two decades later, the presence of Czechs and Russians in the NHL is something less than newsworthy, but back then? It was a highly charged issue—politically, socially, and for the long-term future of the league. The flight of the Stastnys read like something out of a Len Deighton thriller, slipping across borders, ever fearful of being apprehended by security on their way to the free world. The two younger Stastnys—who were later joined by their older sibling, Marian—proved that there was little wrong with the state of the game in Czechoslovakia. As a 24-year-old rookie, Peter Stastny won the 1981 Calder Trophy as the NHL's rookie of the year, scoring 109 points in his inaugural year, the second-highest rookie points total in history.

It didn't take long for the Nordiques to build a contender. In addition to the Stastnys and Michel Goulet, they also drafted and traded wisely. The presence of agitating Dale Hunter, who was later swapped for the draft choice that resulted in Joe Sakic's selection, plus goaltender Daniel Bouchard gave the Nordiques instant credibility and established the foundation for one of the 1980s great rivalries, the Battle of Quebec. Perhaps the seminal moment of the team's Quebec history came in the 1982 playoffs when the Nordiques eliminated Montreal in the best-of-five preliminary round, moving on to the second round while the storied Habs went home. The Nordiques made another splash at the Canadiens' expense when they signed Guy Lafleur as a free agent in 1989, following his bitter falling out with the Montreal organization. Lafleur retired in 1984, at the age of 33, but returned to the NHL four years later with the New York Rangers. Following a year in New York, Lafleur signed with the Nordiques and played two more seasons in Quebec, where he'd starred as a junior, before retiring again at age 39.

On the ice, the Nordiques were struggling by the early 1990s. That, plus a growing Quebec separatist movement, made it difficult to attract English-speaking players to the provincial capital, which was mostly a unilingual francophone city. The problem came into sharp focus in 1991 when the Nordiques drafted Eric Lindros with the first overall pick and he flatly refused to sign a contract with them. Following a year-long stalemate, the Nordiques turned a negative into a positive, acquiring a flotilla of reinforcements from Philadelphia—Peter Forsberg, Steve Duchesne, Kerry Huffman, Mike Ricci, Ron Hextall, Chris Simon, as well as draft choices that produced Jocelyn Thibault—in exchange for Lindros. That group of players, with the talent already on hand, established the base for a decade of on-ice prosperity that carried over into the new millennium.

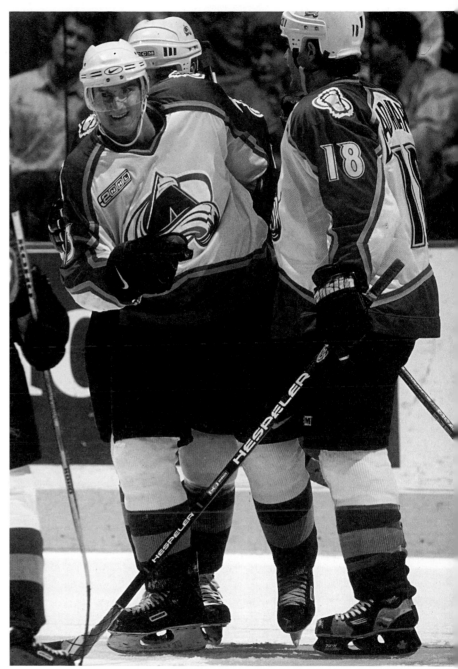

Ray Bourque was acquired from Boston to help the Avalanche in their pursuit of the 2000 Stanley Cup.

Team Records

	Career	Season
Goals	Michel Goulet, 456	Michel Goulet, 57 (1982–83)
Assists	Peter Stastny, 668	Peter Stastny, 93 (1981–82)
Points	Joe Sakic, 1,060	Peter Stastny, 139 (1981–82)
Goals-Against Average	Patrick Roy, 2.37	Patrick Roy, 2.28 (1999–2000)
Games Played	Joe Sakic, 852	

Dallas Stars

Founded 1993

Formerly the Minnesota North Stars, 1967–93

Arenas
Reunion Arena 1993–present

Stanley Cup Wins
1998-99

Award Winners

Calder Trophy
Bobby Smith, 1978–79
Danny Grant, 1968–69

Jenning Trophy
Ed Belfour and Roman Turek, 1998–99

Bill Masterton Trophy
Al MacAdam, 1979–80

Frank J. Selke Trophy
Jere Lehtinen, 1998–99, 1997–98

Conn Smythe Trophy
Joe Nieuwendyk, 1998–99

Brett Hull, one of the most feared goalscorers in the NHL, won the Stanley Cup with the Dallas Stars in 1999.

Profile

Bob Gainey joined the then Minnesota North Stars as their head coach in June 1990 and immediately led the team to the 1991 Stanley Cup finals. He took on the dual role of coach and GM in 1992, the same year he was elected to the Hockey Hall of Fame, and held both positions until 1996, when he turned the coaching reins over to Ken Hitchcock. In Gainey's 16-year playing career with the Montreal Canadiens, the team won the Stanley Cup five times. He was the 1979 Conn Smythe Trophy winner and also won the Selke award as the league's top defensive player in four consecutive years (1978–81). Upon retiring in 1989, he coached a tier-two team in Epinal, France.

Face to Face

He had earned five previous Stanley Cup rings as a player with the Montreal Canadiens, but in 1993, for Bob Gainey, the coach and general manager of the stumbling Minnesota North Stars, it didn't look as if a sixth championship was coming anytime soon.

The team had missed the playoffs and attendance was on the decline. As a result, team owner Norman Green, who had grown tired of trying to sell professional hockey in a market that preferred the college and high-school game, moved his money-losing team to Dallas and renamed it the Stars.

Gainey recalled, "That was an expansion year, which helped us to make a couple of changes in the summer. Teams had protection problems and we were able to pick up a couple of players, so the team we began with in Dallas was really a stronger team than the one we finished with in Minneapolis.

"That year turned out to be a really good entrance year in Dallas. We finished 13 points above .500 and won our opening round of the playoffs.

"We had a lot of anxiety, and rightfully so, about going to a non-hockey environment but it was a good competitive year for us to make an entry into the community."

Dallas represented the NHL's first incursion into Texas, a

Bob Gainey

Kirk Muller (#22) began the 1999–2000 season without an NHL contract. He was eventually signed by the Dallas Stars and proved that he could still be a valuable member of an NHL team.

market so far removed from the league's beaten path that most of the people associated with the Stars had never even visited the city, let alone lived there.

"None of us knew about Dallas," Gainey said. "I remember when I found out we were going to Dallas, I had to go down to a bookstore and get a book and actually place it geographically, because I'd never been there before.

"No one was really sure what was going to happen in Dallas, but within a year, I would say that all those concerns were put aside and everyone could see the change from a much more positive point of view."

During the 1995–96 season, the Stars changed hands. Tom Hicks, a wealthy sports entrepreneur who also owns baseball's Texas Rangers, bought the team from Green, thereby allowing the Stars to compete in the big-money atmosphere that was just staring to make its impact on the NHL.

"I remember being in a meeting with Norm and the guy who did the sales and marketing," said Gainey. "Norm said, 'Now this is the person who spends the money. You have to get the money,' and that was sort of how we worked.

"But when the ownership changed, it wasn't a question of money being able to get you players right away because there weren't any unrestricted players. They just weren't there. You got players through the draft or you got players through trade. There were cases of holdouts because salaries were escalating through the first five years of the nineties, but it wasn't really a case of deciding that you wanted to spend another million dollars to get another player because they just weren't there. That happened a bit later."

Gainey coached the team in those early years in Dallas but in January 1996, Gainey the GM fired Gainey the coach.

"We went through maybe 20 games where we played really well and would lose by a goal," he explained. "When you're a player and that happens, the message that's coming from the coach's office gets to be hard to believe. You're following that message to a T, but the results aren't there.

"Our team had lost its energy for me, but I thought there was still time in the season for us to possibly salvage that year."

That was one of the factors in the transformation of the Stars from just another team to one of the NHL's elite squads. "There were three things and they all happened within a few months there," Gainey said. "One would have been being able to trade for Joe Nieuwendyk. The others were Tom Hicks coming in as owner and Ken Hitchcock coming in as coach. All of that would have happened between November of 1995 and January of 1996."

At the same, time, with Nieuwendyk providing the peer pressure and Hitchcock providing the coaching pressure, Mike Modano began to blossom as a superstar. That too was to be instrumental in the team's emergence.

Realizing that his team had moved into the ranks of the contenders, Gainey began to fill in the gaps, making all the little moves that are needed to build a championship team. He not only wanted the Cup, as all hockey people do, he wanted to establish the Stars in Dallas before the novelty wore off.

"My feeling was that to really penetrate and really become a regular participant in professional sports in the community then you needed to win a championship," he said.

"I base that on teams like the Philadelphia Flyers. They were able to win a championship and root themselves in their community. Pittsburgh floundered for 25 years and then they won championships and then Pittsburgh became a much, much stronger hockey town.

Mike Modano overcame a frightening neck injury at the start of the 1999–2000 season, which had him questioning whether he wanted to continue his NHL career and return to help lead the Dallas Stars to the Stanley Cup Finals. Although they would eventually lose in their bid to repeat as Stanley Cup champions, Modano demonstrated that he had matured into a team leader. Always a sensational offensive player, Modano possesses explosive speed and has developed into an unselfish leader and a solid defensive performer, making one of the most exciting and dependable players in the game today.

Team Highlights

- June 19, 1999: The Stars win their first Stanley Cup over the Buffalo Sabres on a controversial goal scored by Brett Hull.

- July 3, 1998: Dallas signs star winger Brett Hull to a free agent contract.

- April 18, 1998: The Stars win the President's Trophy for most points during the regular season.

Mike Modano

"I felt that in Dallas, if we were going to put down roots that were going to stay for hockey, we really needed to push for a championship. When we did accomplish it, knowing that we had set those goals made it that much more rewarding."

The Stars won the Stanley Cup in 1999, defeating Buffalo in a grueling six-game series that lacked artistry but made up for it in intensity.

Gainey remembers the win fondly, for a number of reasons. When he arrived in the organization in 1990, his son Steven was only 11. Now, he was a grown man and a premier prospect in the organization. Beyond that, there was also the gratification that came with the knowledge that the Stars had been truly accepted in Dallas.

"One of the most rewarding things about the Cup," he said, "was that we had a parade a day or two later. It wasn't anything like the parade that Montreal might have been or maybe that they would have for the Cowboys, but watching the people who were at the parade, it was a completely broad painting of the community.

"It was people with cowboy hats. It was families. It was the Dallas community. We hadn't just touched the hockey fan; we had touched the community."

The Franchise

The Minnesota North Stars made their NHL debut in the 1967–68 season as one of six expansion teams and got off to a disastrous start when Bill Masterton, a popular 29-year-old rookie, died in the middle of their first season after striking his head on the ice in a game against the Oakland Seals. The North Stars had a handful of brushes with respectability in their first decade, but none was more dramatic than the spring of 1971 when they took a pair of games from the heavily favored Montreal Canadiens before falling in six games during the Stanley Cup semifinals. Lou Nanne, the only player to stay with the North Stars for their first 11 years, took over as general manager in 1978 and helped forge perhaps the most consistent period in the team's Minnesota history. A voluble and popular manager, Nanne benefited significantly from a merger in which the money-losing Cleveland Barons (née California) franchise was merged with the North Stars in time for the 1978–79 season. With so many extra bodies under contract, Trader Lou parlayed that extra depth into some important additions, which eventually saw Minnesota evolve into one of the league's most competitive teams through the early 1980s. The high-water mark came in the spring of 1981 when they advanced to the Stanley Cup finals, only to lose to a New York Islanders' team that was in the midst of a four-in-a-row run atop the league. Nanne's provocative trading—he once offered Islanders GM Bill Torrey all of his draft picks for the rights to select Denis Potvin—kept the North Stars competitive for the next five years, but they were unable to get any closer to a championship. Unhappy with slumping attendance in 1990, owners George and Gordon Gund sold the North Stars to a group that included Norman Green and Howard Baldwin. The Gunds were, in turn, granted the San Jose expansion franchise for the 1991–92 season and were able to stock their new teams with 24 players from the North Stars' reserve list. Green made two important hires in 1990, his first year as owner, bringing in former Flyers great Bobby Clarke as GM and Bob Gainey as coach. That management team was in place during the North Stars' astonishing run to the 1991 Stanley Cup finals in which Minnesota, a 16th-place team overcame a 68-point regular season to knock off Chicago, St. Louis, and Edmonton, en route to a Stanley Cup finals appearance against the Pittsburgh Penguins and Mario Lemieux. That was their last trip to the finals in the Minnesota years, but eight years later, they would close out the 20th century as its final Stanley Cup champion.

Ed Belfour has regained the form he demonstrated earlier in his career in Chicago to once again one of the NHL's premier goaltenders.

Team Lowlights

- April 29, 1997: After finishing first in their division, the Stars are upset by the Edmonton Oilers in the first round of the playoffs.

Team Records

	Career	Season
Goals	Mike Modano, 349	Dino Ciccarelli, 55 (1981–82)
		Brian Bellows, 55 (1989–90)
Assists	Neal Broten, 593	Neal Broten, 76 (1985–86)
Points	Neal Broten, 867	Bobby Smith, 114 (1981–82)
Goals-Against Average	Ed Belfour, 1.99	Ed Belfour, 1.88 (1997–98)
Games Played	Neal Broten, 992	

Detroit Red Wings

Founded 1932

Formerly the Detroit Falcons 1930–32; Detroit Cougars 1926–30

Arenas
Louis Arena 1979–present
Detroit Olympia 1927–79
Windsor Arena, 1926–27

Stanley Cup Wins
1997–98, 1996–97,
1954–55, 1953–54,
1951–52, 1949–50,
1942–43, 1936–37,
1935–36,

Award Winners

see page 252

One of the NHL's best defensive forwards, and a dynamic offensive performer, Sergei Federov was the first European to ever win the Hart Trophy in 1993-94.

Profile

Steve Yzerman ranks second in career goals, assists, and points on the Detroit Red Wings' all-time list, behind only the legendary Hall of Famer Gordie Howe. Yzerman joined the Red Wings in the fall of 1983 and, by the end of the 1999–2000 season, was the NHL's No. 6 all-time scorer. He is the longest-serving captain in NHL history when measured by games played, having received the C as a 21-year-old in 1986; he is one of only 7 NHLers to score 100 points in six successive seasons.

Face to Face

The year was 1983. In the days leading up to the National Hockey League's annual entry draft, an 18-year-old Steve Yzerman was mulling over the possibilities. Minnesota or Hartford? The New York Islanders or Detroit? Three of the four teams were bottom feeders and then there were the Islanders, in the midst of a run of four consecutive Stanley Cup championships.

"The Islanders picked third," began Yzerman. "They were my favorite team and Bryan Trottier was my favorite player, so I thought, 'Oooh, it would be awesome to play there.' I didn't know much about Detroit. I'd been there once for a hockey tournament as a kid, but I hadn't seen their team on TV, except when they were playing the Toronto Maple Leafs once in a while. A buddy of mine had been drafted two years earlier by the Red Wings, so I thought that was kind of neat. Once I was drafted, I got into reading about the team and starting to become interested."

What Yzerman soon discovered was that the lean times were not always a permanent fixture in the Motor City. By 1983, the Red Wings had won seven Stanley Cup championships, but the last of them had been in the spring of 1955. That year, the Gordie Howe-led team won the Stanley Cup for the fourth time in a six-year span and looked as if they would rule the league indefinitely. Instead, the bottom slowly fell out of the organization, and by the time Yzerman arrived on the scene, the Red

Steve Yzerman

Wings had missed the playoffs in 12 of the previous 13 seasons.

In Yzerman's draft year, the team was coming off a 44-loss, 57-point season; the once proud franchise had come to be known as the Dead Things or the Gray Wings because they had evolved into an aging, underperforming team. Yzerman turned up in training camp that year and, as an 18-year-old, rattled off an astonishing 87 points, helping the team squeeze into the playoffs. The revival was under way.

The Red Wings brought in one of the league's most charismatic coaches, Jacques Demers, and within four years, they were playing competitive hockey again. Yzerman rattled off six consecutive seasons of 100-plus points and was the catalyst in their turnaround. Unhappily, the presence of the Edmonton Oilers in their conference stood in their way during much of the 1980s. It was only after the Oilers were dispersed around the NHL to meet the financial obligations of their owner, Peter Pocklington, that the Red Wings finally came all the way back. A seminal moment came in 1993 when the Red Wings lured the NHL's winningest coach, Scotty Bowman, away from the Pittsburgh Penguins. Bowman and Yzerman did not always see eye to eye in the early days of their relationship. Bowman thought Yzerman lacked an understanding of the two-way aspects of the game; Yzerman thought Bowman's oppressive tactics were too old-school. Two years after Bowman's arrival, the Red Wings seriously considered moving Yzerman to the Ottawa Senators—at that time, the NHL's worst team—in a one-for-one exchange for Alexei Yashin. The Senators wanted Yzerman because he was a Ottawa native and would

Above: The winningest coach in NHL history, Scotty Bowman, surveys his troops from behind the Red Wings bench.

Next Page: Detroit power forward Brendan Shanahan combines physical strength and goalscoring ability to overpower opposing players.

lend credibility to an organization that had none. The only problem was, Ottawa was so bad, and Yzerman, at 30, knew the prospect of ever winning the Stanley Cup with the hapless Senators was remote in his career.

It was the prospect of leaving a Detroit team, inching ever closer to a championship, to join a team in a rebuilding mode that prompted Yzerman to buy into Bowman's program. Yzerman made his peace with Bowman and gradually gave him what he wanted: a more consistent, two-way game. The 100-point days were over, but gradually, it became clear that this new approach provided a greater opportunity for team success. Yzerman eventually became a proponent of the defense-first hockey preached by Bowman, and even if his scoring totals dropped, his influence in the dressing room and around the league rose.

"I've been very lucky," Yzerman said. "There are a lot of things that have to fall into place for a guy to stay in the same city for a long time. There were a couple of times, on a couple of different occasions, when it was possible that I might be traded for different reasons."

In 1995—for the first time in 29 years—the Red Wings qualified for the Stanley Cup finals, but lost to New Jersey. The next year, they established an NHL record with 62 regular-season wins but were eliminated in the semifinals by Colorado. Finally, in 1997, with Yzerman leading the way, they ended their 42-year championship drought—and did it convincingly, by sweeping Philadelphia in the Stanley Cup finals.

"People look for the rah-rah stuff, for the outpouring of emotion, for the fiery quotes in the paper, but that's not what makes someone a leader," Yzerman said. "It's about the willingness to pay the price, to compete harder than the other guys."

As if they needed to put a punctuation mark on that triumph, the Red Wings successfully defended their title a year later, one of only two teams to do so in the 1990s.

Winning the Stanley Cup twice gave Yzerman more recognition and satisfaction than any other achievement, before or since.

"I went 13 years [without a Stanley Cup win] and you always felt as if you were missing something," he said. "I'd go to All-Star games and see all the guys with Stanley Cup rings.... It's not that you feel inferior, but after you've won it, it's a kind of relief."

Detriot's famed "Production Line," Gordie Howe (left), Sid Abel (center), and Ted Williams (right) finished 1–2–3 in NHL scoring in the 1949–50 season.

Over time, Yzerman grew to appreciate the opportunity to play in hockey-mad Detroit and its rich hockey history.

"Detroit's become my home. It's important to me that I'm playing there. It's a good hockey city with a good background, and the team is well-supported. The game—and what you do—is appreciated by the people in the city. There's always going to be a few guys that get the same opportunity as I did—to stick with their teams, in their cities for their entire careers. A lot of it has to do with luck or timing, rather than anything you do, good or bad."

In the 1999–2000 season, Yzerman became the 10th NHL player in history to record 900 assists and the 11th to score 600 goals. It is an exclusive, eclectic group. Only four other players have ever joined the 600–900 club: Wayne Gretzky, Marcel Dionne, Mark Messier...and Howe.

"It's kind of neat—and it's been that way my entire career—to go into the locker room and see Ted Lindsay in there before practice, working out. Gordie Howe pops in every now and then. That's one of the special things about playing with a team that has a good history—to see some of the older players come around every now and then. And winning those championships? That's really helped me enjoy the whole experience—everything from day one all the way through. So I can appreciate the good and the bad and really feel comfortable that I can enjoy everything and smile about everything that's gone on."

The Franchise

Their logo—the Winged Wheel—is one of the most famous and beloved in the National Hockey League, but it was not the original choice in the Motor City. In 1926, during the NHL's expansion, a group led by former goaltender Percy LeSueur outbid four other competitors for the right to operate a new franchise in Detroit. LeSueur and his backers determined that they would stock their new team with players from the Western Hockey League's Victoria franchise, a prudent move considering they had won the Stanley Cup as recently as 1925. Detroit retained the team's nickname—the Cougars—but couldn't duplicate its success on the ice. In the beginning, the Cougars played their home games in Windsor, Ontario—or until construction could be completed on the Olympia, their new state-of-the-art arena. From 1926 until 1933, the team struggled—on the ice and on the balance sheet. In 1930, the team became the Falcons, but it wasn't until millionaire James Norris purchased the team in 1932 that the Wings turned things around.

For the second time in three years, Norris changed the name and the logo, but this time, he kept the same manager: the legendary Jack Adams. Adams proceeded to wheel and deal the team into contending status. By 1934, they finished in the league and lost in the Stanley Cup finals. After missing the playoffs in 1935, they then ran off two consecutive Stanley Cup championships, beginning a 23-year stretch in which they missed the playoffs only once, won seven championships, and finished as runners-up six times.

These were heady days. Gordie Howe appeared on the scene

Team Highlights

- June 16, 1998: The Red Wings win their second consecutive Stanley Cup and become the first Detroit team to win back-to to-back titles in over 40 years.

- November 10, 1963: Gordie Howe scores his 545th goal to set the all-time NHL record for most goals scored by a single player.

- 1948-49–1954-55: The Red Wings finish first for seven consecutive seasons. They win four Stanley Cup championships during this time.

- 1936–1949: The team makes the playoffs 23 years in a row.

An NHL legend, Gordie Howe played professional hockey until he was over 50 years old. He still holds Detroit team records for most goals, points, and assists. Gordie Howe won four Stanley Cup titles with the Red Wings, played in 23 All-Star games, and won the Hart Trophy six times.

in 1946, and within three years, he and linemates Ted Lindsay and Sid Abel—known as the Production Line—were considered one of the most complete lines, if not the most complete, in the NHL. Howe went on to play parts of four decades with the Red Wings and won the Stanley Cup four times in all. Arguably, the highlight came in 1952—a team some believe is the strongest of all time—when the Wings lost only 14 (of 70 regular-season games) and swept the playoffs in the minimum eight games. The 1951 and 1952 Red Wings were two of only three pre-1967

Federov and blueliner Nicklas Lidstrom celebrate a goal against the Chicago Blackhawks.

expansion teams to earn 100 points. Much of Adams' success in keeping the Red Wings competitive revolved around his ability to tweak the roster, even in times of prosperity. The magic began to dissipate, however, in the late 1950s when he made a series of trades that backfired, dispatching goaltender Terry Sawchuk to Boston and then giving up up-and-coming Johnny Bucyk to get him back. Lindsay's attempts to start a players' union earned him a trip to Chicago. By the mid-1960s, the remaining core of players was aging and the Red Wings began to sink in the standings. The 1970s proved to be the lost decade, as Detroit missed the playoffs in nine of ten years. Their fortunes didn't change until the early 1980s when pizza entrepreneur Mike Ilitch bought the team in 1982 and his choice as GM, Jim Devellano, called out Steve Yzerman's name the following June at the entry draft.

Team Records

	Career	Season
Goals	Gordie Howe, 786	Steve Yzerman, 65 (1988–89)
Assists	Gordie Howe, 1,023	Steve Yzerman, 90 (1988–89)
Points	Gordie Howe, 1,809	Steve Yzerman, 155 (1988–89)
Goals-Against Average	Clarence Dolson, 1.98	Clarence Dolson, 1.43 (1928–29)
Games Played	Gordie Howe, 1,687	

Team Lowlights

- June 13, 1997: Shortly after winning their first Cup championship, the Red Wings' defenseman Vladimir Konstantinov and massage therapist Sergei Mnatsakanov are badly injured in a car crash. Konstantinov's career ends and he never fully recovers from his injuries.

Edmonton Oilers

Founded 1979

Arenas
Skyreach Center Centre 1979–present (formerly the Northlands Colliseum)

Stanley Cup Wins
1989–90, 1987–88, 1986–87, 1984–85, 1983–84,

Award Winners

Jack Adams Award
Glen Sather, 1985–86

Lady Byng Trophy
Jari Kurri, 1984–85
Wayne Gretzky, 1979–80

King Clancy Trophy
Kevin Lowe, 1989–90

Hart Trophy
Mark Messier, 1989–90
Wayne Gretzky, 1986–87, 1985–86, 1984–85, 1983–84, 1982–83, 1981–82, 1980–81, 1979–80

Norris Trophy
Paul Coffey, 1985–86, 1984–85

Art Ross Trophy
Wayne Gretzky, 1986–87, 1985–86, 1984–85, 1983–84, 1982–83, 1981–82, 1980–81

Conn Smythe Trophy
Bill Ranford, 1989–90
Wayne Gretzky, 1987–88, 1984–85
Mark Messier, 1983–84

Vezina Trophy
Grant Fuhr, 1987–88

Profile

Kevin Lowe recorded a number of firsts in his 15-year playing career with the Edmonton Oilers, including the first goal in team history, scored against the Chicago Blackhawks' Tony Esposito on October 10, 1979, at the Chicago Stadium. In 19 NHL seasons, Lowe played 1,254 regular-season games and another 214 playoff games, missing the playoffs only once in that time. Lowe holds Oilers records for most games played in both the regular season (1,037) and playoffs (172) and is one of only 27 players in history to play 1,000 games with the same team.

Face to Face

Lowe was the Oilers' first-ever selection in the National Hockey League entry draft and one of only seven players to play on all five of their Stanley Cup championship teams. He left—as did so many of his peers—for greener pastures in the early 1990s and, in doing so, won a sixth championship with the New York Rangers.

Kevin Lowe

The draw of returning to the organization in which he made his name and reputation, however, was strong for Kevin Lowe. In 1998, upon the completion of his distinguished playing career, he rejoined the Edmonton Oilers as an assistant coach. The next year, he was elevated to the head coaching position.

Considering how much he eventually became a part of Oilers history, it is odd how little Lowe knew about them on the fateful day in August 1979, when he was originally drafted by the Oilers.

Lowe said, "My first reaction was 'Edmonton? They're not in the NHL, are they?' That's exactly what I said to my agent. I mean, I knew nothing about them. Zippo. Nada. I didn't know it existed. I was playing junior in Quebec City and used to go to the Nordiques games. The only thing I knew about Edmonton was they had a team in the WHA. In my last year of junior, I would go down to the Colisée in the mornings and watch the team practice and sit on the bench.

"One time, I actually talked to Slats [Glen Sather, then the

Grant Fuhr, one of the game's best athletes, won four Stanley Cups as the goaltender for the Edmonton Oilers in the 1980s.

Paul Coffey and Mark Messier, two future Hall of Famers, patrol the Edmonton Zone in support of Andy Moog.

team's coach, and later its general manager]. That summer, when I started talking to scouts about where I might end up, I talked to Chicago, Boston, and Minnesota. All three of those teams said the same thing: 'We're definitely going to draft you.' Boston had two picks, Minnesota had two picks. So finally when I got the telephone call to say I was drafted by Edmonton, my agent said, 'You're a first-rounder, that's what you wanted.'"

But Edmonton?

"That's the other funny part," said Lowe. "Playing junior in Quebec City, it can be brutally cold there. I was 19 and remember saying, jokingly, 'I just want to go anywhere farther south than Quebec.' In the end, I got drafted by the only place farther north than Quebec."

Lowe arrived for his first training camp in September 1979 and found a huge contingent of players trying out for the team, one of whom was especially noticeable, a teenager named Wayne Gretzky, who had played for the Oilers the year before in the WHA. So, for that matter, had another member of the WHA, center Mark Messier.

"It was interesting because that team had had success in the WHA," said Lowe, "so there was already some competition between the holdover WHA guys and the expansion-drafted NHLers. The WHA guys were trying to prove they belonged. They were the so-called veterans and the NHL guys said to them, 'Yeah, but you're veterans of a so-called lesser league.'"

In those early days, it was difficult to imagine the championships that would follow. The Oilers were a bunch of eager kids, mixed in with jaded veterans that would eventually do a lot of on-the-job training.

"To envision all that happened from day one?" repeated Lowe. "No, you couldn't have. There were even questions about Gretz. Some people thought he wasn't even going to be able to play in the league, let alone star. Mess was a holdout in training camp. We were all just trying to play in the NHL. We did relatively well in the exhibition season, but it was mainly against ex-WHA teams. Then we slid into Chicago for the first game ever and bang, we were down 2–0 in the first six minutes of the game. I thought, 'This is going to be a long year.'

"But no one could account for what Gretz was going to be. Plus, we had good leadership out of the gate, character guys. You often hear talk about expansion teams and how critical it is to get good leadership out of the gate."

Jari Kurri weaves between a trio of Boston defenders.

Glen Sather was hired as coach and led the team into the playoffs. They were dusted in the opening round by the Philadelphia Flyers, but the foundation was in place and starting to develop. The next summer, they added three more future stars in the entry draft: Paul Coffey, Jari Kurri, and Andy Moog. Additionally, Glenn Anderson, chosen in 1979, turned pro after playing for Canada's Olympic team. In 1981, they added two more key pieces of the puzzle, Grant Fuhr and Steve Smith. In

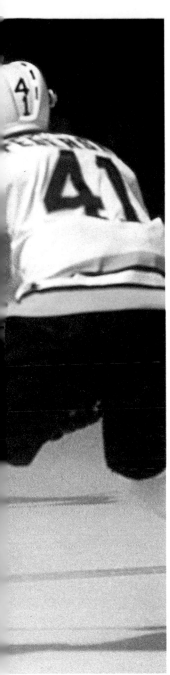

three years, the Oilers' brains trust—Sather and chief scout Barry Fraser—drafted six potential Hall of Famers to join Gretzky in a supporting cast that was soon considered one of the finest collections of talent ever amassed in NHL history.

Improvement came rapidly. The 1981 playoffs saw the 14th-seeded Oilers knock off the third-seeded Montreal Canadiens in the opening round, earning a second-round series against the defending Stanley Cup champion New York Islanders. The boyish Oilers, so new to this process that they were singing on the bench in Long Island, swiped two games from the heavily favored Islanders before losing in six. In 1982, the Oilers made a quantum leap forward in the regular season, improving from 74 to 111 points, but took a disastrous pratfall in the playoffs. They were themselves upset that season by the underdog Los Angeles Kings in the opening playoff round. Learning from that experience, the Oilers went all the way to the Stanley Cup finals the next season, before falling to the Islanders for one last time.

After that, they were virtually unstoppable. Edmonton won its the Stanley Cup for the first time in 1984 and then defended the championship a year later. They lost in the quarter-finals to Calgary in 1986, before winning back-to-back championships again in 1987 and 1988.

By 1988, owner Peter Pocklington's financial problems were growing and, as a result, he began to disperse his talent around the league. Coffey was the first to go in November 1987. Gretzky followed in August of 1988. Enough of the team's core hung around long enough to add one more championship ring in 1990 before they were all cast adrift—Kurri to Los Angeles via Philadelphia in May 1991; Fuhr and Anderson to Toronto in September 1991; Messier to New York in October 1991. Finally, Lowe was himself moved to the Rangers in December 1992.

The Oilers' success, according to Lowe, could be attributed to the fact that their young players came into their prime at roughly the same time. Beyond that, the team also showed

Team Highlights

- May 24, 1990: The Oilers win the Stanley Cup for the fifth time in seven years proving their dominance even in the "post-Gretzky" era.

- February 24, 1982: Wayne Gretzky scores his 77th goal of the season to break Phil Esposito's record for most goals in a year. He ends the season with a record 92 goals.

- 1980s: The Oilers of the 1980s era are one of the greatest hockey teams ever assembled. Led by Wayne Gretzky, they win the Stanley Cup four times in a period of five years.

- November 2, 1978: The Oilers arrange to buy the contract of a young WHA player from Indianapolis Racers. His name was Wayne Gretzky.

positive growth from year to year. Even though they lost to L.A. in the 1982 playoffs, they had moved a dozen places up the NHL ladder that season. Accordingly, there was always progression.

"One part of our success was the willingness of whoever is running the team to keep it together," said Lowe. "Then there was also the willingness of individuals involved to stay as one group and coexist through thick and thin. There wasn't a lot of thin during that period either.

"For me, not until I got to New York in 1994 did it dawn on me what a team that was. I wasn't nostalgic about it the way some of the other guys were until then. The subject was brought up often: 'What if that team had stayed together?' Remember, Wayne was still doing well in L.A., Mess was doing well in New York. Coff was still doing his thing and Fuhrsie and Jari too. It was when we—the Rangers—won in 1994 that I became nostalgic too. I was with guys like Andy and Mess and Mact [Craig MacTavish]. There were seven of us there in New York and not everyone was there when we won the first Stanley Cup, but Andy, Mess, and I were there for the whole run."

It was that affinity for the organization, for the city, and for Sather's management style that lured Lowe home.

"Glen and I, we're still trying to play hockey and run hockey the way it was 10, 12, or 15 years ago."

The Franchise
The beginnings of the Edmonton Oilers' dynasty can be traced, in a roundabout way, to the decision by Indianapolis Racers' Nelson Skalbania in 1978 to offer Wayne Gretzky a seven-year contract worth an astonishing total of $1.75 million to play hockey for the Indianapolis Racers. Happily for the Oilers, even with Gretzky in the lineup, the Racers were a box-office flop. Gretzky lasted eight games, not seven years, in Indianapolis before Skalbania put out the word that Gretzky was available to the highest bidder. Ultimately, Skalbania sold the contract to the Edmonton Oilers' Peter Pocklington, who could outbid the Winnipeg Jets for Gretzky's services. Gretzky arrived in Edmonton, along with goaltender Eddie Mio and forward Peter Driscoll, and proceeded to score 110 points in his one and only WHA season. Under terms of the NHL-WHA merger, the four WHA teams were allowed to protect two skaters and two goaltenders from their existing teams. Wisely, the Oilers used one of their priority selections to retain

"The Great One" was at his greatest as a member of the young Edmonton Oilers. Surrounded by such players as Jari Kurri, Grant Fuhr, Paul Coffey, and Mark Messier, Gretzky and the Oilers were virtually unstoppable in the mid-1980s.

Mark Messier flourished under the guidance of the Oilers coach and GM Glen Sather. On July 13, 2000, Sather was reunited with Messier when he signed with the New York Rangers as a free agent.

Gretzky. For their faith, Gretzky went on to reward them with more than 1,500 points in nine years in Edmonton, a time that also produced four Stanley Cup championships, seven scoring titles, and eight Hart Trophy winners.

The Oilers won the Stanley Cup again in 1990, two years after Gretzky's departure, but the rest of the decade was not especially kind to the once-proud franchise. The next two springs, 1991 and 1992, the Oilers salvaged mediocre regular seasons in which they were only two games above .500 to advance as far as the conference championships. For a time, the legacy of their winning nature spilled over into the post-season.

By 1993, however, the bottom had fallen out. Instead of Gretzky, Messier, et al., the Oilers' leaders were Petr Klima, Todd Elik, Shayne Corson, and a young Doug Weight. They missed the playoffs for four consecutive seasons and then squeezed in as a lower seed for the next three years, twice registering impressive first-round upsets before seeing the magic run out in the second round.

Team Lowlights

- August 9, 1988: Cash-strapped Oilers' owner Peter Pocklington trades Wayne Gretzky to the Los Angeles Kings.

Team Records

	Career	Season
Goals	Wayne Gretzky, 583	Wayne Gretzky, 92 (1981–82)
Assists	Wayne Gretzky, 1,086	Wayne Gretzky, 163 (1985–86)
Points	Wayne Gretzky, 1,669	Wayne Gretzky, 215 (1985–86)
Goals-Against Average	Tommy Salo, 2.33	Tommy Salo, 2.33 (1999–2000)
Games Played	Kevin Lowe, 1,037	

Florida Panthers

Founded 1993

Arenas
National Car Rental Center
  1998–present
Miami Arena 1993–98

Stanley Cup Wins
0

Award Winners

Maurice "Rocket"
  Richard Trophy
Pavel Bure, 1999–2000

In December 1997, John Vanbiesbrouck became only the second American goalie to win 300 NHL games.

Profile

An "original Panther" and a member of their 1996 Cup finalist team, Scott Mellanby was claimed in the 1993 expansion draft from Edmonton. He made his reputation as a two-way forward with the Oilers, and before that as a Philadelphia Flyer. He has seven 20-goal seasons to his credit and almost 100 playoff games and appeared in his 1,000th regular-season game during the 1999–00 season. He was born in Montreal, raised in Toronto, and played at the University of Wisconsin before the Flyers drafted him in the second round in 1984.

Scott Mellanby

Face to Face

Prominently placed on the mantel of Scott Mellanby's home in Coral Springs, Florida, sit two black plastic rats.

Ah, if those rodents could talk....

They have special significance for the Panthers, for South Florida, and for Mellanby, the holder of seven club records for scoring and longevity and one of just three players remaining from the 1993–94 expansion team. They represent the wonderful ride the club took to the 1996 Stanley Cup playoffs, an amazing feat for a team built from scraps just three years before.

"That was such a great year," Mellanby said. "To play such a big role in getting the rat thing started with the fans, and to create an unusual mascot like that was a lot of fun."

The bizarre rat tale started in the Panthers' dressing room at the old Miami Arena on October 8, 1995, Florida's home opener that season. The vermin somehow found its way into the room and, in an attempt to hide, came skittering straight at Mellanby. With the follow-through that saw him rack up 274 NHL goals, he one-timed it off the wall to rat heaven. It proved to be a great warmup drill, because that same night, Mellanby fired two goals in a 4–3 home-opening win over the Calgary Flames.

With reporters clustered around Mellanby, teammate John Vanbiesbrouck dubbed his eventful evening "a rat trick," and the episode got lots of play around the sports world. Within a few weeks, Panther fans were showering imitation rats of all kinds onto the ice any time the team scored.

Team Highlights

- January 17, 1999: Florida management pulls off a blockbuster deal that brings Pavel Bure, one of the league's most exciting players, to the Panthers.

- June 1, 1996: The Panthers beat the Pittsburgh Penguins to advance to the Stanley Cup finals for the first time.

- April 14, 1994: The Panthers set a record for most wins by an expansion team with 33 in their inaugural season.

"I was playing in the All-Star game in Boston that year," Mellanby said, "and a little boy came up to me for an autograph. He looked at me really wide-eyed and asked, 'Are you the Rat Man?'"

Eventually, the rat-tossing rave reached epidemic levels and to speed up games, the league had to threaten to penalize the Panthers if the fans didn't abstain.

Mellanby has certainly seen it all in the franchise's short history.

In the most talked-about liftoff in NHL history, the Panthers compiled a record of 33–34–17 in their inaugural season. The 83 points were 10 more than 22 NHL expansion outfits have managed before or since. Mellanby, who was claimed from the Edmonton Oilers, led the Panthers with 30 goals and 60 points as the club came within two points of making the playoffs.

"I wish I knew the answer to such quick success, because I'd bottle it and sell it to every expansion team," Mellanby said.

"I think a lot of the credit has to go to [president] Bill Torrey and general manager Bobby Clarke. Their plan going into the expansion draft was to get the players with the most experience possible. They got some really competitive people in there right away.

"Part of it was luck, no doubt, when you're trying to find some chemistry. Getting John Vanbiesbrouck was probably the biggest factor. He'd been in Mike Richter's shadow in New York and he provided us with some good leadership in net."

Mellanby was among a group of Panthers he describes as the "perfect age...guys who'd played a few years who were experienced enough to assume [high-profile] roles. They were third- and fourth-line guys from around the league: Dave Lowry, Brian Skrudland, Mike Hough, Tom Fitzgerald, and myself.

"The first time any of us really met was in the summer of 1993 during a promotional tour with about six or seven of us. There was a mutual respect right away."

Florida tied Chicago 4–4 in its opening game, with Mellanby scoring the first goal from Rob Niedermayer and Evgeny Davydov. They were five games over .500 at one point, before a late-season fade cost them a playoff spot.

Mellanby had gained Clarke's respect during a five-year NHL orientation with the Flyers. On March 22, 1986, Mellanby stepped on the ice against the Rangers for his first big-league game, straight from the campus of the University of Wisconsin.

His youth was spent in the hockey-mad cities of Montreal and Toronto, where his Emmy-award winning father Ralph was producing "Hockey Night in Canada." Scott proved a perfect ambassador for the game in South Florida, although the thousands of transplants from Canada and the northeastern United States have made the Panthers' job much easier.

"A lot of people had missed the game of hockey by the time we got there," Mellanby said.

The customers certainly didn't mind that coach Roger Neilson employed the plodding trap as a game plan, since it allowed the Panthers to make such a huge leap in year one.

"We had the good first-year numbers, and fans in this area welcomed a team that gave it everything they had," Mellanby said.

In short order, the pieces were added for a playoff-caliber team. Doug MacLean, who had a wide-ranging background in

Pavel Bure charges in on Philadelphia goaltender, John Vanbiesbrouck, a former member of the Panthers.

Blessed with an incredible combination of strength, speed, and offensive imagination, Pavel Bure is one of the game's most explosive performers. In the 1999–2000 season, he won the Maurice Richard Trophy for the league's leading goal scorer.

Team Lowlights

the game as a coach, scout, and minor league executive, came aboard and had the Panthers challenging for first place at the halfway point of 1995–96.

The sandpaper players from the first two seasons were augmented by youth, such as Robert Svehla, Ed Jovanovski, and Radek Dvorak.

"We were a team ready to take on a bigger challenge," Mellanby said. "I don't think I've ever played on a team that knew how to play the score of a game better."

Three huge obstacles stood in the Panthers' way as the 1996 playoffs began, but they beat the Bruins in six games, out-muscled Eric Lindros and the Flyers, and put the clamps on the explosive Penguins to win the East.

However, they lost the Cup finals in four straight to an equally good Cinderella story, the Colorado Avalanche. They fired 63 shots at Colorado's Patrick Roy in a Game 4 loss that went three overtimes at Miami Arena before Avs defenseman Uwe Krupp ended it.

Mellanby had nine points in 22 playoff games, as he made it back to the finals for the first time since his rookie year with the Flyers.

A couple of lean years followed, but in the interim, team ownership realized a dream with the construction of a state-of-the art facility in Sunrise, north of Miami. General manager Bryan Murray made a bold trade during the 1998–99 season, luring Russian Rocket Pavel Bure from contractual limbo in Vancouver. Bure has since responded with 71 goals in 85 games, and won 1999–00's Rocket Richard Trophy with 58 goals

"It's been fantastic since he's arrived," Mellanby said of the international acclaim his signing brought the Panthers, not to mention the power of his movie idol looks.

"Pavel's really something special to watch on the ice. This is a big place and very diverse, so he can just go and hide. In Canada, that would be a lot tougher to do."

Mellanby had a personal milestone to celebrate in 1999–00, when the Leafs came to town on March 1. It was his 1,000th NHL game, coming against the team he watched as a kid, with a number of friends and family on hand at the National Car Rental Center.

"I've played more than 500 of those games in Florida and I'm always going to be proud of that," he said. "This is my home now."

The Franchise

Two proven winners in businessman H. Wayne Huizenga and hockey maven Bill Torrey made an indoor sport a hit in the Sunshine State.

Huizenga, head of the Blockbuster video stores chain among other endeavors, added the Panthers to his growing sports stable when Miami was granted an NHL franchise in December 1992. Torrey was involved in the 1967 expansion Oakland Seals and then built the Islanders from doormats to Cup dynasty.

They put together a team that was in the playoff hunt its first year and challenging for the Cup an astonishing three years after the expansion draft. Using more liberal draft rules that weren't available to predecessors Tampa Bay and Ottawa, the Panthers assembled a team ripe with skill and character, led by Brian Skrudland and Scott Mellanby and backstopped by former Ranger John Vanbiesbrouck. Coach Doug MacLean was runner-up to Scott Bowman as coach of the year in 1995–96.

South Florida didn't have any minor league hockey background, but the fans, many of them northern transplants, supported the club's early achievements. They followed the team to the Fort Lauderdale area after they departed aging Miami Arena for the National Car Rental Center, one of the most picturesque in the league.

In the last couple of years, the Panthers have been evolving into a more dynamic team, starting with the acquisition of Pavel Bure, whose 58 goals netted him the 1999–00 Maurice Richard Trophy. The Panthers were back in the playoffs after a two-year hiatus, and several draft picks and trades from their early years, such as Robert Svehla and Jaroslav Spacek, are maturing.

Ray Whitney led the Panthers in scoring in 1998-99 and was selected as a member of the 2000 All-Star Team.

Team Records

	Career	Season
Goals	Scott Mellanby, 153	Parel Bure, 58 (1999–2000)
Assists	Scott Mellanby, 188	Viktor Kozlov, 53 (1999–2000)
Points	Scott Mellanby, 341	Parel Bure, 94 (1999–2000)
Goals-Against Average	John Vanbiesbrouck, 2.58	John Vanbiesbrouck, 2.29 (1996–97)
Games Played	Scott Mellanby, 512	

Los Angeles Kings

Founded 1967

Arenas
Staples Centre 1995–
present
Great Western Forum
1967–1995
Los Angeles Sports Arena
1967

Stanley Cup Wins
0

Award Winners

Jack Adams Award
Bob Pulford, 1974–75

Lady Byng Trophy
*Wayne Gretzky, 1993–94,
1991–92, 1990–91*
Butch Goring, 1977–78
Marcel Dionne, 1976–77

Calder Trophy
Luc Robitaille, 1986–87

King Clancy Trophy
Dave Taylor, 1990–91

Hart Trophy
Wayne Gretzky, 1988-89

Bill Masterton Trophy
Dave Taylor, 1990–91
Bob Bourne, 1987–88
Butch Goring, 1977–78

Norris Trophy
Rob Blake, 1997–98

Art Ross Trophy
*Wayne Gretzky, 1993–94,
1990–91, 1989–90*
Marcel Dionne, 1979–80

Profile
Luc Robitaille trails only Hall of Famer Marcel Dionne on the Los Angeles Kings' career goal-scoring list, and he was 16th overall in NHL history following the 1999–2000 season. Robitaille was the 12th-fastest player in NHL history to score 500 goals and is the only left winger ever to score 40 goals or more in eight consecutive seasons. Five times a first-team NHL All-Star, Robitaille also holds the league's single-season records for goals (63) and points (125) by a left winger.

Face to Face
He was 18 years old the day he sat in the Montreal Forum, watching round after round of the National Hockey League's entry draft go by, without hearing his name called.

It got to be the ninth round, and a disappointed Luc Robitaille—his dreams gradually crumbling in front of his eyes and those of friends and family—wondered if it wasn't time to go home.

Luc Robitaille

Robitaille stayed, mainly at the urging of his father, and finally, in the ninth round, the Los Angeles Kings called out his name. One hundred and seventy other players were drafted ahead of Robitaille, including the Kings' own fourth-round choice, who turned out to be a pretty fair baseball player named Tom Glavine.

Yes, the Kings were drafting pitchers before they were prepared to gamble on Robitaille, a gifted and accomplished scorer who, in the words of his hometown newspaper, skated slower than the Zamboni.

They called him Lucky now, but even with his perpetual smile and his *GQ* good looks, you have to know that Robitaille made his own luck. The 1987 Calder Memorial Trophy winner as the NHL's rookie of the year, he became a Los Angeles fan favorite almost from the moment he joined the team—and even now, a dozen years later, is serenaded with the long, drawn-out chant of "Luuuuuc, Luuuuuuc," whenever he scores a goal.

Robitaille turned up in L.A. during the last days of Marcel Dionne, one of the most prolific scorers in NHL history. Dionne made a promise to Robitaille's parents: that he would look after

A dominant force, when healthy, Los Angeles captain Rob Blake is capable of controlling a game with both his offensive and defensive play. Blake won the Norris Trophy in 1997-98.

young Luc in the City of Angels. True to his word, the Dionnes arranged for Robitaille to move in with his family during the latter's rookie season, and they proceeded to show the shy youngster from Montreal how to open a bank account, where to buy a car, and how to negotiate freeway traffic in the all-day rush hour. Dionne also arranged for Robitaille's fellow rookie Jimmy Carson to live next door, and that year, 1987, the two kids were known as the Gold-dust Twins. It wasn't babysitting exactly, but the move from old-world Montreal to L.A.'s urban sprawl represented a huge culture shock for Robitaille, one that Dionne's steadying influence helped to mitigate.

Robitaille was there for years, achieving individual honors on a Kings team that accomplished little of significance until Wayne Gretzky arrived on the scene in the summer of 1988. Gretzky's presence changed everything. Suddenly, hockey—a fringe sport that appealed only to a small hardcore fan base—began to attract a larger following. Suddenly, it was "in" to support hockey. Soon, Hollywood's glitterati came out to the aging no-longer Fabulous Forum, to watch Gretzky, Robitaille, Dave Taylor, and Bernie Nicholls put on a dazzling offensive show. In Gretzky's fifth full season—1992–93—the Kings advanced to the Stanley Cup finals, the brightest moment in the franchise's 33-year history.

Eventually, Gretzky and Robitaille would find their way to the New York Rangers. Gretzky was in his twilight, Robitaille in a two-year, injury-plagued funk. Taylor, by then the Kings GM, had a bright idea before the start of the 1997–98 season: trade underachieving Kevin Stevens to the Rangers for the slump-ridden Robitaille. Perhaps a change of scenery would inspire both players to return to their previous forms.

Stevens never did. But Robitaille, returning to the franchise for which he starred, eventually blossomed again. He struggled at times in his first year back, mainly because of a hernia that finally required surgery, but then in the next two seasons, he was magically resurrected. For two years running, he was among the NHL's top goal scorers.

"The biggest thing for me is that I went for eight or nine years and never got injured," said Robitaille. "In the last year I was in L.A., I broke my ankle and it was tough coming back. After that, in New York, I had injuries every year. Even my first year back in L.A., I had the hernia surgery. So I went four or five years where something happened to me every year. You always try to

Marcel Dionne, one of the most prolific goalscorers in NHL history was a member of the Los Angeles Kings from 1975 until 1987. He finished his career with the New York Rangers and retired in 1989 with a total of 1,771 points.

Team Highlights

- August 9, 1998: Kings owner, Bruce McNall acquires Wayne Gretzky from the Edmonton Oilers.

- March 23, 1994: Wayne Gretzky scores his 802nd career goal, breaking Gordie Howe's record for most goals in a career.

- May 29, 1993: The Kings defeat the Toronto Maple Leafs and advance to the Stanley Cup finals vs. the Montreal Canadiens.

play with injuries, but a lot of times, you find out you can't and that you're not playing really good. When I came back from my [hernia] operation, I got into a different workout program. I got bigger. That's been the biggest thing for me. Now, I'm a little quicker and stronger. That's helped me the most."

L.A. is now home. His wife, Stacia, hails from there. His sons, Jesse and Steven, are in school there.

"It's been a good city for me. There's always been a fan base of 10-, 12-, 15,000. These are people who really know the game. Then when you start winning, you sell out. That's the key. In L.A., you gotta win. If you win there, people will follow you. It's not a basketball town. Nobody goes to see the Clippers. It's a winning town. You're nowhere if you don't win."

Over the years, Robitaille has slid seamlessly in and out of the L.A. social whirl. For whatever reason, film stars tend to gravitate towards athletes, and Robitaille counts among his acquaintances dozens of celebrities whom he can call upon for

his charity work. In the early 1990s, everyone from former president Ronald Reagan and John Candy to Sylvester Stallone and Goldie Hawn were fixtures at Kings games. Nowadays, a new generation of stars—from Jason Priestley to Cuba Gooding Jr.—turn up at the new Staples Center.

"I wouldn't say I'm friends with celebrities," said Robitaille, "but I do know a lot of them. I have tons of acquaintances. Throughout the year, they all come to the games and they come into the locker room every once in a while, so you get to meet a lot of people. That's one part of L.A. that's definitely different. What you realize is that everybody's just people first. They're just like us. I own some hockey rinks in the area, and we sometimes give ice time to celebrities and they just love it."

Robitaille is now a senior statesman on the team and tries to make the transition easier for the team's younger players, in the same way Dionne helped him get established.

"The way I look at it, I enjoy every day," he said. "That's the

The famed Triple Crown Line consisting of Charlie Simmer, Marcel Dionne, and Dave Taylor was one of the most dangerous offensive forces in the entire NHL, during the early 1980s.

biggest thing—not to take it for granted. We make a lot of money to play the game, but when we go on the ice, we play the same game I was playing when I was 12 years old—except the guys are a lot bigger, a lot quicker, and they hurt more. Sometimes, when you're younger, you complain about stupid things or take things for granted. Then, as you get a little older, you realize this is the greatest life you can have."

The Franchise

Jack Kent Cooke, a transplanted Canadian, received the rights to operate the Los Angeles Kings as part of the NHL's 1967 expansion and thought he had the makings of a sound investment. After all, Los Angeles was home to a colony of expatriated Canadians, not to mention all the Americans from the industrial northeast who had resettled in southern California. After six not-so-great seasons, including four consecutive playoff misses, Cooke was forced to conclude: "Now I know why they came to California. They hated hockey." In their eighth season, under coach Bob Pulford, the Kings executed a major on-ice turnaround, accumulating 105 points, a team record that still stands today. As a player, Pulford was a defensive specialist and his team took its cue from him, surrendering only 185 goals, an astonishingly low total for that era. Unhappily, the Kings' fine regular season was spoiled when they were upset in the preliminary, best-of-three playoff round by the underdog Toronto Maple Leafs. That summer, the Kings engineered a trade for Marcel Dionne, the disgruntled Detroit Red Wings star. Dionne stayed for 12 years and in that span accumulated 1,307 points in a Los Angeles uniform. For much of the early 1980s, Dionne, Dave Taylor, and Charlie Simmer—the Triple Crown line—was one of the most productive in the game.

Cooke eventually sold the team to Los Angeles Lakers owner Jerry Buss who, in turn, took on as a partner in 1986 coin dealer and would-be movie producer Bruce McNall. Eventually, McNall persuaded Buss to sell him control of the team. McNall, knowing the value of a marquee name in the L.A. marketplace, engineered what is arguably the biggest trade in NHL history, acquiring Wayne Gretzky, in the prime of his career, from the Edmonton Oilers for two players, three first-round draft choices, and $15 million. In Gretzky's first season in Los Angeles, the Kings met the Oilers, the defending Stanley Cup champions, in the opening playoff round and proceeded to eliminate them from the playoffs. The Kings made the playoffs in Gretzky's first five seasons and in

1993 rode his scoring feats all the way to the Stanley Cup finals, the one and only time they've ever made it that far. Many believe the Kings were on the verge of the championship when they won the opening game of the final series in Montreal and were nursing a one-goal lead in the dying seconds of the second game. That's when Canadiens coach Jacques Demers asked that the stick of Kings defenseman Marty McSorley be measured. It was found to be illegal, and with McSorley in the penalty box and Canadiens goaltender Patrick Roy on the bench to allow a sixth attacker, the Canadiens tied the game in regulation time and won in overtime. Disheartened by the loss of a game they had well in hand, the Kings promptly dropped three consecutive games and finished as the runners-up. The disappointment spilled over into the next year and beyond, as Los Angeles missed the playoffs five times in the next six seasons.

Gretzky was eventually traded to the St. Louis Blues. McNall, meanwhile, found his financial empire crumbling around him, and he was finally forced to sell the team. In time, he was found guilty of fraud and sentenced to a six-year prison term. The Kings' fortunes took a turn for the better in 1995 when Denver real estate magnate Philip Anschutz and his partner, Edward Roski, purchased the team and broke ground on a new arena in downtown Los Angeles, the Staples Center, which is now the team's home.

Dave Taylor is the Kings all-time leader in games played at 1,111.

Team Lowlights

- June 7, 1993: The Kings lose their third straight overtime game to the Montreal Canadiens, who win the Stanley Cup two nights later.

Team Records

	Career	Season
Goals	Marcel Dionne, 550	Bernie Nicholls, 70 (1988–89)
Assists	Marcel Dionne, 757	Wayne Gretzky, 122 (1990–91)
Points	Marcel Dionne, 1,307	Wayne Gretzky, 168 (1988–89)
Goals-Against Average	Jamie Storr, 2.51	Rogie Vachon, 2.24 (1974–75)
Games Played	Dave Taylor, 1,111	

Montreal Canadiens

Founded 1917

Arenas

Molson Centre 1996–
   present
Montreal Forum
   1926–1996
Mount Royal Arena
   1917–1926

Stanley Cup Wins

1992–1993, 1985–86,
   1978–79, 1977–78,
   1976–77, 1975–76,
   1972–73, 1970–71,
   1968–69, 1967–68,
   1965–66, 1964–65,
   1959–60, 1958–59,
   1957–58, 1956–57,
   1955–56, 1952–53,
   1945–46, 1943–44,
   1930–31, 1929–30,
   1923–24, 1915–16,

Award Winners

see page 253

Shayne Corson first
played with the
Montreal Canadians
in 1985-86 and soon
developed into one of
their toughest players
and leading scorers.
Traded to Edmonton
in 1992 he would
return to play in
Montreal from 1996
through 1999–2000.
In July 2000 he signed
as a free agent with
the Toronto Maple
Leafs.

Profile

Guy Lafleur (aka the Flower) joined the Montreal Canadiens as the first overall choice in the 1971 entry draft, but needed three full seasons to become an overnight sensation. Lafleur's breakthrough year came in 1974, and he was the game's most dominant player for the next five seasons, leading the Canadiens to four consecutive Stanley Cup championships (1976–1979), the last time in the 20th century that they would ice a hockey-playing dynasty.

Guy Lafleur

Face to Face

Of the tens of thousands of National Hockey League games played in the 20th century, only a handful attain legendary status—and live on forever in the minds of the players who played in them and the fans who watched them.

The legend of Guy Lafleur was solidified—and his Hall of Fame credentials rubber-stamped—on one of those memorable nights.

It was May 10, 1979, and the Montreal Canadiens were on the verge of seeing their Stanley Cup dynasty end after three consecutive years as champions. The Boston Bruins, a team that

Ken Dryden uses his size to cover the whole net and kick a puck away.

had been nipping at their heels for most of the decade, were leading in the seventh and deciding game 4–3—and time was running out.

Then, in what was arguably the most famous minor penalty in history, the Bruins were flagged for too many men on the ice, setting the stage for Montreal's tying goal. It was a gaffe that haunts Bruins coach Don Cherry even to this day—and after more than 20 years, Lafleur's recollection of that moment remains crystal clear.

"Everybody was shaking their heads because we knew we didn't have much time left," said Lafleur. "The only thing that could really save us was a penalty. There was a minute and a half before the end of the game and they got caught with too many men. Everybody said, we have a chance. You never know how things are going to work out. I went out with Jacques Lemaire and Steve Shutt. I came from behind and Lemaire dropped it back and—without thinking, without even looking—I just let it go. Gilles Gilbert was the goalie. I scored."

He scored.

Then Montreal's Yvon Lambert scored the overtime winner, enabling the Canadiens to advance to the Stanley Cup finals against the New York Rangers, a series the Habs won in five games.

That moment—Lafleur's goal—was a landmark achievement on two different levels. First, it set the stage for the 21st Stanley Cup championship in team history. Second, it marked the end of an era. From 1917 until 1979, the Canadiens won more championships than any other NHL team: 21. They would later add a 22nd championship in the 1980s and a 23rd championship in the 1990s, but it would never be the same again. In the six-team NHL, in the 12-team NHL, even in the 17-team NHL, the Canadiens were special, a franchise that was alternately charmed and savvy. It was as if the hockey gods had given a special dispensation to the Flying Frenchmen, granted them a divine right to win Stanley Cups, even if other teams were equally deserving. In 1979, there was little to choose from between Montreal and Boston—and yet, the Canadiens found a way to win.

As Lafleur says now, "Everybody was very, very happy about it . . . and surprised at the same time. We never expected to win that game three minutes earlier."

It was a seminal moment for Lafleur and for the Canadiens

Team Highlights

- June 7, 1993: Left winger John LeClair scores an overtime goal to give the Canadiens their third straight overtime win, and a Stanley Cup victory over the Los Angeles Kings.

- 1970–1979: Montreal puts together one of the most dominant teams in NHL history. Comprised of Hall of Famers such as Ken Dryden, Serge Savard, Larry Robinson, and a host of other greats, the Canadiens win the Cup six times in the 1970s, dominating the decade as few others ever have.

- October 19, 1957: Maurice "Rocket" Richard becomes the first NHL player to break the 500-goal mark.

organization as well. Until that frozen moment in time, the Canadiens inspired awe—and sometimes fear—in their opponents, something that worked to their advantage on the ice. In 1980, following the retirement of Ken Dryden and Jacques Lemaire and the decision of coach Scotty Bowman to move on to the Buffalo Sabres, they lost their quarter-final series—and their chance to win a fifth championship—to the Minnesota North Stars, a heretofore unspectacular expansion team.

Some of the mystique drained out of the Canadiens team right there—and continued to do so over the next two decades. The tradition associated with their colors and their crest remains the same, but their results no longer speak of myth, only today's overcrowded NHL reality.

Lafleur was the second-to-last superstar developed by the Canadiens and the last who wasn't a goaltender (Patrick Roy). Nor were things especially easy for Lafleur in his early days with the team. The Canadiens' wily general manager, Sam Pollock, chose Lafleur first overall in the 1971 entry draft, using the California Golden Seals' No. 1 pick that he had acquired the previous year in a trade. Then, just to ensure the Seals did finish last overall, Pollock dispatched player help to the Los Angeles Kings—most notably, Ralph Backstrom—in a bid to shore up their playoff run.

A star and budding legend with the junior Quebec Remparts, Lafleur arrived as Jean Beliveau retired in 1971 following the Canadiens' 17th Stanley Cup championship. The plan was for Lafleur to slide seamlessly into the void created by Beliveau's departure. It wouldn't be enough for Lafleur to quietly produce offense, he needed to do it with style and panache. After all, it wasn't just winning that mattered in Montreal, you needed to win with passion and grace, lifting people out of their seats.

Lafleur eventually did just that, but not before he spent three difficult seasons learning the NHL ropes. All the time, he found his every play dissected under the microscope of the unrelenting public eye. Just about everybody in Quebec, waiting impatiently for Lafleur to develop, eventually learned everything there was to know about him—from his day-of-game rituals to the brand of cigarette that he chain-smoked. Lafleur will concede now that playing in Montreal, before its demanding crowd, made the transition from junior to the NHL all the more complicated for him.

"One of the reasons was because of all the guys who played

before us," said Lafleur. "The other reason was, in Montreal, they didn't want to send you on the ice just to send you on the ice. They wanted to send you on the ice when they thought you were ready. That's why guys like Yvan Cournoyer played three years on the bench. I also played on the bench for three years, which was different compared to other guys who would play 35, 40 minutes right away—like Marcel Dionne, who went to Detroit."

Dionne was a junior rival of Lafleur's who was drafted by a struggling team. In Detroit, Dionne was essentially all the Red Wings had offensively. By contrast, Lafleur had to share ice time with Cournoyer, Henri Richard, Jacques Lemaire, the Mahovlich brothers, and others in Montreal. In a city impatiently waiting for their next superstar to develop, it made the transition difficult for Lafleur.

A Canadian legend and an icon in his home province of Quebec, Maurice "Rocket" Richard was one of the greatest players hockey has ever seen. Widely considered to be the best player of all time from the blue line in, The Rocket will forever be remembered for his legendary intensity and incredible goalscoring ability. Maurice Richard died on May 27, 2000.

The Vezina Trophy, awarded to the top goalie in the NHL each year was named after legendary Montreal Canadiens goaltender, Georges Vezina. The Canadiens organization created the trophy in his honor in 1926, shortly after he died of tuberculosis.

Lafleur was asked: In the end, which system is better?

"It's better for your production to play more," replied Lafleur, "but team-wise? I'm not so sure any more. An organization like Montreal, Toronto, Boston, they were not just thinking about the present, they were thinking about the future of the organization."

Following three respectable but not overwhelming seasons, Lafleur broke out with a 119-point campaign in the 1974–75 season. That year, he discarded the helmet he had worn in his first three NHL years, a change that gave him a new, pleasing look. For years to come, Lafleur's trademark was his long blond hair, flapping in the breeze, as he accelerated up the ice. He followed his breakthrough season by winning the scoring championship in 1975–76 and then led the Canadiens to the Stanley Cup in the playoffs. Lafleur duplicated those results in the following two years—following up an Art Ross Trophy win as the regular-season scoring champion with the Stanley Cup, symbol of post-season triumph.

Lafleur had arrived on every level—as an eye-popping individual star and as the leader of the suddenly resurgent Canadiens' dynasty. In a span of six seasons, from 1974–75 until 1979–80, he scored an astonishing 766 points and collected four championship rings.

The expectations of Lafleur were high—but over time, he met them all.

"In Montreal," began Lafleur, "because of the dynasties and because of the guys we were playing with—who had won Stanley Cups before we arrived—they kept us going by telling us, 'It's important here, for the Montreal fans and for the province of Quebec, to keep on winning the Stanley Cup.' They would say, 'It was part of the heritage that Maurice Richard and Toe Blake and Aurel Joliat gave to the players.' We were so proud to be Montreal Canadiens and said to ourselves, 'We can do it, we have the talent to do it, let's go after it. We might not win the Stanley Cup every year, but we're going to give it a shot.' That's why everybody was motivated in that sense."

Lafleur's career in Montreal began to ebb in an injury-filled 1980–81. He missed 14 more games the next year and 12 more the year after that, a period that coincided with Montreal's three consecutive first-round playoff exits. By the 1984–85 season, at the age of 33, Lafleur abruptly retired following the 19th game of a season that saw him produce only five scoring

Ken Dryden led the Canadiens to the Stanley Cup in 1971 after having played only six regular regular-season NHL games. A Hall of Fame goaltender, Dryden backstopped the Canadiens to the Stanley Cup six times in his brief but brilliant NHL career. One of the sport's great thinkers, after his retirement from hockey Dryden went on to successful careers as a best best-selling author and president of the Toronto Maple Leafs.

points. Lafleur then spent the next three seasons chafing idly on the sidelines, unsure if he'd made the correct decision, before the New York Rangers lured him back in the lineup for the 1988–89 season. By then, he had already betoen enshrined in the Hockey Hall of Fame. Lafleur followed up his single season in the Big Apple with two more years as a Quebec Nordique, enabling him to return to his junior hockey roots, before he finally retired for good.

Looking back on his career in Montreal, Lafleur describes the highlight as "being raised as a hockey player—if you could call it that—by the old guys, like Henri Richard and Jim Roberts and Frank Mahovlich. They showed me how important it was to perform, to put on a good show for the fans and never let down, even if there was only a minute left in the game. We proved that in 1979. As long as the game is on, there's still hope. As long as you're within a goal or two, you never know. These guys were my idols as a kid and to me, I feel very lucky to have played with them. I learned a lot."

Others who followed into the Montreal Canadiens learned a lot from watching and listening to Lafleur repeat those same lessons. Lafleur was considered a controversial figure in his time, in part because he spoke his mind—and there were always reporters on hand, to chronicle his every utterance.

"We had a fantastic team spirit," continued Lafleur. "Everybody was like a family. Everybody stuck together when things were going bad. We always won the Stanley Cup as a team, as a big family. Our fans were a part of that big family."

That family extended around Canada. As the NHL expanded west—to Winnipeg and Edmonton, and Calgary—the Canadiens' loyal followers would turn out in full force, usually to watch Lafleur. It was an odd sensation to hear a home crowd salute the opposition's top star—as they chanted, "Guy, Guy, Guy" whenever he wound up for a rush.

"Montreal and Toronto were the only teams in Canada, so it's tough to ask for a fan to cheer for a new team, even if it's in your own city. It's always nice to have fans all over the place like that. You don't realize it when you play, but when you're retired and people are talking about the past, it's amazing how many fans know everything about you, even kids who are only 10 or 11 years old. Their parents must be good teachers."

The Franchise

Trying to pinpoint a defining moment in Montreal Canadiens history is a thankless task, largely because there have been so many triumphs and championships during their existence that is difficult to distill them down to one or two. The only certainty is that the Canadiens came by the sobriquet Les Glorieux honestly.

Established in 1909, the Canadiens won their first Stanley Cup championship seven years later—in 1916, by defeating the Portland Rosebuds of the Pacific Coast Hockey Association. In 1917, the Canadiens joined the new National Hockey League and two years later, as NHL champions, earned the right to play the Seattle Metropolitans for the Stanley Cup, which was then a challenge trophy.

The Canadiens traveled west, only to find the tournament canceled as a result of the Spanish influenza epidemic that cost defenseman Bad Joe Hall his life. It took the Canadiens until the 1923–24 season to win their next Stanley Cup championship, a team that boasted the legendary Georges Vezina in goal and future Hall of Famers Howie Morenz, Aurel Joliat, and Sprague Cleghorn as skaters. The Canadiens won only two championships in the 1930s (1929–30 and 1930–31) and then waited another 13 years before their glory days began. In the 1943–44 season, as war raged in Europe, undermining the dominant clubs of the era, the Canadiens built a team around Toe Blake, Maurice Richard, Elmer Lach, Butch Bouchard, and goaltender Bill Durnan that went on to win the Stanley Cup twice in a three-year span. No decade was as good to the Canadiens as the 1950s, however, which saw them add six more championships in eight years, beginning in the 1952–53 season and ending with the 1959–60 team. That 1959–60 team capped a remarkable five-year run that saw

Team Records

	Career	Season
Goals	Maurice Richard, 544	Steve Shutt, 60 (1976–77)
		Guy Lafleur, 60 (1977–78)
Assists	Guy Lafleur, 728	Peter Mahovolich, 82 (1974–75)
Points	Guy Lafleur, 1,246	Guy Lafleur, 136 (1976–77)
Goals-Against Average	George Hainsworth, 1.78	George Hainsworth, 0.92 (1928–29)
Games Played	Henri Richard, 1,256	

the Habs become the only team in NHL history to win the Stanley Cup five consecutive times. Twelve players, plus coach Toe Blake, had their names engraved on the Cup for all five championship seasons. The 1955–56 team, considered by many to be the team of the century, also boasted a dozen future Hall of Famers: Plante, Beliveau, Bouchard, Bert Olmstead, Bernie Geoffrion, Doug Harvey, Dickie Moore, Henri Richard, Maurice Richard, Tom Johnson, plus Blake and GM Frank Selke Sr.

The year before the Canadiens won the 1956 Stanley Cup, they were again involved in one of the more memorable, if unpleasant, moments in NHL history: the Richard riot. It happened in the spring of 1955 in the aftermath of a game between the Canadiens and Bruins, in which Maurice Richard, after getting high-sticked by Hal Laycoe, clubbed the Bruins defenseman over the head with his stick.

NHL president Clarence Campbell responded swiftly, suspending Richard for the balance of the regular season and playoffs. On the night of St. Patrick's Day, Campbell was attacked in his Montreal Forum seat by a Habs fan. Police were called in after someone set off a tear-gas bomb at the end of the opening period; and angry Habs fans took to the streets, running amok in the downtown area. Only a call for calm by the Rocket himself quieted the rioting after 24 raucous hours.

The 1960s proved to be another successful decade for the Canadiens, as they won four more championships. Beliveau, Henri Richard, and Claude Provost, members of their 1950s dynasties, were part of all four of their 1960s championships as well.

A new set of heroes emerged in the 1970s, from goaltender Ken Dryden to a trio of skilled defensemen—Serge Savard, Guy Lapointe, and Larry Robinson—to key six additional Stanley

Cup championships, including four in a row from 1976 to 1979.

In 1986, rookie goaltender Patrick Roy picked up the torch from Dryden and took home the Conn Smythe Trophy for the playoffs' most valuable player as the Canadiens—an underdog that year—interrupted the Edmonton Oilers' mid-1980s dynasty by defeating the Calgary Flames in the Stanley Cup finals. Seven years later, with Roy playing a key role again in backstopping the team to 10 consecutive overtime wins, the Canadiens duplicated their 1986 Stanley Cup championship, knocking off the Wayne Gretzky-led Los Angeles Kings in the final.

Current Montreal goaltender Jeff Hackett drops to his knees to stop a low shot.

Nashville Predators

Founded 1998

Arenas
The Gaylord Entertainment
Center 1998–present

Stanley Cup Wins
0

Predators captain Tom Fitzgerald is chased by Doug Weight, captain of the Edmonton Oilers.

Profile
The former captain of the Florida Panthers, Tom Fitzgerald, was a major contributor to their run to the Stanley Cup finals in 1996. Known as a solid player and respected leader, he was a perfect fit as the first captain of the Nashville Predators when he joined the franchise in 1998.

Face to Face
When you've listened to country music as much as Tom Fitzgerald has, you start seeing connections to life in the NHL.

Good times, bad bounces, hurtin' tunes, crops, Cups, pucks, guitar pluckers, and the loneliness of the road.

"They are songs about blue-collar people with a pick-up truck, talking about everyday lives," the Nashville Predators' captain said. "The people here are so down to earth, just like most hockey players you'd meet."

As the Massachusetts-born Fitzgerald became a country convert, so have Nashville sports fans gradually identified with the Predators. A minor league team called the Nashville Knights kept the spirit alive for years. But after lots of talk in the mid-1990s about putting an NHL team in the new 20,000-seat Gaylord Entertainment Center, the Predators were born in 1998.

Tom Fitzgerald

They achieved 63 points their first year, better than 10 other post-1967 expansion teams. A seven-point improvement in their second year put them on the verge of playoff contention.

Fitzgerald was a logical addition as team captain when the fledgling Predators out-bid teams such as the Maple Leafs for the right winger's services. As a charter member of the Florida Panthers in 1993, he had the blend of youth and experience that had helped propel his former club into the playoff hunt almost immediately.

"We had a team meeting with [general manager] Bobby Clarke before that first season in Florida," Fitzgerald recalled. "The message was clear: We were not going to be a doormat

Team Highlights

- 1999–2000: Center Cliff Ronning sets a team record, scoring 62 points in the season.

- June 27, 1998: Nashville uses the No. 2 pick overall to select future star David Legwand in the NHL entry draft.

- June 25, 1997, The NHL announces that Nashville will be awarded an expansion franchise for the 1998–99 season.

The Predators took a chance in a trade with Phoenix when they selected the speedy Cliff Ronning. Focusing on skill and quickness over size and strength, the Predators surprised many in their inaugural season with their competitiveness. Ronning has developed into the team's leading scorer and finished the 1999–00 season with a team high 62 points.

Goalie Mike Dunham snares a high shot above the Nashville goal.

team and if you think we are, we don't want you. I tried to bring that same approach to Nashville."

Fitzgerald was part of the Panthers' amazing Rat Race to the 1996 finals and Predators general manager David Poile knew the value of getting someone with Cup credentials. Fitzgerald, wife Kerry and sons Ryan, Casey, and Jack were up for a challenge. Kerry helped form the Predators' Foundation Board, which quickly gave the team a face in many worthy community projects.

"It was a risk putting a hockey team in Nashville," Tom Fitzgerald said. "It's a game they knew from television, but in person, it's even better and we had to sell that.

"But now that we're established, they've been so enthralled and the energy they bring to the rink is unbelievable. It's a nice feeling that you're doing something to help the game grow."

Nashville, a city of more than half a million in middle Tennessee, still has its ties to the north through transplants, and Fitzgerald can pick out many Red Wings sweaters on game night. A lot of Canadians have made their home in the area as well. Fitzgerald's cousin, Keith Tkachuk, was in similar pioneer circumstances with the Phoenix Coyotes.

"We're the baby here," Fitzgerald said. "It's a chance to build a base of fans."

Not to use country music as a marketing tool would have been a waste. Gaylord Entertainment, the club's owners, have a huge stake in the industry through their holdings of Country Music International Television, Grand Ole Opry Radio, and Acuff-Rose Music Publishing.

"I'm always asked what it's like living in the heart of country music, and I say it's like a miniature Los Angeles," Fitzgerald said. "Vince Gill and Barbara Mandrell are at a lot of our games."

In May 1999, "The Late Show with David Letterman" did a special Nashville edition of the show in which a few hundred residents were flown to the studio. Fitzgerald read Letterman's famous Top 10 List of Favorite Predators' Pick-up Lines.

On the ice, the Predators were built slightly differently than most 1990s expansion clubs, with an eye to speed and skill in anticipation of the NHL reducing obstruction. Poile, the long-time Washington Capitals boss, was wheeling and dealing from the moment the 1998 expansion draft started. Without giving up too much of the future, Poile acquired some immediate help.

"He got us Sergei Krivokrasov, Greg Johnson, and Tomas

Team Lowlights

- March 1, 1999: Nashville loses to St. Louis 5–1. It is the Predator's ninth straight home game without a win, a streak that includes eight losses and one tie.

Vokoun for next to nothing," Fitzgerald said. "David is quite a businessman."

Nashville didn't get the easiest route into the NHL as they were placed in the Central Division with perennial powerhouse Detroit and the best regular-season team in the circuit in 1999–00, the 114-point St. Louis Blues. But they've avoided the blowouts many predicted would be a consequence of expansion. Fitzgerald has back-to-back 13-goal seasons, three of them shorthanded, making the Predators one of the top penalty-killing teams in the league.

"I think if you took a poll of every team that has played us,

you'd find all of them dislike us," Fitzgerald said. "We worked at establishing a hard-working reputation and now we've added people such as Cliff Ronning [their ageless leading scorer] and David Legwand [second overall pick in the 1998 draft]. We're in the same position as a lot of more established teams are right now, not far away from a turnaround season."

The Franchise
Though it's not considered a traditional hockey market, Nashville quickly came to prominence in the mid-1990s with construction of the Gaylord Entertainment Center. The state-of-the-art arena and rabid sports fans in the Music City area made it the subject of many relocation rumors for other franchises.

But in 1997, businessman Craig Leoipold teamed with the country music industry giant Gaylord in a successful expansion bid. Jack Diller, a former vice president of the New York Rangers, was appointed president.

The team was named the Predators after the prehistoric saber-toothed tigers whose fossils were found in the Nashville area. Dark blue, silver, orange, and gold, which include the recognized colors of a couple of college football teams in the area, are featured on the sweaters.

The owners chose Washington Capitals' long-time general manager David Poile to run the hockey operation. Poile's father, Bud, had overseen two other expansion clubs, in Philadelphia and Vancouver.

After a 63-point inaugural season, with 28 wins ranking it third in NHL expansion history, coach Barry Trotz's team posted a seven-point improvement in 1999–00. Thanks to 62 points by Cliff Ronning, in his second year at the top of club scoring, the Predators expect to be in playoff contention in coming seasons.

David Legwand struggles to control a rolling puck. He was the second overall pick in the 1998 NHL entry draft, and the Predators hope Legwand will be the centerpiece of the team's future.

Team Records

	Career	Season
Goals	Cliff Ronning, 44	Cliff Ronning, 26 (1999–2000)
Assists	Cliff Ronning, 71	Cliff Ronning, 36 (1999–2000)
Points	Cliff Ronning, 115	Cliff Ronning, 62 (1999–2000)
Goals-Against Average	Tomas Vokoun, 2.86	Tomas Vokoum, 2.78 (1999–2000)

New Jersey Devils

Founded 1982

Formerly the Colorado Rockies 1976–82; Kansas City Scouts 1974–76

Arenas
Continental Airlines Arena 1982–present Present (formerly known as the Meadowlands Arena.)

Stanley Cup Wins
1999–2000, 1994–95

Award Winners

Jack Adams Award
Jacques Lemaire, 1993–94

Calder Trophy
Scott Gomez, 1999–2000
Martin Brodeur, 1993–94

Jennings Trophy
Martin Brodeur, 1997–98
Martin Brodeur and Mike Dunham, 1996–97

Bill Masterton Trophy
Ken Danyeko, 1999–2000
Glenn Resch, 1981–82

Conn Smythe Trophy
Scott Stevens, 1999–2000
Claude Lemieux, 1994–95

Martin Brodeur watches the puck as it heads back up the ice.

Profile

Ken Daneyko has been a Devils player since 1986 providing defensive stability along New Jersey's blue line. A key contributor to their Stanley Cup victory, Daneyko was instrumental in the Devils' push to recapture the Cup in 2000. In addition to winning the Cup, Daneyko also captured the Bill Masterton Trophy at the end of the season.

Face to Face

As young man, he would often introduce himself by saying, "My name is Ken Daneyko, and I'm going to play in the NHL." Not only was the young man right, but he would spend his career as a rarity, a player who stayed with one team year after year.

One June 9, 1982, every first-round pick in the NHL draft was at the Forum in Montreal, except for one. Daneyko stayed home because his agent wasn't sure where he'd be picked. He didn't have to wait long to find out—Daneyko was selected 18th overall by the New Jersey Devils, who had just moved east from Colorado.

"They called me at 7:15 in the morning in Edmonton and told me I'd been drafted," Daneyko remembered. "I forgot to ask them who had taken me." Finally, he was told he'd been selected in the first round by the Devils. "Great," he replied. "Where's New Jersey?"

Daneyko went back to junior hockey for a year, and then joined the Devils as a 19-year-old in the fall of 1983. Eleven games into the season he broke his leg, which spared him from playing in the most embarrassing game in franchise history. In his hometown of Edmonton, Daneyko watched in horror from the press box as the Oilers demolished New Jersey 13–4, after which Wayne Gretzky called the Devils a "Mickey Mouse organization."

"We took it personally," Daneyko said. "But coming from the greatest player in the game, you had to think maybe he's got a point, maybe there are some things we could do differently around here."

Ken Daneyko

Team Highlights

- April 17, 1997: New Jersey goalie Martin Brodeur scores a goal in a play-off game vs. the Montreal Canadiens.

- June 24, 1995: The Devils complete a four-game sweep of the Detroit Red Wings to win their first Stanley Cup title.

- September 3, 1991: The Devils are awarded rock-solid defenseman Scott Stevens as compensation for the St. Louis Blues' signing of Brendan Shanahan. Stevens goes on to become the Devils' captain and is named MVP after the Devils win the 1999–2000 Stanley Cup,

It took a while, but things did change. By the 1987–88 season, with new general manager Lou Lamoriello in charge, and a young nucleus that included John MacLean, Pat Verbeek, and Kirk Muller, the Devils went unbeaten in their last eight games to grab a playoff spot. The clincher, on the final day of the regular season, came when MacLean scored in overtime against Chicago.

"It's funny to look back on it now," Daneyko said, "but at the time, it was like winning the Stanley Cup, and when we got into the playoffs, we came within a game of getting to the Stanley Cup finals."

The Devils appeared to be on their way, but they would have to endure the first of a seemingly endless list of contract squabbles. In the summer of 1989, Pat Verbeek got into a public spat with Lamoriello and was promptly dealt to Hartford. Daneyko also held out briefly in training camp, but owner John McMullen intervened and convinced Daneyko to go back to work. "They were very fair with me," Daneyko said. "Lou could have traded me, but Mr. McMullen convinced him not to, thank goodness."

Since then, Daneyko has watched a long line of Devils stars go nose to nose with Lamoriello and lose. After Verbeek, Muller was traded to Montreal in 1991, and other key players like Scott Niedermayer have tested the team's resolve, only to discover that Lamoriello and the Devils will not back down. Bill Guerin ended his holdout late in 1997, but began sobbing at his first practice. He was promptly traded to Edmonton.

"It's tough for the superstar, because we have that team concept," Daneyko said. "Lou's going to pay a **third-line player** with eight goals as much as a first-line player with 30 goals if he believes they have the same value to the team." Daneyko, who describes himself as old school, added: "I'm a firm believer in that, absolutely."

The Devils do not promote individual players, and the team-

A rock on the New Jersey blue line, captain Scott Stevens led the Devils to Stanley Cup victory in 1999–2000, winning the Conn Smythe Trophy for his efforts.

first philosophy rankled many offensive players, who felt constrained in New Jersey's tight checking system. Steve Thomas, who later played in Toronto, likened his three years in New Jersey to being "shackled."

But in 1995, the teamwork paid off. The Devils tore through the playoffs and swept the Red Wings, to win the Stanley Cup. For Daneyko, MacLean, and Bruce Driver, who had been together for more than a decade, the win was especially sweet.

"It was something special," Daneyko said, still smiling five years later. "We had come full circle from the early years, from being the doormats, the 'Mickey Mouse organization,' coming so close the year before and then finally winning it, we really took it to heart."

To an outsider, Daneyko appeared to be on top of the world. He was a key player for a championship team, and it was hard

Superpest Claude Lemieux leans into a slap shot. An abrasive competitor, Lemieux is at his best in the playoffs.

to imagine how things could have been better. The truth was, things were quickly going downhill. Privately, Daneyko was drinking heavily and having difficulty at home. Finally, in 1997, he stepped forward and sought treatment.

"That was the hardest decision in the world. I was as scared as anybody," Daneyko said. "I was on the fence for a couple of years, but finally, something had to give."

For Daneyko, who wore his heart on his sleeve in every game, the emotional roller coaster had become too much. "I did everything off the ice just as hard as I did on the ice. I took wins and losses home with me—the highs were too high, and the lows were too low."

With the full support of Devils management, Daneyko checked into a treatment program and received counseling to help him where he needed it most, away from the ice. "It's funny," Daneyko says now, "the reason I loved playing so much was that it was the only three hours I didn't have to worry about what was going on inside me."

Today, Daneyko is still an intense, gritty player—with a difference. "I still bring all that emotion to the rink, but when I leave, I leave it there." Daneyko is deeply thankful to John McMullen, who he says "has been like a father to me." Lamoriello helped too, although Daneyko says, "There was a lot of tough love there, believe me."

In the 1999–2000 season, Daneyko played his 1,000th NHL game, becoming only the 16th player in league history to accomplish the milestone while playing for only one team. In describing himself, today's Ken Daneyko very much resembles the one who wasn't sure he was good enough to be drafted in the first round in 1982.

"I'm not a star player who does fancy things," he says. "I'm just a guy who plays his heart out."

The Franchise
That a hockey colossus could rise out of the swamps of New Jersey is improbable enough. That the Devils could do it after failing miserably in two other places stands as one of the most remarkable turnarounds in the business of sport.

The Devils began their hockey life in 1974, as the Kansas City Scouts. Badly watered down by expansion and facing fierce competition for players from the World Hockey Association, the NHL couldn't have picked a worse time or place to locate a

Jason Arnott finally reached his potential in 1999-2000 and emerged as one of the league's premier power forwards. Arnott used his strength and scoring ability to become one of the most important contributors to New Jersey's second Stanley Cup victory.

franchise. Rising oil prices and a falling commodity market were devastating America's breadbasket, and the market for pro hockey, especially bad pro hockey, was limited.

The Scouts weren't nearly as bad as their expansion cousins in Washington, but after two unsuccessful years on and off the ice, they headed for the hills—literally. The Scouts moved to the mountains of Colorado, became the Rockies, and hoped to cash in on a marketplace that had a long hockey history.

Denver did have a long history with the game, the college game, and while the NHL's Avalanche would later flourish in Colorado, the Rockies did not. The team made the playoffs in its second year in Denver, but almost everyone did in those days. The Rockies were hilariously inept, with players like goaltender Hardy Astrom, who had a legendary penchant for being beaten on long shots. One day at practice, Bobby Schmautz tried to help

Astrom by shooting pucks at him from the blue line. The first four beat him cleanly.

In 1979–80, the team hired Don Cherry as coach, and while the former boss of the Bruins quickly made "Rocky hockey" fashionable, he feuded with ownership, missed the playoffs, and was fired after one season.

Meantime, the ownership was in chaos. The team had changed hands twice in four years and finally, in the spring of 1982, it was sold to Dr. John McMullen, a New Jersey shipping magnate who said he had "big plans" for the franchise. He did, but those plans had nothing to do with Colorado or Denver. McMullen announced that the team would be moving to New Jersey immediately.

The move did not appear to make sense. Although the team would be playing very close to New York City, the newly christened Devils would be surrounded by hockey powerhouses. To the east there were the Rangers and Islanders, and to the west there were the Philadelphia Flyers. McMullen would have to compensate all three teams for invading their territory, then try to make a go of it in eastern New Jersey.

As expected, the Devils fared poorly at first. The only sellouts at the Meadowlands came when the Rangers visited, and long-time fans who could not get tickets in New York crossed the Hudson. On the ice the franchise was still terrible, in the midst of a streak that would see it miss the playoffs nine straight times, an unofficial NHL record.

The team hit bottom in 1983–84. In November of that year, the Devils were trounced 13–4 by the powerhouse Edmonton Oilers, as goaltender Ron Low was torched by Wayne Gretzky and company. A friend and former teammate of Low's, Gretzky was visibly angered afterwards, calling the Devils a "Mickey Mouse organization." It would take New Jersey a long time to live that one down, and while Gretzky later acknowledged the misstep, he has also privately maintained that he was absolutely right, which he was.

By 1987, the franchise was nearly a decade removed from its last playoff appearance. Two general managers (Billy MacMillan and Max McNab) and three coaches (MacMillan, Tommy McVie, and Doug Carpenter) had been unable to lift the team into the post-season.

On April 30, 1987, McMullen stunned the hockey world again, hiring Lou Lamoriello from Providence College as the team's pres-

The winner of the Calder Trophy for Rookie of the Year in 1994, Martin Brodeur was instrumental in New Jersey's Stanley Cup victory in the 1994–95 season. A perennial All-Star, his consistently solid goaltending ensures that year in and year out, the Devils have to be considered among the league's top Cup contenders.

ident. Lamoriello, who named himself GM just prior to training camp that fall, had never played or managed in the NHL, and was largely unknown outside the U.S. college community.

Lamoriello inherited a team with rising young stars like Kirk Muller and John MacLean, and in the spring of 1988, the Devils finally made their mark, in a big way. With Jim Schoenfeld having replaced Carpenter behind the bench in mid-season, the Devils surged down the stretch, going undefeated in their last eight games. On April 3, in the final game of the regular season, MacLean scored the overtime winner in Chicago, securing the Devils a spot in the playoffs. And they weren't done there.

After upsetting the Islanders in the first round, the Devils took out Washington in seven games to advance to the Conference final. The series against the Bruins featured an infamous altercation between Schoenfeld and referee Don Koharski, in which Schoenfeld uttered the immortal line "Have another doughnut, you fat pig!" Angry that Schoenfeld was not severely disciplined, the NHL's regular officials refused to work Game 4. Amateurs refereed the contest wearing yellow practice sweaters, and while the Devils won the game, they went on to lose the series in seven.

Over the next several years, the Devils were unable to duplicate that success, but the team was forging an identity for itself. Lamoriello was becoming known as a shrewd dealer, and his patient building philosophy was paying dividends. Believing strongly in the draft and player development, Lamoriello's Devils would become the blueprint for other teams to follow, and while his tough negotiating policies would alienate many top players, Lamoriello's teams were competitive despite a payroll that annually put them in the bottom half of the league.

In the summer of 1993, having watched his team bow out in the first round of the playoffs for the fourth straight year, Lamoriello made another bold move, hiring Jacques Lemaire as the team's coach. In his first season behind the bench, Lemaire guided the Devils to the Conference final, losing a seventh-game heartbreaker in double overtime to the Rangers.

The following year, the NHL season was shortened to 48 games due to a league-wide lockout of the players. The Devils, who were among the hard-liners in the dispute with the Players Association, wound up being extremely grateful the season wasn't canceled.

With Scott Niedermayer and Scott Stevens patrolling the

blue line, budding superstar Martin Brodeur playing brilliantly in goal, and veteran Claude Lemieux leading up front, the Devils cruised through the first three rounds of the playoffs, losing only four games. They didn't lose a game in the finals, sweeping Detroit to capture the franchise's first Stanley Cup championship.

The celebration was typically New Jersey. Since the team's arena isn't located in an actual community, there was no home city in which to hold a parade. The Devils settled for a rally in the parking lot at the Meadowlands, a far cry from the Rangers celebration on Broadway a year earlier.

But if the franchise suffers in comparison to more glamorous teams in the NHL, the people who run the Devils don't seem to mind a bit. Lemaire didn't flinch when his team was criticized for being dull and defensive, and with the full backing of McMullen, Lamoriello has continually held firm in contract talks with star players, coming away the victor each time. The Devils' draft record remains one of the NHL's best, its development system turns out a steady diet of NHL regulars, and the team remains competitive year after year.

If Lamoriello's patience has been rewarded, so too has McMullen's. In the spring of 2000, he negotiated the sale of the Devils to a group headed by New York Yankees owner George Steinbrenner. Once the poor cousins of the New York area sports scene, the Devils are now the cornerstone of a cable television empire destined to rival the biggest in the United States.

It's been a long journey in less than 20 years, and while NHL historians will point out that the franchise is really older than that, the Devils make little mention of their humble beginnings. In the team's media guide you'll find no references to those two years in Kansas City, or Hardy Astrom and "Rocky hockey." When you think about how far they've come, the Devils do indeed seem very far removed from those early days.

Team Lowlights

- November 19, 1983: Following a 13–4 drubbing by the Edmonton Oilers, the Devils franchise suffers their its lowest moment when Wayne Gretzky publicly declares that they are "a Mickey Mouse organization."

Team Records

	Career	Season
Goals	John MacLean, 347	Pat Verbeek, 46 (1987–88)
Assists	John MacLean, 354	Scott Stevens, 60 (1993–94)
Points	John MacLean, 701	Kirk Muller, 94 (1987–88)
Goals-Against Average	Martin Brodeur, 2.20	Martin Brodeur, 1.88 (1996–97)
Games Played	Ken Daneyko, 1070	

New York Islanders

Founded 1972

Arenas
Nassau Veterans Memorial
  Coliseum

Stanley Cup Wins
1982–83, 1981–82,
  1980–81, 1979–80,

Award Winners

Jack Adams Award
Al Arbour, 1978–79

Lady Byng Trophy
Pierre Turgeon, 1992–93
Mike Bossy, 1985–86,
  1983–84, 1982–83

Calder Trophy
Bryan Berard, 1996–97
Mike Bossy, 1977–78
Bryan Trottier, 1975–76
Denis Potvin, 1973–74

King Clancy Trophy
Bryan Trottier, 1988–89

Hart Trophy
Bryan Trottier, 1978–79

Jennings Trophy
Billy Smith and Roland
  Melanson, 1982–83

Bill Masterton Trophy
Mark Fitzpatrick, 1991–92
Ed Westfall, 1976–77

Norris Trophy
Denis Potvin, 1978–79,
  1977–78, 1975–76

Art Ross Trophy
Bryan Trottier, 1978–79

Conn Smythe Trophy
Billy Smith, 1982–83
Mike Bossy, 1981–82
Butch Goring, 1980–81
Bryan Trottier, 1979–80

Vezina Trophy
Billy Smith, 1981–82

Profile

Mike Bossy is the only player in NHL history to produce 50 or more goals in each of his first nine seasons in the league, a record of goal-scoring consistency that may never be duplicated. A back injury prematurely ended Bossy's career at age 30, but only after he had produced 1,126 points in just 752 games. Eight times an All-Star, including five first-team selections, Bossy was on four Stanley Cup championship teams and won three Lady Byng Trophies, plus the 1982 Conn Smythe Trophy and the 1978 Calder Trophy.

Face to Face

Much about the legend of Mike Bossy is already known: how the New York Islanders were one of the worst teams in the National Hockey League for their first two seasons, but had already started to turn the corner by the spring of 1977, the year they drafted him. How 14 teams passed over Bossy, a brilliant goal scorer, but a player who hockey scouts thought might struggle with the intimidating tactics of the era. How Bossy, after weighing an offer from the Quebec Nordiques of the rival World Hockey Association, eventually signed with the Islanders—and then promptly informed general manager Bill Torrey that he planned to score 50 goals as an NHL rookie. And finally how Bossy actually scored 53 goals and won the Calder Trophy as the league's rookie of the year.

No, Bossy never lacked confidence as a player and always found a way of backing up his words.

"I actually did say that," Bossy confirms now, "but there was a little prodding from my agent involved in that too. When I look back on that today, just the fact that I agreed to say something like that to Bill Torrey was a little ridiculous, a little preposterous. I can imagine what was going through his mind. 'Here's this guy that's been drafted 15th, so 14 teams don't think he has a chance of playing in the National Hockey League ever. Then all of a sudden, he's in here telling me he can score 50 goals.' I guess, at the time, I hoped that by agreeing to say something like that, that he would think I had confidence in myself and that I wanted to not just make

Mike Bossy

Bryan Trottier won six Stanley Cups during his 18-year NHL career. He spent four years playing for the Islanders.

the team, but make the team and score goals at the same time."

Bossy proved to be a nice fit on an Islanders team that already boasted plenty of grit and will, but not enough pure scoring talent. Bryan Trottier, the consummate two-way player and playmaker, had come along two years previous and the two forged a partnership that ultimately anchored four Stanley Cup championship teams. In the end, the quality Bossy brought to the Islanders was the quality they were looking for. On a young and improving team that was getting close to putting all the pieces together, Bossy was the final core piece added by Torrey.

Bossy arrived in the 1977–78 season and even though he had a spectacular first season, the Islanders were upset in their opening round by the Toronto Maple Leafs. The next year, as Bossy scored an eye-popping 69 goals, the Islanders were eliminated by the crosstown rivals, the New York Rangers, in their second round. They were enduring growing pains or, more precisely, a learning period, as Bossy puts it.

"They had been to the semifinals three times before I got there and we lost in our first or second round the first two years I was there. But at the same time, I do believe that by the way I played and the attitude I had, it sort of let others start to express themselves as far as players. Because of the success I was having, they let themselves get out of the strict defensive mode that [coach] Al Arbour had and be a little more creative—but at the same time, playing his style.

"A lot of credit goes to Al for letting the players do that. It would have been easy to clamp down on Bryan Trottier or the others and say, 'Let him do his thing, but I want you guys at the blue line or the red line or staying back.' My first training camp, I hounded Al. I kept asking him, 'Where should I be? What should I do? How should I be playing this?' He said, 'Forget about all that. Play the way you played in junior and we'll teach you the rest as time goes on.'"

Bossy was a productive player in the Islanders' first championship year—1979–80, when they defeated the Philadelphia Flyers in a stirring six-game series—but Trottier received the nod as playoff MVP. The next year, Bossy established playoff records for both points (35) and power-play goals (nine), but saw Butch Goring take home the Conn Smythe. It wasn't until 1982— when the Islanders brushed aside the underdog Vancouver Canucks in four consecutive games—that Bossy was rewarded with the MVP award. That year, Bossy scored seven goals in the

four-game finals, tying Jean Beliveau (1956) for the modern record for goals in a finals series. In 1983, Bossy produced another solid playoff, leading the league in playoff goals with 17 for the third spring in a row. This time, it was goaltender Billy Smith—the fourth different Islanders player in four years—who took home the Conn Smythe, a measure of how much the Islanders, despite all their individual talents, won as a team during their Stanley Cup reign.

In looking back on that unprecedented run—the Islanders remain the only U.S.-based team to win the Stanley Cup four successive times—Bossy said, "The first one stands out because it was the first—and we had struggled the two previous years in

Pat LaFontaine scored 54 goals in the 1989-90 season joining Mike Bossy and Bryan Trottier as the only Islanders to have scored 50 or more goals in a season. In the 1992–93 season, Pierre Turgeon also joined the 50-goal club when he scored 58.

As a member of the Islanders, Bryan Trottier won four Stanley Cup championships and finished his career as one of the highest scoring players in league history. A key member of the Islanders' dynasty of the early 1980s, along with players such as Mike Bossy and Denis Potvin, Trottier was more than an offensive center—he was also a standout defensive player. Trottier was voted into the Hockey Hall of Fame in 1997.

the playoffs before we were able to win. So that was very gratifying. The fourth was special because we weren't supposed to win that one. The Oilers were supposed to be this great young team—and although they were a great young team, they still had to go through the same kind of growing pains we went through before we won our first Stanley Cup. On top of that, to beat them four straight was something special."

Bossy played until the 1986–87 season, by which time the Islanders were a good but no longer great team. For his part, Bossy found the wear and tear of going into the traffic areas had exacted a severe toll on him and led to chronic back problems. Missing 17 games in his final season cost Bossy a chance to become the only player in NHL history to score 50 goals every season in which he played.

"When I hurt my back and finished the season with 38 goals,

that was probably the most disappointing part of my hockey career," said Bossy. "I was gunning for 50 goals every year. Not being able to get them that 10th year was disappointing to me. I realized my back wasn't going to get better; knowing I was probably going to have to go through another season with the same kind of pain that I had and the same disappointments as the previous year was difficult.

"That last year, there were times when I shouldn't have played, but played anyway and risked getting seriously injured because I didn't have the mobility I had before that. All those things together—and knowing down deep that 50 goals was out of the question, wasn't a possibility any more—was probably the main reason that I stopped playing.

"Being 43 now and looking back and realizing that I've been retired for so long, a little part of me regrets that I left so early and that I wasn't able to accept from myself that I could have gone out and contributed in some way—at a lesser scale maybe. Part of me regrets that I didn't do that, that I decided to be the stubborn guy that I am."

How is his back today?

"I cope with it. My back hurts 24 hours a day, from the time I get up until the time I go to bed. You just get used to living with the aggravation. I can't say it's always pain because it depends upon what I do. I play golf, yes, but I play golf hurt.

"At this stage now, because I've lived with it so long, it's more aggravation than pain—but then again, that depends upon what I do, and I have to say I don't do very much. I know whatever I do, my back's going to hurt—so I keep away from a lot of things.""

The Franchise
For the New York Islanders, the less said about the first two years of the franchise, the better. Joining the NHL as an expansion team for the start of the 1972–73 season—which coincided with the beginning of the rival World Hockey Association—the Islanders won just 12 and 19 games in their first two seasons. That early futility paid off with high selections in the annual amateur draft, and the Islanders chose wisely, selecting Denis Potvin first overall in 1973 and Clark Gillies fourth overall in 1974. Their presence in the lineup helped New York begin a relatively rapid journey to respectability. They made the playoffs in Year 3, making an extraordinary 58-point regular-season improvement in a 24-month span—and the best was yet to come. In the spring of 1975, the Islanders

Team Highlights
- 1998: Zigmund Palffy is selected to the NHL All-Star game and goes on to score 45 goals for the season.

- April 18, 1987: Pat Lafontaine scores in the fourth overtime in the final game of a seven-game series to advance the Islanders past the Washington Capitals to the second round of the playoffs.

- May 17, 1983: The Islanders hold off the young Edmonton Oilers to win their fourth straight Stanley Cup title.

became only the second team in NHL history to recover from a 3–0 deficit and go on to win a playoff series. That happened in the second round against the Pittsburgh Penguins and they almost did it again in the third round, versus Philadelphia, overcoming a 3–0 deficit to get to 3–3 before finally dropping the seventh game.

The Islanders were on their way and they would add two more important pieces of the puzzle in the next three seasons. First, center Bryan Trottier and then right winger Mike Bossy would join a team that already had excellent goaltending in Billy Smith, a go-to defenseman in Potvin, plus grit and toughness in Gillies, Bob Nystrom, and Bob Bourne.

Improving every year, the Islanders exceeded the 100-point mark for four consecutive seasons—from 1975–76 to 1978–79—but could not get beyond the semifinals.

Curiously, it was the year that they slipped back a touch—to a 91-point regular season that they finally won the Stanley Cup. As critics wondered if the Islanders would ever meet their early expectations, they advanced to the Stanley Cup finals and knocked off the Philadelphia Flyers in six games, with Nystrom scoring the overtime game winner on a play that may go down in history as the most famous missed offside of all time.

Once they got over the hump, the Islanders effectively cruised to their next two championships. In 1981, they defeated a Minnesota North Stars team that recorded only 87 regular-season points. In 1982, they knocked off a Vancouver Canucks team that qualified for the finals, despite the fact that they'd lost more regular-season games (33) than they won (30). The next real challenge came against the maturing Edmonton Oilers, a team that boasted Wayne Gretzky, Mark Messier, and the rest of their future Hall of Fame cast. In a clinical display of their trademark grit and tenacity, the 1983 Islanders knocked off the Oilers in four consecutive games, putting a punctuation mark on a dynasty of their own.

That fourth championship would prove to be their last hurrah, however. The Oilers, learning something about the sacrifices individual players needed to make to win in a team sport, knocked off the defending champions in the 1984 playoffs. They were a team on the rise, the Islanders—though it wouldn't become apparent for a few more seasons—a team in decline. The Islanders slipped back into the NHL pack over the next four years, but remained competitive, always winning more games than they lost. The bottom fell out in the 1988–89 season when they slipped back to 61 points and missed the playoffs for the first time since their second year.

Unhappily, in the 1990s, the Islanders made more headlines for what they did off—as opposed to on—the ice. In all, they missed the playoffs in seven of 10 years, as ownership issues came to the fore. John Pickett, the team's owner during the championship years, tried to sell the team in 1997 to would-be entrepreneur John Spano, who turned out to be something of a fraud—and eventually relinquished the team back to Pickett before heading to prison. A year later, Pickett sold the team again—to New York Sports Ventures, a group that included Steven Gluckstern and Howard Milstein. They, in turn, tried to get the Nassau Coliseum condemned as unsafe and threatened to play home games in nearby Hartford. That ploy didn't work, however.

Faced with declining attendance and poor on-ice results, the Islanders purged the team of virtually all but a handful of their top players—Ziggy Palffy, Felix Potvin, Robert Reichel, Bryan Smolinski, Trevor Linden—turning them into draft choices and cheaper youngsters. Eventually, Gluckstern and Milstein found another willing buyer, software tycoon Charles Wang, chairman of Computer Associates International, who completed the purchase of the team in the spring of 2000.

Zigmund Palffy attempts to kick the puck out of his skates as an Ottawa defender dives headlong into his knees.

Team Records

	Career	Season
Goals	Mike Bossy, 573	Mike Bossy, 69 (1978–79)
Assists	Bryan Trottier, 853	Bryan Trottier, 87 (1978–79)
Points	Bryan Trottier, 1,353	Mike Bossy, 147 (1981–82)
Goals-Against Average	Chico Resch, 2.56	Chico Resch, 2.07 (1975–76)
Games Played	Bryan Trottier, 1,123	

New York Rangers

Founded 1926

Arenas
Madison Square Garden
    1926–present

Stanley Cup Wins
1993–94, 1939–40,
    1932–33, 1927–28,

Award Winners

see page 253

Acrobatic goalie Mike
Richter had 16
playoff wins for the
Rangers when they
won the Stanley Cup
in 1993-94.

Profile

The captain of the New York Rangers from 1997 to 2000 and a two-time Norris Trophy winner, Brian Leetch holds or shares more than 30 club records for regular season and playoffs. He had 102 points in 1991–92 and was a member of the Rangers' 1994 Stanley Cup team, when he also won the Conn Smythe Trophy. Drafted in the first round in 1986, Leetch is slated to play in his 900th NHL game during the 2000–01 season.

Face to Face

Brian Leetch is a real-life New York City ghostbuster. But the specter he helped slay had a number, not a name.

"Nineteen-forty," said Leetch, now able to laugh at the mention of the Rangers' second-last Stanley Cup. "They used to start chanting it in warmups during road games on Long Island and New Jersey. It was kind of a killer for us every game.

"To have our fans hear it . . . well, there wasn't really any good comeback they had for it."

Like every Ranger who suited up from World War II to the Clinton administration, Leetch endured that grating chant. The difference was, he was able to exorcise it and bring the longest Cup drought in NHL history to a close in 1994.

"I was raised in Massachusetts as a Red Sox fan and I knew the feeling, that everyone almost expects something to go wrong every year. But the best thing about winning it was that a lot of the guys who'd been there from other years, such as Rod Gilbert and John Davidson, were still involved with the team. They were as excited as we were to end the curse."

Leetch, a six-foot defenseman blessed with outstanding offensive skills, came to the Rangers six years earlier, after the completion of the 1988 Olympic tournament in Calgary. The ninth overall pick in 1986, he spent a year at Boston College and jumped to the U.S. National team.

The "Miracle of '88," Leetch's facetious term for the Americans' poor seventh-place showing in Calgary, was quickly forgotten when the call came to get to New York.

"I went to the team hotel and knocked on Mark Hardy's

Brian Leetch

Team Highlights

- June 19, 1994: Led by stars such as Mark Messier and defenseman Brian Leetch, the Rangers beat Vancouver to win their first Stanley Cup in 54 years.

- October 4, 1991: Searching for leadership, the Rangers acquire the legendary Mark Messier from the Edmonton Oilers.

- April 7, 1928: With the Rangers goalie injured, 44-year-old coach Lester Patrick plays goal and leads New York to an overtime win in game two of the Standly Cup final.

door," Leetch recalled. "He told me we were getting a lift to the game with Marcel Dionne after we had a rest. I don't think I slept at all. I was walking around saying, 'I can't believe I'll be in a car with Marcel Dionne.'"

Leetch made his Ranger debut on February 29, 1988, at Madison Square Garden against the St. Louis Blues.

"The first person I met was Chris Nilan. He came up and gave me a hard time about Calgary because he was an American. Then I was standing on the bench during the national anthem, looking around, listening to the crowd and it was unbelievable. Then the game starts and Nuck [Nilan] gets into a fight right away. That's when it hit me; welcome to the Big Apple, Brian, welcome to The Show."

He assisted on a Kelly Kisio power-play goal that first game, the trigger for 781 regular season points to date. The Rangers missed the playoffs that season, but Leetch's 14 points in 17 games were a sign of great things to come. In his first full season, he had 71 points and captured the Calder Trophy, only the second Ranger in 35 years to be named top rookie.

"It's a great place to play because of the fans," he said. "You almost expect to have 100 fans around your car every night. I can't imagine playing somewhere where there isn't that [attention]. You really notice the Ranger [mystique] on the road. Every city either has a transplanted New Yorker or a Ranger fan who drove down to the game."

The fans always saved their worst receptions for Denis Potvin, captain of the hated Islanders. Leetch vividly recalled Potvin's last game at Madison Square Garden, just a few days after he'd joined the Rangers.

"The crowd was yelling at him out on the blue line during the anthem, booing, waving signs, unfurling banners," Leetch said. "Potvin's just standing there and I thought, 'This guy is something special to be taking all of this abuse.' Man, they were vicious."

There was a tremendous old guard presence in New York when Leetch broke in: Dionne, Guy Lafleur, Ron Greschner. The club finished in first place twice in the Patrick Division in two of Leetch's first four years. He set a number of club records for assists in a single season and in 1991–92 became the first Ranger since Harry Howell to win the Norris Trophy, getting 102 points. General manager Neil Smith, whose ascent began just after Leetch's arrival, was making the Rangers a younger, more

Rod Gilbert overcame a broken back suffered in junior hockey to make it to the NHL with the New York Rangers. In his 15 years with the Rangers he would set no fewer than 20 club scoring records.

dynamic team, but needed someone who had been around the block with the Cup.

In October of 1991, Smith brought steely-eyed general Mark Messier from Edmonton in exchange for Bernie Nicholls, Steven Rice, and Louie DeBrusk.

"Mark was a tremendous asset to me and the team, in the way he played and the way he spoke," Leetch said. "It wasn't that he scored a lot of goals, it was that they were always big ones. He made that one great pass or that one great shot that changed the course of a game."

After a hiccup saw the Rangers miss the playoffs in 1992–93, Smith named Mike Keenan coach. The Islanders, Oilers, Canadiens, Flyers, and Penguins had dominated the Cup since expansion, but now at last, it was the Rangers' time.

"We had a so-so start and suddenly we got rolling," Leetch said. "Mike Richter didn't lose a game in net for 20 starts [16–0–4] and as a team, we put together some streaks.

"At the trade deadline [in 1993 and 1994], we got ourselves some more experience and depth with Craig MacTavish, Glenn Anderson, and Esa Tikkanen. If those guys didn't score, they used their bodies in some way to make them a pain in the neck to play against. We won the President's Trophy that year [with a team-record 112 points].

"Any time you're on a good team such as that, it rubs off. Jeff Beukeboom and I got lots of ice time on power play, penalty killing, just about every key situation."

Many star players have clashed with Keenan, but he and Leetch enjoyed a prosperous relationship.

"He was a different coach than what I was used to, a real psychological motivator. It was an adjustment, but the winning was most important. He kept everyone on edge. I'm glad we had 52 wins that year, because I wouldn't like to have been around him if we'd lost that many."

The final 16 victories to get the Cup were not without peril. Those were the days when the first overall team was usually a fat target for a playoff upset.

"We opened against the Islanders, who had absolutely nothing to lose while we were still a little scared. But we came on like gangbusters in that series, won a couple of games 6–0 and we just built from there."

Messier's stirring speeches received all the attention in the seven-game double overtime conference finals against the

Devils, but by then, the whole team was in overdrive. The last speed bump was in the final series, when the Rangers looked like they were about to give up a 3–1 lead to Vancouver.

"Coming all the way back from Vancouver after Game 6 without the Cup...that was a long flight. There was definitely tension in the air in New York. You could feel how tight the building was in Game 7. Fortunately, we got an early goal [Leetch's 11th of the playoffs] and got the crowd into it."

Signed by the Rangers as a free agent before the 1999–2000 season Theo Fleury was expected to add much needed scoring power to the New York offense.

The 3–2 final put the city on its ear. Leetch not only got to hoist the Cup, he was named winner of the Conn Smythe Trophy, the first American ever to win it, for 11 goals and 23 assists, with 11 points coming in the finals.

"What a blur that last game is now," Leetch said. "All I remember afterwards is doing so many interviews, then going to a friend's restaurant to celebrate. I only got about four hours sleep I was so excited."

A fan's sign at the game that night read "Now I Can Die in Peace" as the party continued around town for days afterward.

Leetch and teammates were invited to bring the Cup everywhere: to David Letterman's show, Conan O'Brien's, Howard Stern's, as well as a baseball game at Yankee Stadium. The traditional ticker-tape parade was also a highlight.

The Rangers have yet to win another Cup, but Leetch hasn't slowed down. He passed Gilbert in playoff scoring the next year, was a second-team All-Star in 1995–96, and won his second Norris the season after that. Keenan and Messier would eventually move on, but the club was invigorated again by the acquisition of Wayne Gretzky in the summer of 1996.

"I used to listen to Mess talk to him on the phone through the door, trying to catch what they were saying," Leetch said. "I'd ask Mark, is there any way you could get him here? When he did come, it was incredible. I would just listen to them tell stories all the time. Wayne was such a class act and he fit in our team right away."

Gretzky's 2,857th and final professional point was an assist on a Leetch goal against Pittsburgh on April 18, 1999, the emotional Madison Square Garden farewell.

"His decision to leave when he did turned out to be the right thing, I believe. If we'd been a top team, he'd have stayed, so that's disappointing that we couldn't have played better for him.

"But he didn't want to play another year and maybe lose his passion for the game. We had to understand that."

Leetch could certainly understand what's lured Gretzky, Messier, and a host of stars to the Rangers' banner.

"You realize you're part of something big," Leetch said. "Something that's been around for a long time before you and something that will still be there long after I'm gone."

Andy Bathgate was one of the Rangers most productive players of the 1950s and 60s. He won the Hart Trophy in 1958-59 and tied Bobby Hull for the league's scoring title in 1961-62 with 84 points.

The Franchise

Flamboyant sportsman George Lewis (Tex) Rickard assembled the Madison Square Garden Corporation in 1925, erecting a huge new hall for various forms of entertainment. One was an NHL team, the New York Americans, who were renting the facility.

The enthusiastic response to hockey in town convinced Rickard to bring in his own team, which the media dubbed Tex's Rangers, in recognition of his Lone Star State roots.

In preparation for their 1926–27 debut, Rickard and Madison Square Garden president Colonel John S. Hammond selected Toronto-born Conn Smythe to be the manager. Using the scouting grapevine he'd nurtured as coach at the University of Toronto, Smythe assembled a team that included future Hall of Famers Bill and Bun Cook. Together with Frank Boucher, they emerged as one of the best forward lines of their era, nicknamed the A Line, for the Eighth Street "A" train that ran nearby. Smythe rounded out the team with goaltender Lorne Chabot and defensemen Taffy Abel and Ching Johnson.

Smythe wasn't there to see his handiwork win the Stanley Cup in 1927–28. He was fired in a row with the equally obstinate Hammond on the eve of the 1926–27 season and went home to buy the team that became the Maple Leafs and, later, build Maple Leaf Gardens.

Lester Patrick was waiting in the wings to replace Smythe. Patrick had a wealth of experience in the Pacific Coast Hockey Association and got the club off on the right foot. On November 16, 1926, the Rangers debuted with a 1–0 win over the Montreal Maroons. Within two years, they had qualified for the Cup finals and even taken some headlines away from the powerful Yankees baseball team of the Babe Ruth era.

Patrick became a huge story himself during one of those first championship games against the Maroons, filling in for Chabot when he was injured and a replacement couldn't be found. The 44-year-old emergency substitute help tie the series 1–1 and the Rangers went on to their first Cup.

In 1933, with several of Smythe's players still on the team, the Rangers beat the Leafs in four games. The graying team was transformed as the 1930s wore on under a new president, General John Reed Kilpatrick. Boucher moved behind the bench to coach a new Cup caliber team that included the Bread Line, Max and Neil Colville and Alex Shibicky. Before the demands of

World War II had stripped the NHL of its best players, the Rangers built a 1939–40 team that lost only once in a stretch of 25 games and beat the Leafs in six games for the Cup.

It was the last time for decades that the Rangers could celebrated. One theory held that the Rangers had desecrated the Cup by burning the Madison Square Garden mortgage in its bowl, thus putting a curse on the team.

For whatever reason, the team entered a Dark Ages phase, either missing the playoffs or making a quick exit, eventually leading to Boucher's departure in 1955.

At least a strong farm team had developed with the Guelph Biltmores, who sent the Rangers' future stars Harry Howell and Andy Bathgate to finish up the 1950s. A bright new general manager, Emile (the Cat) Francis emerged, building a team that boasted Jean Ratelle, Rod Gilbert, and Ed Giacomin. They peaked with an appearance in the 1972 Cup loss to the Bruins.

Before the crosstown Islanders dynasty was set up, the Rangers almost stole their thunder in 1979, but lost the Cup to the Canadiens in a five-game final.

It wasn't until the 1990s that the Rangers put themselves in a position to win it all. Top draft pick defenseman Brian Leetch was joined by Edmonton's feared and respected leader, Mark Messier, who had an even sterner man behind the bench in Mike Keenan. Resolved to win, the Rangers withstood a 3–2 series' deficit against the New Jersey Devils and finished a seven-game championship set with Vancouver with a 3–2 win.

It was the Rangers' first Cup since 1940. Manhattan would also be the backdrop for Wayne Gretzky's last fling in the NHL, including two 90-point seasons as part of his three years there. He skated into the sunset in April of 1999, with 2,857 NHL points.

Team Records

	Career	Season
Goals	Rod Gilbert, 406	Adam Graves, 52 (1993–94)
Assists	Rod Gilbert, 615	Brian Leetch, 80 (1991–92)
Points	Rod Gilbert, 1,021	Jean Ratelle, 109 (1971–72)
Goals-Against Average	Lorne Chabot, 1.61	John Ross Roach, 1.41 (1928–29)
Games Played	Harry Howell, 1,160	

Ottawa Senators

Founded 1992

Arenas
Corel Centre 1996–present
Ottawa Civic Centre
  1992–96

Stanley Cup Wins
0

Award Winners

Jack Adams Award
Jacques Martin, 1998–99

Calder Trophy
Daniel Alfredsson, 1995–96

Alexei Yashin leads the rush as Adams Graves chases him from behind.

Profile

Even before he played his first-ever NHL game, Wade Redden had the peculiar distinction of being traded from the New York Islanders, where he was the second overall pick in 1995, to the Ottawa Senators for Bryan Berard, the first overall pick in 1995. Only 23, with four NHL seasons under his belt, Redden is one of the NHL's rising stars, with two world junior championships (1995 and 1996) to his credit, plus a bronze medal from the 1999 world hockey championships.

Wade Redden

Face to Face

The growing pains— and in the Ottawa Senators' first four years, there were a lot of growing pains— were pretty much over by the time defenseman Wade Redden arrived on the scene. The highly rated Redden was chosen by the New York Islanders second overall in the 1995 entry draft, one behind the Ottawa Senators' first choice, defenseman Bryan Berard. Berard saw a Senators team that had won just nine games in the lockout-shortened 1994–95 season that was not ready to accede to his contract demands. He demanded a trade and, following a change in management—Randy Sexton out, Pierre Gauthier in—received his wish. Berard, a New York kind of guy anyway, joined the Islanders. Redden, a small-town Saskatchewan kid, came to hockey country. In many ways, Ottawa turned out to be a much better fit than the Islanders on a number of levels, including the quality of the hockey team. The Senators started winning almost as soon as Redden arrived in October 1996 for his first training camp.

"They were last in the league, but they had just made a lot of changes in the front office," said Redden. "My agent, Don Meehan, knew more about it than me and he said, 'Things are turning around there.' I was excited to be a part of it. There were 12 new guys who came in the previous year and in my first year, there were 11 more new players. The whole team changed its face.

"The way things have worked out, I've been really happy here the last four years. The organization is making strides to get better and they've shown lots of improvement. It's good to

Team Highlights

- April 12, 2000: The Senators begin to resurrect the "Battle of Ontario" when they meet the Toronto Maple Leafs in the first round of the Stanley Cup playoffs.

- May 2, 1998: The Senators beat New Jersey 3–1 to win their first playoff series.

- October 8, 1992: The Senators win their first game, beating future rivals, the Montreal Canadiens 5–3.

Ottawa goaltender Tom Barrasso stops a rolling puck in front of the Ottawa net. The Senators traded for the controversial goaltender, known for his abrasive personality, at the trade deadline of the 1999–2000 season.

be part of something like that. I want to be a winner. It's good to be around that atmosphere."

In Redden's first year, the 1996–97 campaign, the Senators qualified for the playoffs for the first time in their history and pushed the Buffalo Sabres to seven games in the opening round. The next year, the Senators squeezed into the playoffs again as the No. 8 seed but, against long odds, upset the top-seeded, 107-point New Jersey Devils in the opening round.

"That playoff series is our biggest thrill to date," said Redden. "Just winning a round and getting that feeling was unbelievable because it's so tough to win in the playoffs. We won the one series and there were three more to go and we couldn't follow through after that, but that little taste was a great feeling. We want to duplicate that and win more."

It didn't happen in 1999, however, when the Senators completed their best regular season to date—a 103-point campaign and a No. 2 playoff seed—only to be upset themselves by Dominik Hasek and the Buffalo Sabres. More uncertainty followed that defeat as Senators majority owner Rod Bryden, arguing that he couldn't continue to run the money-losing team without government support, threatened to sell the team to U.S.-based interests if help didn't come. After the Canadian government approved—and then rescinded—a support package for the six Canadian-based NHL teams, Bryden held a season-ticket drive that generated enough support to keep the team in Ottawa for the foreseeable future. Through that—and a season-long holdout by star center Alexei Yashin—the Senators produced a wholly respectable

1999–2000 season, qualifying for the playoffs for the fourth year in a row.

"We didn't want to pick up and leave," said Redden, "especially when you consider the support we receive. In some cities, they don't get any fans at all. It would just be a shame if the team left on that note. It's good to see it's staying on. I want to play wherever I can and be part of a winner, but I want that to be Ottawa now.

"Playoffs is where you really make a name for yourself. That's where it means the most. We were proud of our season in 1999. It fell apart at the end and playoffs were bad, but we had something to build on. We ended up making the playoffs and improving every year points-wise. We'll keep building, I guess. The end goal is the Stanley Cup. That's still in our sights, but we still have a long way to go."

The Franchise
Sometimes it looked as if the Marx Brothers were running the Ottawa Senators in their first four NHL seasons. Conceived as a real estate project by a trio of local land developers, the Senators received the last expansion franchise ever awarded to a Canadian city in 1992, in part because they were willing to pay the $50-million franchise fee, with no questions asked. Mel Bridgman, a member of the Philadelphia Flyers during the Broad Street Bullies era and more recently a graduate of the Wharton business school, became the first general manager in team history. He made an inauspicious debut during the expansion draft to stock Ottawa and Tampa by drafting a trio of ineligible players. Bridgman lasted just one year, a 24-point season that included only 10 wins. Just before Bruce Firestone sold his share of the team to Rod Bryden, he told reporters that the team deliberately lost games down the stretch so as to guarantee itself the first choice in the 1993 entry draft. The Senators were fined $100,000 by the league, but they were not obliged to forfeit the pick. Sexton, who replaced Bridgman as GM, turned around and selected Alexandre Daigle with their first choice, passing up future stars Chris Pronger, Paul Kariya, and others. Compounding the error, the Senators then offered Daigle a ground-breaking five-year, $12.5-million contract, a staggering sum for an entry-level player and millions more than the going rate. The Daigle contract, along with a handful of others, started the NHL's dizzying 1990s salary spiral, but what made it all the more painful

Senators captain Daniel Alfredsson is one of a growing number of talented young Swedes assuming leadership roles for their respective NHL teams.

Wade Redden tries to outmuscle another player for the puck.

from Ottawa's perspective was how little Daigle returned for their investment. Following five years, 301 games, and only 74 goals, Daigle was traded to the Philadelphia Flyers. The Senators fared much better with Alexei Yashin, their top choice in the 1992 entry draft, whenever Yashin was of a mind to play for them. He held out before the 1994–95 season, again before the 1995–96 season, and then missed all of the 1999–2000 season when he refused to honor the final year of a five-year, $13-million contract, negotiated early in 1996 by general manager Pierre Gauthier. Gauthier had replaced Sexton midway through that season and made an astute move, firing coach Dave Allison and replacing him with Jacques Martin who, in less than four seasons, oversaw the move to respectability.

Team Records

	Career	Season
Goals	Alexei Yashin, 178	Alexei Yashin, 44 (1998–99)
Assists	Alexei Yashin, 225	Alexei Yashin, 50 (1998–99)
Points	Alexei Yashin, 403	Alexei Yashin, 94 (1998–99)
Goals-Against Average	Ron Tugnutt, 2.32	Ron Tugnutt, 1.79 (1998–99)
Games Played	Alexei Yashin, 422	

Team Lowlights

- 1999–2000: The season is mired in controversy as the team suspends star center Alexei Yashin for the entire season after he fails to honor his contract, and team owner, Rod Bryden, threatens to move the team due to the lack of support from the Canadian federal government.

Philadelphia Flyers

Founded 1967

Arenas
*First Union Center
   1996–present
The Spectrum 1967–1996*

Stanley Cup Wins
1974–75, 1973–74

Award Winners

Jack Adams Award
*Mike Keenan, 1984–85
Pat Quinn, 1979–80
Fred Shero, 1973–74*

Hart Trophy
*Eric Lindros, 1994–95
Bobby Clarke, 1975–76,
   1974–75, 1972–73*

Jennings Trophy
*Bob Froese and Darren
   Jensen, 1985–86*

Bill Masterton Trophy
*Tim Kerr, 1988–89
Bobby Clarke, 1971–72*

Frank J. Selke Trophy
*Dave Poulin, 1986–87
Bobby Clarke, 1982–83*

Conn Smythe Trophy
*Ron Hextall, 1986–87
Reggie Leach, 1975–76
Bernie Parent, 1974–75,
   1973–74*

Vezina Trophy
*Ron Hextall, 1986–87
Pelle Lindbergh, 1984–85
Bernie Parent, 1974–75,
   1973–74*

Profile

Inducted into the Hockey Hall of Fame in 1990, Bill Barber is one of only four players in Philadelphia Flyers' history to have his number (7) retired. A member of their Stanley Cup championship teams in 1974 and 1975, Barber also made the NHL All-Star team three times. In a 12-year career that prematurely ended at age 32 because of knee problems, Barber scored 883 points in 903 games.

Bill Barber

Face to Face

In the year that Bill Barber broke in with the Philadelphia Flyers—1972—he was wishing and hoping that they would select him in the NHL's amateur draft. It had nothing to do with a love of their orange and black color scheme or any precognition that the team was on the verge of a pair of Stanley Cup championships.

No, Barber's desire came from the most pragmatic of reasons.

"Being young, what I was a little concerned about was having an opportunity to play," said Barber.

Rightly so, too. That year, the Montreal Canadiens—a talent-rich organization that frequently asked their players to spend three or more seasons in the minors—had three selections in the top eight, Nos. 4, 6, and 8. Barber slipped through the cracks at No. 7, going to a Flyers' team that was nicely rounding into shape.

Philadelphia had selected its future captain, Bobby Clarke, three years previously in the second round of the mostly undistinguished 1969 draft. In May 1973, the Flyers remedied an earlier mistake by reacquiring goaltender Bernie Parent from Toronto, a player they had originally sent to the Maple Leafs just 27 months previously.

In Barber, Clarke, and Parent, the Flyers developed the necessary talent component to challenge for the Stanley Cup. Talent alone, however, is only one element of a championship formula and Flyers—in semi-pioneering style—determined that toughness would be equally valuable. Taking their cue from the Boston Bruins' teams of the early 1970s, the so-called Big Bad Bruins, the Flyers loaded up the bottom half of their lineup with some of the finest emerging pugilists in the game: Dave Schultz,

At the end of the 1999–2000 season Eric Lindros's future with the Flyers was in doubt. Suffering from a series of career-threatening concussions and an irreparable relationship with GM Bobby Clarke, it is unlikely the superstar will ever play for Philadelphia again.

Team Highlights

- June 30, 1992: The Flyers acquire future superstar Eric Lindros in a blockbuster draft day trade with the Quebec Nordiques.

- June 7, 1976: Bobby Clarke wins the Hart Trophy as the league's most valuable player for the third time.

- May 19, 1974: During an era of unprecedented physical hockey, the "Broad Street Bullies" win their first Stanley Cup title over Boston's "Big Bad Bruins."

John LeClair was acquired by Philadelphia from Montreal on February 9, 1995. LeClair has blossomed in Philadelphia and is a fixture among the league's top scorers. He scored over 50 goals in both the 1995–96 and 1996–1197 seasons.

Don Saleski, Bob Kelly. The Flyers selected as their coach Freddie "The Fog" Shero, who had spent 13 years in the minor leagues, most recently with the New York Rangers' top affiliate in Omaha. Shero's presence behind the bench acted as a catalyst and after an undistinguished first season—66 points, not good enough to qualify for a playoff spot—the Flyers began a rapid upward ascent. They earned 85 points the following season, getting all the way to the semifinals, and then won it all the next year—1974—to become the first of the 1967 expansion teams to carry off the Stanley Cup.

Barber joined the Flyers in Shero's second year and knew exactly what to expect from him, thanks to his brother, who played for Shero in both Buffalo and Omaha.

"He told me Freddie gave young players a chance," recalled Barber, "and that's all I ever wanted. As my first season went on, my role expanded and then it expanded again the following year."

Barber evolved into the consummate two-way player, who scored 34 goals in each of the team's two Stanley Cup seasons. There was a league-wide fascination in the 1970s with the Montreal Canadiens' Bob Gainey, considered the era's prototypical defensive player, who won four Selke trophies as a result. Barber was asked to check as well, and he evolved into a 50-goal scorer.

"Our chemistry was right," analyzed Barber, "and how we played was right for the city. We had a lot of identifiable players because helmets weren't in [general use] back then. We were an aggressive team that pursued the puck hard and would do anything to win. That's what won the city over. We had a lot of fans from south Philadelphia. They're hard-nosed, but real quality people and die-hard fans.

"It had been such a long time since any sports team had won in the city of Philadelphia, so by winning back-to-back championships and the Stanley Cup parades, the city just really warmed up to the team. That established a tradition and as time went on, the tradition got stronger. The second year we won again, and then the third year we went to the finals again. We maintained a high tradition of play. That was probably the key."

The funny thing about so many players who pass through the Philadelphia organization is that they come to think of themselves as Flyers first and NHLers second. To wear the Flyers logo once brings you into a black and orange world, with its own ethic and identity.

As good as the Flyers were in the spring of 1974, the fact that they were able to defeat the Bruins of Bobby Orr, Phil Esposito, Ken Hodge, and Wayne Cashman in the finals caught the NHL establishment by surprise. It just didn't seem right that an expansion team could win the Stanley Cup only seven years into their new incarnation, not against the identifiable powerhouse that the Bruins iced back then.

"The league had a good heads-up the year before, in my first year of pro, when we went to the semifinals with Montreal," said Barber. "They knew this team would contend and be tough to compete against. Maybe it was a little bit of a surprise, us

A three-time Hart Trophy winner, Bobby Clarke's emotional style of play inspired a generation of hockey fans. Clarke was the leader of the legendary Broad Street Bully teams that won two Stanley Cups in the mid-1970s.

beating Boston, but we knew we could play with them. We had good balance on our team. We had the right youth, the right leadership and the good chemistry going along with it.

"I don't think there was any doubt in our dressing room the following year about what was going to happen—that we were going to win again. Even the third year, we had numbers that were second to none, but fell a little short in the Stanley Cup finals there.

"We established a lot of tradition during that period of time. When new players showed up, they saw how the players competed and what it meant to wear a Flyers uniform. It wasn't just a given. It was a privilege."

Eventually, Barber settled in as the No. 1 left winger on a line with Clarke and Reggie Leach, who joined the Flyers in a deal with the California Golden Seals the summer after their first championship win. In the 1975–76 season, the trio put together one of the most memorable individual years that any line ever had. Barber scored 50 goals in 80 games and finished with an astonishing plus-minus rating of plus–74. Clarke had a league-leading 89 assists, en route to 119 points and a third Hart Trophy as NHL most valuable player. Leach led the NHL in goals with 61 and then added 19 more in only 16 playoff games to win the Conn Smythe Trophy as post-season MVP, despite the fact that the Canadiens won the Stanley Cup that season.

Barber's finest post-season moment came in the 1974 finals against the Bruins when he scored the winner in the fourth game to put Philadelphia ahead 3–1 in the series.

"It was one of those freaky things that happened. The puck came off the sideboards and I half-snapped, half-slapped the puck. Bobby Orr was standing there, and it went right over his shoulder and past the goaltender. I don't even think he saw the puck, and it ended up being the winning goal."

The Bruins obliterated the Flyers in the fifth game back in the Boston Gardens, which left the Flyers with one more opportunity to win on home ice—in the sixth game. That night, Rick MacLeish scored early, and goaltender Bernie Parent made his goal stand up for a heart-stopping 1–0 victory.

Barber remembers watching Parent play for the Maple Leafs during his final junior year in Kitchener and thus had a pretty good idea of the caliber of player the Flyers were getting when he rejoined Philadelphia at the start of their championship year.

"Bernie's style complemented how we played," said Barber.

Philadelphia's star goaltender in the mid-1970s, Bernie Parent was a key factor in the Flyer's back-to-back Stanley Cup victories. Parent was awarded the Conn Smythe Trophy, as the most valuable player of the playoffs, for both the 1973–74 and 1974–75 seasons.

Team Lowlights

- March 27, 2000: After months of public infighting, Flyers General Manager Bobby Clarke strips star center Eric Lindros of his captaincy for publicly criticizing the team's medical staff and trainers.

"We played a pretty tight system. They call it a trap now, but we called it a one-four then. If we had a chance to pursue the puck, we did. Obviously, when we didn't, defense came first. That's how you win championships. If you're solid defensively, you have a chance to win. We kept shots down to under 20 per game. It worked out very well."

Barber detected no complacency setting in with the Flyers following the 1974 championship, something he attributes to the era.

"Times have changed," said Barber, now coach of the Flyers' No. 1 minor league affiliate, the Philadelphia Phantoms. "In our situation, all we wanted to do was win. I don't think it was a job for any of us. Obviously, salaries were not at the level they are today. I believe money was not even a factor. We were just playing for the love of the game and the chance to get your name on the Stanley Cup. That's how we viewed it as a team. We had a good enough team to stay on top."

The Franchise

The Philadelphia Flyers, one of six teams to join the NHL in the 1967–68 expansion, were not exactly an overnight success story, on the ice or at the box office. Only 2,100 season tickets were sold for their inaugural year and only 7,812 fans turned up for the Flyers' original home opener, against the Pittsburgh Penguins, a desultory 1–0 victory. The Flyers inched along that season, trying to build a following in a city known primarily as a football town when the fates conspired to put them in the headlines for all the wrong reasons. In February 1968, during a matinee performance of an ice show, large sections of the Spectrum roof literally blew off in a ferocious windstorm. Two weeks later, just as repairs were completed and sanity was restored, it happened again—and this time, the city shut the building down indefinitely. As a result, the Flyers were forced to play home games on the road—in New York, in Toronto, and then finally in Quebec City, home of their top minor league affiliate. In an ultra-tight race for top spot, the Flyers grew together on the road and won the first-ever Western Division regular-season crown. They moved back into the Spectrum in time for the playoffs and eventually lost their opening playoff round to the St. Louis Blues in a hard-fought seven-game series. It may have been an artistic failure, but the Flyers' spirit had captured the city's imagination. Even as the next handful of seasons featured a series of ups and downs, fan support gradually built.

A seminal moment came in the 1969 amateur draft when the Flyers gambled that a 20-year-old from Flin Flon named Bobby Clarke would be able to have a successful NHL career, despite the fact that he had diabetes and was forced to take daily insulin shots. Clarke's relentless work ethic and his unbridled passion came to epitomize the Flyers' style and many of the team's finest achievements came during Clarke's reign as the team's undisputed leader. There were the two Stanley Cup championships (1974 and 1975) and two other trips to the finals (1976 and 1980). In addition, the Flyers also established an NHL record 35-game undefeated streak in the 1979–80 season, a magical 84-day run that included 25 victories and a win over every NHL team, except the Washington Capitals. The Flyers couldn't cap that season off with a championship—they lost a six-game Stanley Cup finals to the New York Islanders—but they were able to sustain a relatively high standard for much of the 1980s.

In an eight-year span between 1979–80 and 1986–87, they

John LeClair is one of the NHL's premier power forwards and is consistently among the top goalscorers in the league.

won five Patrick Division championships and finished with 97 or more points seven times. That period included two more trips to the finals under coach Mike Keenan—1985 and 1987—where they were defeated both times by Wayne Gretzky and the talented Edmonton Oilers. Clarke's departure in 1990 to become the Minnesota North Stars' general manager coincided with the darkest days in franchise history. In all, the Flyers missed the playoffs for five consecutive years (1990 to 1994). Clarke eventually returned in 1994 as general manager after his astute stewardship of the expansion Florida Panthers ultimately allowed them to qualify for the Stanley Cup finals in only their third year of existence. In Clarke's absence, the Flyers had engineered arguably the biggest trade in NHL history, surrendering a total six players, two draft choices, and $15 million to the Quebec Nordiques for the rights to budding superstar Eric Lindros.

The 1990s were dominated by Lindros's presence. He led the team to consecutive Atlantic Division titles in 1995 and 1996 and then took them all the way to the Stanley Cup finals in 1997, a year in which it looked as if he'd finally lived up to the expectations and hype that had surrounded him since he was a teenager. That year, however, the Flyers bowed out in four consecutive games to the Detroit Red Wings. In the next three years, despite solid contributions whenever he was in the lineup, Lindros ran into a series of injuries—knee problems, a collapsed lung, a quartet of concussions—that limited his effectiveness in the 1998 playoffs and kept him out of the playoffs in 1999 and for all but two games in 2000.

Mark Recchi is a talented offensive player who set a career high for goals with 53 goals during the 1992-93 season. Renowned for his durability, Recchi rarely misses a game and is a valuable performer for Canada in international competition.

Team Records

	Career	Season
Goals	Bill Barber, 420	Reggie Leach, 61 (1975–76)
Assists	Bobby Clarke, 852	Bobby Clarke, 89 (1974–75 and 1975–76)
Points	Bobby Clarke, 1,210	Mark Recchi, 123 (1992–93)
Goals-Against Average	Bernie Parent, 2.42	Bernie Parent, 1.89 (1973–74)
Games Played	Bobby Clarke, 1,144	

Phoenix Coyotes

Founded 1996

Formerly Winnipeg Jets, 1979–96

Arenas
America West Arena
   1996–present

Stanley Cup Wins
0

Award Winners

Jack Adams Award
Bob Murdoch, 1989–90
Tom Watt, 1981–82

Calder Trophy
Teemu Selanne, 1992–93
Dale Hawerchuk, 1981–82

King Clancy Trophy
Kris King, 1995–96

After proving himself as one of the top goalies in the NHL in 1998–99, Coyotes goaltender Nikolai Khabibulin sat out the 1999–2000 season after failing to reach a contract agreement with Phoenix management.

Profile

As recently as the 1996–97 season, the Phoenix Coyotes' Keith Tkachuk led the NHL in goal scoring with 52 and his team in penalty minutes, with 228, only the second American-born player to record at least 50 goals and 200 penalty minutes in the same season. He has been alternately nicknamed Walt (after former New York Ranger Walt Tkachuk) and Reg (after the Paul Newman character in *Slapshot*). Tkachuk is third in franchise history in point scoring, second in goals, and first in penalty minutes.

Face to Face

He joined the organization in their Winnipeg Jets' days as a 19-year-old kid from Boston. Talk about culture shock. Here was Keith Tkachuk, a rough-and-tumble teenager from working-class Jeffrey's Point, a Boston suburb, arriving in a small Canadian city that adored hockey. The Jets' tradition was all speed and flow, beginning with its WHA days, when Bobby Hull joined a pair of Swedish pioneers, Anders Hedberg and Ulf Nilsson, on what was clearly the best line outside the NHL. For years, the Jets were thought of as a stylish and skilled team. Then along came Tkachuk, who eventually evolved into the NHL's prototype power forward, one of a handful of players to score 50 goals in the same season that he earned 200 penalty minutes.

There were many other personal highlights in Tkachuk's first decade as an NHLer—a 1996 World Cup championship with Team USA, signing what was then an unprecedented five-year, $12-million offer sheet with the Chicago Blackhawks—but ask about team achievements and Tkachuk's voice begins to trail off.

"The highlight of the franchise on the ice?" he repeated. "That is hard to say. The most satisfying thing you can ever imagine is winning the Stanley Cup—and yet, we haven't got out of the first round. We've had some confidence builders, where we've come out of the gate strong and were in first place overall and people were talking about us, but we haven't been able to sustain it. That's frustrating. Even going back to the Winnipeg days, the people get so excited about the playoffs and we haven't even won a series."

Keith Tkachuk

Phoenix captain Keith Tkachuk bulls his way to the front of the Islanders net as teammate Travis Green awaits a pass.

More precisely, in the franchise's first 20 years, the team has only ever won two first-round playoff series—in 1985 and in 1987, both before Tkachuk arrived on the scene. The team missed the playoffs six times and lost in the first round on 13 other occasions. On the plus side, there have been some dramatic, memorable close calls. Three times, the team had an oppo-

nent on the ropes—ahead 3–1 in the series—only to lose three consecutive games and the series. It happened most recently in the 1999 playoffs when the Coyotes were on the verge of eliminating an extremely competitive St. Louis Blues team. Instead, St. Louis won three consecutive games, including two in overtime, to win the series. On the final night of their season, the Coyotes battled the Blues (and future Hall of Fame goaltender Grant Fuhr) through four scoreless overtime periods before eventually losing a 1–0 decision in the seventh game. That type of defeat, piled on top of the team's previous playoff failings, proved difficult for long-time players such as Tkachuk to accept.

"If you play with the right guys and you play a lot, you get the opportunities to score 50 goals," said Tkachuk. "I've done that. Now, I need that ultimate, the Stanley Cup. As a player, you want to be associated with winning. That's the toughest part. There have been years when we should have gone to at least the second round and haven't. Sometimes, I hear people compare us to the Boston Red Sox, not winning the World Series. It's tough."

Tkachuk arrived in the NHL in the spring of 1992, fresh off an appearance with the U.S. Olympic hockey team, and made a splashy debut in the final quarter of the season. By his second full year, 1993–94, he was already a 40-goal scorer. Along with Teemu Selanne and Alexei Zhamnov, the team looked as if it had a big upside, possessing three of the brightest young scoring stars in the game, all of them in their early 20s. Selanne had established an NHL record by scoring 76 goals in his rookie year, a mark that may never be duplicated. Zhamnov was considered one of the slickest playmakers in the league and finished as high as third overall in the scoring race in the 1994–95 season.

A six-time All-Star, Jeremy Roenick again represented Phoenix at the All-Star game in the 1999-2000 season. A former 100-point scorer with the Chicago Blackhawks, Roenick no longer posts those types of numbers but has become one of the game's best two-way forwards. Hampered by injuries in recent years, including a broken jaw from a Derian Hatcher elbow just before the start of the 1999 playoffs, Roenick displayed his toughness by missing only a few playoff games and returning to play in a specially designed protective helmet. Roenick scored 78 points in 1999-2000 and was invaluable to the Coyotes on the powerplay and as a leader in the dressing room.

Rick Tocchet backs out of the way of Jeremy Roenick's slap shot. A rejuvenated Roenick scored 34 goals and totaled 78 points in 1999–2000. His competitive edge added a much needed spark to his team.

Team Highlights

- October 10, 1997: The Coyotes play their very first game at home and beat the San Jose Sharks 4–1.

- April 12, 1996: Keith Tkachuk scores his 50th goal of the season during the Jets final home game in Winnipeg.

- 1991–1992: Teemu Selanne sets a new rookie record when he scores 76 goals in his first NHL season.

Unhappily, the Jets were in the throes of an ownership crisis by then. For a time, government assistance from the province of Manitoba kept the team afloat. Indeed, Manitoba taxpayers contributed heavily to Tkachuk's 1995–96 salary of $6 million, which he received after the Jets matched the Blackhawks' offer sheet. It looked as if the team were heading for the United States following the lockout year, but a spirited community rally kept them alive for another year—the 1995–96 campaign, the first of Tkachuk's consecutive 50-goal years. By the summer of 1996, however, with no new arena deal on the horizon, the team was transferred from Barry Shenkarov to a group led by Richard Burke, a former chairman of United HealthCare Corporation. Burke was himself looking for new investors in the spring of 2000 as—in a wholly ironic development—a poor lease agreement with his landlord, the America West Arena in Phoenix, kept the franchise bleeding red ink. The Coyotes' attempts to quietly shop Tkachuk's NHL rights became an ugly, front-page issue that same year when one prospective suitor, the Carolina Hurricanes, made the news of Tkachuk's availability public. It's not that the Coyotes had soured on Tkachuk as a player, they were frightened by the prospect of paying him over $8 million per season, a contract that they were having difficulty fitting into their tight payroll.

"I loved being a Winnipeg Jet and I love being a Phoenix Coyote," said Tkachuk. "About the only disappointing thing has been the lack of stability. There's always been ownership problems and there have been a lot of changes. It's unfortunate we didn't have one big owner where money wasn't an issue, because Winnipeg was a great place to live and a great place to grow up. I was a 19-year-old kid, out on my own for the first time. Then moving to Phoenix, it's just the best place to live. Six years ago, I didn't know anything about the city, they've really turned it into a hockey town. When we first got down there, it was different. It's a different crowd than goes to basketball games. People go there to have fun and they're learning the game along the way. They're excited about hockey and it's a great atmosphere. You get a lot of transplants from the northeast that have come down there to live. Obviously, we've not had the success that we wanted to—to get to the Stanley Cup finals and maybe winning the Stanley Cup—but you can see where it's heading. Every place deserves a winner—and we want to deliver that.

"No matter what happens down the road for me, after I'm finished playing hockey, my family and I are going to live there. It's totally different place than Boston, where I grew up. Arizona is incredible—and it's just getting better and better."

The Franchise
Admitted to the NHL in 1979 as one of four teams involved in the WHA merger, the Jets earned early notoriety as one of the worst clubs ever in league history. In their second season, which they began under popular coach Tom McVie, the Jets won only nine games and finished with 32 points, one of only a handful of times in the expansion era that a team couldn't reach double digits in the wins column. Gradually, the team began to turn its fortunes around on the ice, thanks to the emergence of Dale Hawerchuk, their No. 1 choice in the 1981 draft, who would lead the team in scoring for eight consecutive years in the 1980s. Even so, the presence in their division of an Edmonton Oilers team that won the Stanley Cup five times between 1984 and 1990 established a playoff roadblock that they couldn't overcome. Indeed, their only two post-season wins ever came at the expense of the less intimidating Calgary Flames. The NHL lockout of 1994–95 produced its share of casualties, including small-market Winnipeg, a team playing in an ancient arena, without the key modern-day, revenue-generators—luxury boxes and seats. An inability to attain financing for a new arena eventually led to the transfer of the franchise to Phoenix, a development that officially occurred July 1, 1996. Six weeks later, the Coyotes made a bold move, acquiring Jeremy Roenick from the Chicago Blackhawks. The Coyotes' breakout 1998–99 season was highlighted by the presence of four players in the All-Star game: Roenick, Keith Tkachuk, Teppo Numminen, and Nikolai Khabibulin—but once again, post-season success failed them.

Team Lowlights
- 1997–1998: Despite having four players selected to the NHL All-Star game in 1998, the Coyotes failed to win a playoff series.

Team Records

	Career	Season
Goals	Dale Hawerchuk, 379	Teemu Selanne, 76, (1992–93)
Assists	Thomas Steen, 553	Phil Housley, 79 (1992–93)
Points	Dale Hawerchuk, 929	Teemu Selanne, 132 (1992–93)
Goals-Against Average	Nikolai Khabibulin, 2.75	Nikolai Khabibulin, 2.13 (1998–99)
Games Played	Thomas Steen, 950	

Pittsburgh Penguins

Founded 1967

Arenas
Pittsburgh Civic Center
1967–present

Stanley Cup Wins
1992–93, 1991–1992

Award Winners

Lady Byng Trophy
*Ron Francis, 1997–98,
1994–95*
Rick Kehoe, 1980–81

Calder Trophy
Mario Lemieus, 1984–85

Hart Trophy
*Jaromir Jagr 1999–2000,
1998–99*
*Mario Lemieux, 1995–96,
1992–93, 1987–88*

Bill Masterton Trophy
Mario Lemieux, 1992–93
*Lowell MacDonald,
1972–73*

Norris Trophy
Randy Carlyle, 1980–81

Art Ross Trophy
*Jaromir Jagr, 1999–2000,
1998–99, 1994–95*
*Mario Lemieux, 1996–97,
1995–96, 1992–93,
1991–92, 1988–89,
1987–88*

Frank J. Selke Trophy
Ron Francis, 1994–95

Conn Smythe Trophy
*Mario Lemieux, 1991–92,
1990–91*

Profile

Joe Mullen was the first American-born player to break the 1,000-point mark in the NHL and the first to score 500 goals. He was with the Pittsburgh Penguins when they won the Stanley Cup twice and was the winner of the Lester Patrick Trophy for contributions to hockey in the United States in 1995.

Face to Face

Joe Mullen has been seeing double since he came to Pittsburgh.

He has two Stanley Cup rings. He achieved two scoring milestones for an American-born player. He's played with two of the greatest players of the NHL's modern era, Mario Lemieux and Jaromir Jagr.

Not to mention witnessing two miracles by Lemieux to resurrect the franchise, on and off the ice.

First, Lemieux put the Penguins back on the map with a mittful·of scoring records in the late 1980s and early 1990s. Then, with a moving van sitting outside the Civic Arena in March of 1999, he stick-handled his way through bankruptcy court as the head of a new ownership group.

"I don't think anyone doubted that when Mario put his mind to something, it would get done," said Mullen, the Penguins' alumni and community relations associate since 1997. "Look at the smart way he operated on the ice. He saw the whole picture in a very short time and always made the right decisions.

"He could make a lot of things happen when it looked like there was nothing there."

But for many years, the Penguins franchise wondered if it would ever turn the corner. Not even the arrival of the much-heralded Lemieux as the first overall pick in the 1984 draft did much at first to end six consecutive losing seasons.

In fact, from their 1967–68 expansion season until Mullen's arrival in a trade with Calgary in June of 1990, the Pens either failed to qualify for playoffs or couldn't advance beyond the second round.

Joe Mullen

Jaromir Jagr has emerged in recent years as the most dominant offensive player in the NHL. In 1999–2000, he lost to St. Louis's Chris Pronger in the closest Hart Trophy vote in league history.

- 1991–92, 1990–91: Led by superstars Mario Lemieux, Ron Francis, and a young Jaromir Jagr, the Penguins use a wide-open, exciting brand of hockey to win back-to-back Stanley Cup titles.

- December 31, 1988: Mario Lemieux scores five goals in a game against the New Jersey Devils. This effort marks the first time in league history that a player has scored a goal in all possible situations: even strength, short-handed, power play, penalty shot, and open net.

- February 3, 1968: In a game against the Toronto Maple Leafs, the Penguins sell out the Civic Arena for the very first time.

Matthew Barnaby's aggressive style makes him one of the most loathed players in the NHL. His antics on the ice make him a favorite target of both fans' and opposing players' abuse.

Mullen was brought to the team on the advice of "Badger" Bob Johnson, his one-time Flames coach, a deal worked by another old acquaintance, general manager Craig Patrick.

"In that year, we brought in myself, Bryan Trottier, Larry Murphy, Jiri Hrdina...and Badger was a positive influence on all of us," Mullen said. "But the big deal was at the deadline that year for Ron Francis, Ulf Samuelsson, and Grant Jennings. That put us over the top.

"Badger wasn't just a good X's and O's coach, he kept practices interesting, he kept guys skating. He would keep telling guys, 'You'll get 40 goals, because this guy or that guy will be setting you up.' He just kept saying it and guys bought into that kind of confidence."

Johnson's methods would also light a fire under Lemieux, who for his first few years, carried the label of an underachiever and a man unhappy to be in Pittsburgh.

"I thought Badger gave him a lot of direction," Mullen said. "He told Mario he would be getting on the ice no matter the situation and he should be prepared for anything. I think guys like myself, Ronny, and Trotts gave him an appreciation for defensive play, once the playoffs started.

"Mario realized he had to work harder."

Lemieux missed 50 games in that inaugural Cup year, following back surgery, but came back with a three-assist night in his January return and amassed 45 points in 26 games, before going wild in the playoffs. Beating New Jersey, Washington, Boston, and then Minnesota in the finals, the Penguins became only the fifth post-expansion team to win the Cup. Lemieux's 44 points were the second-highest in one playoff year in Cup history. The city went crazy and the Cup, as part of the club's post-season frolic, wound up briefly in the bottom of Lemieux's pool.

But the title celebrations wrapped up on a tragic note. Johnson was diagnosed with brain tumors that summer and died a few months later.

"It was probably the saddest thing I ever saw in hockey," Mullen said. "He finally got what he wanted so much in life, the Stanley Cup, and he didn't get a chance to enjoy it."

But there would be no stopping the well-oiled Pittsburgh machine, which went on to more glory in 1991–92 with Scotty Bowman behind the bench. Lemieux and Kevin Stevens had 100-point seasons, and Mullen set a record with back-to-back four-goal games. The Pens lost just 10 games between February

Pittsburgh acquired veteran goaltender Ron Tugnutt at the trade deadline of the 1999–2000 season, only to lose him to free agency in July of 2000, when he signed with the Columbus Blue Jackets.

29 and winning the Cup for the second time.

Lemieux bravely survived a bout of Hodgkin's disease in 1992–93 to win another scoring title, but as the 1990s went on, fans began marking the progress of Jaromir Jagr, dubbed "Mario Jr."

"It was very hard on Jaromir when he first came over [as a first-round pick] in 1990–91," Mullen said. "He spoke a different language and it was a little frustrating for him trying to deal with the coaches. He was the third right winger on the team and at times you could tell by looking at him he was thinking, 'What am I doing here?'

"One of the smartest moves we made was getting Jan Hrdina that season. Jaromir needed another Czech player to settle him down."

Jagr was named to the NHL's all-rookie team and blasted off on his own distinguished career. He joined Lemieux as the only Penguin to have won the Hart, Lester Pearson, and Art Ross trophies in the same season in 1998–99, and followed that up with his third straight scoring title in 1999–2000.

"I saw him up close every year but one over the past 10 seasons and I think he's becoming much better at handling fame and everything that's gone on in Pittsburgh," Mullen said.

The storied careers of Lemieux and Jagr tend to overshadow what some of the other Pens accomplished. Pierre Larouche, Jean Pronovost, Francis, Mark Recchi, Stevens, Rob Brown, and Paul Coffey have all enjoyed 100-point seasons. Mullen had 325 points in 379 games for the Pens as well as contributing to two Cup wins.

But the native of New York's tough Hell's Kitchen will be most revered in American hockey lore for his scoring exploits. His assists on February 7, 1995, in Florida made him the first Yankee to reach 1,000 points in a career that began with the Blues in 1981.

Late in 1996–97, his final NHL season, he scored in

Colorado to give him another American first, 500 goals.

"I always felt I would be comfortable in Pittsburgh," Mullen said. "You never come into the league thinking you'll reach such milestones. I was a kid who grew up playing roller hockey [on school asphalt around the corner from Madison Square Garden] and though it's everyone's dream to play pro, I didn't skate until I was 10 years old."

Joe and younger brother Brian played in the New York Met League, beating the odds to play college hockey and go on to the NHL.

"The records, they just sort of crept up on me," Mullen said.

Now Mullen is part of Lemieux's revitalization of the franchise. The cover of the Pens' 1999–2000 media guide showed Lemieux in his business suit and Jagr in team uniform, symbols of a new era in Pittsburgh hockey.

"Mario will always have a place in the fans' hearts in Pittsburgh, and it was only fitting he be involved now," Mullen said. "He put his heart on the line for the franchise and people are thrilled that hockey is going to survive here."

The Franchise

The Penguins were actually Pittsburgh's second foray into the National Hockey League.

A club called the Pirates, named after the city's more famous baseball team, competed in the American Division from 1926 to 1931, before moving to Philadelphia for a year and then disappearing.

Pittsburgh's great minor league tradition—the Hornets were an American Hockey League power—put the city in good stead for acceptance in the 1967 expansion. The wife of one of the team's original investors thought the name "Penguins" would be cute, because the new team would play out of the Civic Arena, dubbed The Igloo.

It's now the oldest rink in the NHL after the Maple Leafs left the Gardens in 1999.

After a cost of $2 million U.S. for expansion fees, the Pens played their first home game on October 11, 1967, losing 2–1 to the Montreal Canadiens before 9,307 people. Andy Bathgate had the first Pittsburgh goal.

Stocked initially with many aging veterans, the Pens missed the playoffs five of their first seven years. Their first breakthrough was 1974–75 when Pierre Larouche, Syl Apps Jr., Ron Schock, Jean Pronovost, and Gary Inness led Pittsburgh

When Mario Lemieux retired, Pittsburgh fans didn't have to wait long for another dazzling offensive performer. Jaromir Jagr assumed the mantle of scoring leadership and was widely considered to be the best player in the NHL in the late 1990s and early 2000s. Jagr has twice won the Hart Trophy as the league's most valuable player and has led the NHL in scoring four times in his career.

On his first NHL shift on October 11, 1984, Mario Lemieux, considered to be one of the leagues most skilled players ever, scored his first NHL goal.

through a wonderful season, only to lose a 3–0 series lead to the Islanders.

A few years later, the Pens tried to change their luck by switching from predominantly blue uniforms to the black and gold that had made the Pirates and football Steelers so successful and recognizable in their respective sports. Unfortunately, when first overall pick Mario Lemieux was asked to come to the team table and put the jersey on at the 1984 draft, he refused. Lemieux eventually warmed to the idea of playing there, winning the Calder Trophy his first year, scoring 100 points, and being named All-Star game most valuable player.

Though the team was still struggling to make the post-season, Lemieux had 98 assists in 1987–88 and became the first Penguin to win the Hart Trophy. An incredible 199-point campaign for Lemieux followed as the Oilers dynasty peaked and Pens began putting the finishing touches on their championship roster.

Jaromir Jagr was drafted in 1990 and new general manager Craig Patrick and coach "Badger" Bob Johnson put together a division title team with a record of 41–33–6. The key acquisitions were Joe Mullen from Calgary and Ron Francis and Ulf Samuelsson from Hartford. Beating New Jersey, Washington, and Boston, the Pens met the Minnesota North Stars in the finals and with Lemieux capping his Conn Smythe Trophy season, they won the Stanley Cup in six games.

Pittsburgh became the 15th team since 1920 to repeat as champions, knocking off the Chicago Blackhawks in 1992. But two terrible events shook the franchise: Johnson's death from brain tumors in November of 1991 and the discovery in January of 1993 that Lemieux had Hodgkin's disease. He came back at the end of the season, but the team's third title bid was halted by the Islanders.

The power shift on the team gradually moved to Jagr as Lemieux's battles with injuries eventually led to his retirement in 1997. Jagr won the Hart Trophy himself, but financial constraints on the team changed it into a more defense-oriented club on the ice and eventually threatened its very existence.

Lemieux, the team's largest creditor, stepped forward in 1999 with a bankruptcy reorganization plan that was approved by the NHL. The team continued its winning ways, with a couple of playoff upsets for good measure, while season's ticket sales and overall attendance went up under the Lemieux group.

Team Lowlights

- November 26, 1991: Pittsburgh coach Bob Johnson dies suddenly after leading the Penguins to their first ever Stanley Cup title.

Team Records

	Career	Season
Goals	Mario Lemieux, 613	Mario Lemieux, 85 (1988–89)
Assists	Mario Lemieux, 881	Mario Lemieux, 114 (1988–89)
Points	Mario Lemieux, 1494	Mario Lemieux, 199 (1988–89)
Goals-Against Average	Al Smith, 3.07	Tom Barrasso, 2.07 (1997–98)
Games Played	Jean Pronovost, 753	

San Jose Sharks

Founded 1991

Arenas
San Jose Arena 1993–
 present
Cow Palace 1991–1993

Stanley Cup Wins
0

Award Winners

Bill Masterton Trophy
Tony Granato, 1996–97

Ron Sutter's work ethic and determination set the tone for the Sharks, a team struggling to rise out of obscurity.

Profile
Jeff Friesen, the 11th player chosen in the 1994 entry draft, joined the San Jose Sharks as an 18-year-old during the lockout-shortened 1994–95 NHL season and became an instant hit. The youngest player in the league, Friesen won a place on the NHL's post-season all-rookie team. Six years later, Friesen, a chiseled 6-foot, 205-pounder, had become the highest-scoring player from his draft year and led the Sharks in virtually every career statistic, from games played to points scored. A fitness fanatic, Friesen is the undisputed leader of the team's talented, emerging kiddie corps.

Face to Face
Geographically, San Jose, California, is situated smack in the middle of Silicon Valley, which provides the United States with virtually all of its computer hardware and an uncommon number of PhDs. It's a funny place to find a hockey town. And yet . . . .

Of all the NHL's forays into the southern states, hockey fever has gripped San Jose like no other city. After nine years and nine losing seasons, the novelty could easily have worn off. Instead, here are the Sharks, continuing to fill their arena on a nightly basis, with some of the loudest fans in the league.

Sometimes, Jeff Friesen wonders what will happen if the Sharks ever do make that quantum leap into the NHL's upper echelons.

"It would be an amazing thing to see," began Friesen, "if we could ever get on a good playoff run or start moving forward in the standings, how good a hockey town this could really be. I mean, it is already. The building is so loud and the fans are so great. They're just dying for us to make a great playoff run. I think it would be a lot of fun."

Friesen arrived on the scene in 1994, just in time for the Sharks' fourth NHL season. Their first two years—played in the ancient Cow Palace, in nearby Daly City—were largely forgettable. Indeed, Year 2 saw them win just 11 games and tie an

Jeff Friesen

Team Highlights

- June 21, 1997: Sharks forward Tony Granato wins the Bill Masterton Trophy after recovering from brain surgery to play again in the NHL.

- January 18, 1997: At the All-Star game played in San Jose, Owen Nolan provides one of the more memorable moments in All-Star history by pointing to the top corner of the opposing net before ripping a shot directly into the spot he had called.

- April 30, 1994: The Sharks upset the first-place Detroit Red Wings to win their first playoff series.

Owen Nolan was resurgent in 1999–2000 scoring 44 goals, 40 assists and greatly improving his defensive play.

NHL record, by registering 17 consecutive defeats. The good news was that the next year, under coach Kevin Constantine, the Sharks registered statistically the most compelling turnaround in league history, improving from 24 to 82 points. It didn't stop there either. As a No. 8 playoff seed, the Sharks then proceeded to knock off the heavily favored Detroit Red Wings in the opening round and then had the Toronto Maple Leafs on the ropes in the second round, ahead 3–2 in the series. Ultimately, they couldn't take that final step and ended up losing to the Leafs in a stirring seven-game series. The next year, the Sharks virtually duplicated their playoff magic, knocking off a No. 2 seed, the Calgary Flames, in the first round.

Two monumental upsets in consecutive years gave the Sharks a taste for what it took to win in the post-season, but Friesen will concede that the team wildly overachieved to record those stunning victories. In the end, there wasn't enough talent in place in order to sustain it over the long haul.

"Knocking off Calgary in double overtime of Game 7 was the biggest highlight for me," said Friesen, "but things were different then than they are today. At the time, we felt we matched up pretty well against Calgary, but then we lost badly to Detroit. It was pretty much of a walkover. It just didn't seem as if we had enough. It's not like now. Now, we think we have a team that can get past the first round. I'd like to think the best moments for our team are still ahead of us."

Friesen is an acknowledged leader of what may be the best young team in the NHL. A happy byproduct of nine consecutive losing seasons is a series of high draft choices, many of whom are now budding NHL stars. A player blessed with great speed and acceleration, Friesen is determined to lift himself—and his team—to a higher plane. His devotion to health and fitness borders on fanatical.

"There's such a fine line between just being in the league and being a good player; between being a good player and a great player; and between being a great player and a superstar. All those steps are a challenge and if you don't take care of yourself,

Tony Granato races after a loose puck sliding through the Islanders' crease.

you're just hurting your game. I look at the Sakics and Kariyas and Yzermans. They're dedicated to what they do. That's the main thing—to be dedicated and take advantage of the opportunity that's ahead for you.

"It's amazing how quickly you can lose your status in this

Team Records

	Career	Season
Goals	Jeff Friesen, 137	Owen Nolan, 44 (1999–2000)
	Owen Nolan, 137	
Assists	Jeff Friesen, 177	Kelly Kisio, 52 (1992–93)
Points	Jeff Friesen, 314	Owen Nolan, 84 (1999–2000)
Goals-Against Average	Mike Vernon, 2.39	Steve Shields, 2.22 (1999–2000)
Games Played	Jeff Friesen, 448	

league. That's just the most important thing I've learned. Every day, you've got to come to the rink prepared to work or there's going to be someone ready to take your job, or a player will fill your role if you're not playing as well as you can. There's so much turnover in hockey. Players come and players go. You don't want to be one of those types. You want to be someone who's a winner. That's why every day is a challenge in the NHL."

The Franchise
The birth of the San Jose Sharks was arguably as odd as any in NHL history. The NHL granted George and Gordon Gund the rights to an expansion franchise to operate in the San Francisco Bay Area in May 1990, after the Gunds sold their interest in the Minnesota North Stars. As part of their agreement to unload the Stars, the Gunds retained 24 players from the North Stars' reserve list—including future All-Star Arturs Irbe—and another 10 players from existing NHL teams. The Sharks enjoyed an exceedingly good first draft, plucking Pat Falloon, Ray Whitney, and Sandis Ozolinsh with the first 30 picks. The Sharks won 17 games in their inaugural season but slipped back the next year to record only 11 victories. Since then, the Sharks have flirted with respectability, for all but the disastrous 1995–96 season, a year that saw them earn only 47 points in 82 games and culminated with a major front-office upheaval. When the dust had settled, a pair of coaches—Kevin Constantine and his interim replacement, Jim Wiley—had both been fired, as was Chuck Grillo, who was effectively sharing the general manager's duties with Dean Lombardi. Lombardi emerged as the clear winner in the power struggle and, after trying out Al Sims as coach for a year, eventually settled on former Chicago Blackhawks player and coach, Darryl Sutter, the man designated to lead the franchise to the next level.

San Jose captain, Owen Nolan, is one of the best power forwards in the NHL. A bruising checker, he also possesses a hard shot and a nose for the net. He holds the team record for goals in a season with 44 during the 1999–2000 season.

Team Lowlights
- 1992–93: The Sharks set an NHL record for futility in their second season, losing 71 of their 84 games.

St. Louis Blues

Founded 1967

Arenas
Kiel Center 1995–present
St. Louis Arena 1967–1995

Stanley Cup Wins
0

Award Winners

Jack Adams Award
Joel Quennville,
  1999–2000
Brian Sutter. 1990–91
Red Berenson, 1980–81

Lady Byng Trophy
Pavol Demitra,
  1999–2000
Brett Hull, 1989–90
Phil Goyette, 1969–70

King Clancy Trophy
Kelly Chase, 1997–98

Hart Trophy
Chris Pronger, 1999–2000
Brett Hull, 1990–91

Bill Masterton Trophy
Jamie McLennan, 1997–98
Blake Dunlop, 1980–81

Norris Trophy
Chris Pronger, 1999–2000
Al MacInnis, 1998–99

Frank J. Selke Trophy
Rick Meagher, 1989–90

Conn Smythe Trophy
Glenn Hall, 1967–68

Vezina Trophy
Glenn Hall and Jacques
  Plante, 1968–69

Profile

Brian Sutter spent the first 16 years of his National Hockey League life with the St. Louis Blues. A second-round pick in the 1976 amateur draft, Sutter played 12 seasons for the Blues, before a back injury forced him to prematurely retire at age 31. He coached the Blues for an additional four seasons before going behind the bench with the Boston Bruins (1992 to 1995) and the Calgary Flames (1997 to 2000). The Blues' captain for nine of his seasons, Sutter remains third on the team's all-time scoring list, first in penalty minutes, and the winningest all-time coach (153) in team history.

Brian Sutter

Face to Face

Brian Sutter didn't arrive in the St. Louis Blues' organization until they'd been in the National Hockey League for the better part of 10 years, but the aura of the people who preceded him cast a long shadow.

In the late 60s the Blues roster was a who's who of aging, former NHL greats—from Glenn Hall and Jacques Plante to Dickie Moore and Jean-Guy Talbot. They also installed in the front office a series of young up-and-comers—Al Arbour, Scotty Bowman, Cliff Fletcher—who all eventually made their marks as coaches and administrators around the league.

By the time Sutter arrived, Bowman was winning championships in Montreal, Arbour was on the verge of winning championships in New York, and Fletcher was on the brink of building a dynasty in Calgary.

"These people who passed through St. Louis in the early days were the benchmark for class, for heart, and for integrity," said Sutter, "so when you got there, you had a high standard to live up to."

Eventually, the aforementioned trio built some of the model NHL organizations. The Blues, by contrast, were forced to live a hand-to-mouth existence for much of Sutter's 16-plus seasons in the organization. Until stability returned in the mid-1990s, the Blues were always a better franchise on the ice than off.

On the ice, they have qualified for the playoffs every year since the 1978–79 season, currently the longest active streak in the league. Off the ice, they always seemed to be moving

Bernie Federko played 13 seasons for the St. Louis Blues and was the first player in NHL history to record 50 or more assists for ten consecutive seasons.

In 1980-81, his second season with the Blues, Mike Liut finished second to Wayne Gretzky in Hart Trophy voting but won the Lester B. Pearson Award, voted on by players for their pick as league MVP.

somewhere, either because they were underfinanced or subject to indifferent ownership. The parade of owners was never-ending. First came the Solomons, Sid Jr. and Sid III. Then came Ralston Purina, who took over the franchise more out of a sense of community responsibility than any great urge to own a hockey team. When they put it up for sale, it took until the 11th hour before entrepreneur Harry Ornest came along and rescued the team, which otherwise was heading for Saskatoon, Saskatchewan. Ornest was a businessman through and through and ran his operation on a shoestring.

In an era when salaries were rising and players began to expect any number of amenities, the Blues were an anomaly, a team that was run as a for-profit enterprise by an owner who has been characterized alternately as both a skinflint and a visionary in the cold light of history.

"Say what you want to say about Harry Ornest," said Sutter, "but he kept the team there. I know they were scraping nickels together to survive. We sacrificed a lot of things. We didn't get sticks like everybody else did. We figured that's the way it was everywhere else around the league. I went for years with them owing me a lot of money. You never said anything, because you wanted to see hockey stay there. Eventually, you always did get paid."

As captain, Sutter believed it was his responsibility to keep things positive, even in the face of adversity. He recalls the early 1980s as a time when it was a daily battle just to get the requisite 20 players on the ice at any given time.

"There were years when we had 23 players in St. Louis and three others on our farm team in Montana and that was it," said Sutter. "Calgary used to have 60-some players under contract and we played them in the Stanley Cup semifinals [in 1986]. I remember I was hurt and maybe shouldn't have played, but I did—because there weren't any other choices. Rob Ramage, Bernie Federko, we were all very young, and we never bitched or complained. We thought we were lucky to be in the NHL. We'd go to one city and sometimes stay in eight or nine different hotels in one year."

Because they were looking for the cheapest rate?

"Because they didn't pay bills in the one we stayed in the last time," answered Sutter. "Sometimes we'd leave at 8:30 in the morning to catch a connecting flight, when other teams might leave their cities at three in the afternoon. There were no direct flights out of St. Louis, so you always had to go someplace else first, usually Chicago. Needless to say, over the years, we figured out where all the little bars and hotdog stands were in the Chicago airport. Some guys really complained, but we stuck together as players. Nothing was ever as bad as it seemed."

The highlight of the Blues' history came in the 1986 playoffs when they advanced to the Stanley Cup semifinals and pushed the heavily favored Calgary Flames to the seventh game. In Game 6, the Flames were comfortably ahead 5–2, but the Blues staged a miraculous third-period comeback and forced overtime. Then Doug Wickenheiser scored the game winner and it became known as the Monday Night Miracle. The Blues had the Flames on the ropes, but in the end, they lost a nail-biter, 2–1, in the seventh game.

"That series was a classic," said Sutter. "We were the underdogs and we were counted out over and over again. Me, I believed right until the final buzzer that we were going to win that [seventh] game. I'll never forget that night. There were 20 seconds to go and we were down a goal and the puck was chipped into their corner. I hooked somebody down and went to the front of the net. Dougie Gilmour got the puck out of the corner and he had so much time to make a play, you couldn't believe it. I was in front and [Flames defenseman] Al MacInnis turned away from me, but Dougie's pass hit him right on the blade of the skate and deflected away. I couldn't believe it—because I knew I was going to score the tying goal. I didn't care if there were three Mike Vernons in the net, that puck was going in.

"The scary part was, we knew we were going to beat Montreal in the finals too—because we had beaten them all year. Plus, by then, Calgary had all our best players."

In 1986, the Flames had acquired Joey Mullen from the Blues in a one-sided February trade, motivated largely by Mullen's contract demands. The next season, they added Rob Ramage and Rick Wamsley. In September 1988, they picked up Gilmour and Mark Hunter as well. All five played for Calgary on its 1989 Stanley Cup championship team.

"Every time we developed a good, young player, you knew they were going to get traded," said Sutter. "It just broke your heart. Whenever I saw [Flames player personnel director] Al MacNeil around, he was like the plague. It meant we were going to get raped again. They were in town to steal somebody—and they always did. It was all about money. We had a young Rob Ramage and a young Joe Mullen and a young Bernie Federko and a young Mike Liut and we felt we were in control of things. We felt we could keep hockey there. We were broken-hearted whenever they said they were leaving, but eventually we got used to it.

"I can't remember how many times [trainer] Tommy Woodcock called me and said, 'Sudsy, come and collect your sweater. I want you to have your sweater.'"

Sutter believes the Blues' off-ice distractions prevented players such as him and Federko from ever getting the recognition they deserved.

Pierre Turgeon grapples with Scott Niedermayer of the New Jersey Devils.

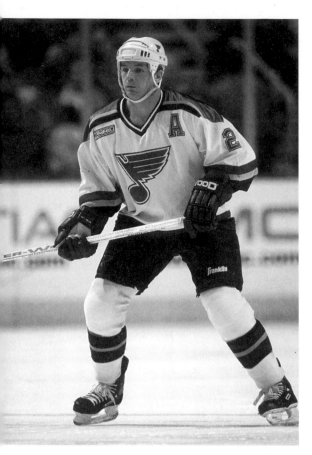

St. Louis defenseman Al MacInnis is a perennial Norris Trophy finalist although in 1999–2000 that honor went to his teammate Chris Pronger.

Team Highlights

- April 9, 2000: The Blues win the President's Trophy for most wins during the regular season.

- 1990–91: Brett Hull scores 86 goals and wins the Hart Trophy as the NHL's most valuable player.

- 1967–70: The Blues shock the NHL by making it to the Stanley Cup finals in each of their first three seasons.

"We never got the respect from anybody," he said. "I played with so many players who were far better than the ones that eventually won the [NHL] awards. Bernie Federko deserves to be in the Hall of Fame. Next to [Wayne] Gretzky, Bernie was the best player in the game for the 10 years we played together. He was typical of the franchise. We didn't put personal accolades ahead of team goals. We did everything we could to win—and did everything we could away from the rink to have fun. We were very, very serious when we got to the rink.

"I was there 16 years and we never won the Cup and it always drove me nuts. We were always right there."

Nowadays, the Blues play in the Kiel Center, but Sutter remembers the old arena gave them something extra in terms of a home-ice advantage. It could get as loud as the Chicago Stadium there during the playoffs.

"The old building was something special. It was the last building in the league not to have air conditioning. It leaked on game days. And it was loud. It had a tremendous hockey atmosphere. St. Louis is a real working-man's city, a small-town, big city, if you know what I mean by that. There's a big difference between St. Louis and Chicago or New York.

"There was no show to be put on there. They took a lot of pride in their hockey team. They had KMOX radio there and my parents could listen to it in central Alberta. We had Dan Kelly, Jack Buck. Bob Costas passed through there. I was associated with some of the best people you could possibly be associated with, and yet, they had the same morals and values I was raised with.

"Every guy who wore that sweater was proud of it. It was really a gratifying place to play."

The Franchise
Of the six teams that entered the NHL in its landmark 1967 expansion, none had a more immediate impact than did the St. Louis Blues. The Blues qualified for the Stanley Cup finals in each of their first three seasons, thanks largely to the presence of a young general manager and coach named Scotty Bowman, who had been plucked out of the Montreal Canadiens organization. Much of the ethic that Bowman introduced to the Blues, he co-opted from his former club. Bowman convinced the legendary Dickie Moore to end his two-year retirement and play again, if only for the leadership qualities he could bring to the team's dressing room. This

established a pattern that would become Bowman's trademark wherever he subsequently worked—a preference for older, established NHLers over younger, but mistake-prone up-and-comers. Bowman's 1971 departure, to return to the Montreal organization, coincided with a decline in the team's on-ice fortunes, finishing sixth of eight in the 1973–74 season. By then, the effects of the World Hockey Association on the team's bottom line were being felt—and soon set in motion a series of changes at the ownership level. From 1976 until 1987, the team passed through the hands of the Solomon family to the Ralston Purina Corporation to Harry Ornest to Michael Shanahan—and once, almost ended up in Saskatoon, Saskatchewan. Shanahan's group brought in the volatile Ron Caron, another Canadiens alumnus. As GM and he helped restore some of their early glories. Following the 1978–79 season, the Blues became the only NHL team to qualify for the playoffs in each of the final 21 years of the millennium. Caron's most astute deal was pilfering a young Brett Hull from Calgary, reversing the flow of talent that had, up until then, been a one-way parade of players from St. Louis. Hull didn't win a championship in St. Louis, but when he left the organization in 1998, after 11 seasons and 744 games played, he was their all-time goal-scoring leader, with 527, and second in points (936) behind Bernie Federko (1,073). The 1990s saw more turbulence in St. Louis with the arrival of Mike Keenan as GM in 1994, fresh off his first Stanley Cup championship with the New York Rangers. Keenan's short and controversial stay saw huge increases in the team's payroll and many player transactions, some of which failed miserably (adding Wayne Gretzky for 18 games in the 1995–96 season), but others (Chris Pronger, Pavol Demitra) which established the foundation for their first-ever overall league championship, won in the 1999–2000 season.

Team Records

	Career	Season
Goals	Brett Hull, 527	Brett Hull, 86 (1990–91)
Assists	Bernie Federko, 721	Adam Oates, 90 (1990–91)
Points	Bernie Federko, 1,073	Brett Hull, 131 (1990–91)
Goals-Against Average	Roman Turek, 1.95	Roman Turek, 1.95 (1999–2000)
Games Played	Bernie Federko, 927	

Tampa Bay Lightning

Founded 1992

Arenas
Ice Palace 1996–present
Thunderdome 1993–1996
Expo Hall 1992–1993

Stanley Cup Wins
0

Award Winners
Bill Masterton Trophy
John Cullen, 1998–99

Rob Zamuner's strong defensive play as a member of the Tampa Bay Lightning won him recognition around the league and a spot on the Canadian Olympic Team at Nagano in 1998.

Profile: A Stanley Cup winner as both a coach and a player, Terry Crisp played on Cup-winning teams in Philadelphia in 1974 and 1975 and coached the Calgary Flames when they won the Cup in 1989. Crisp has been head coach of Tampa Bay as well as Calgary and was an assistant coach on Canada's Olympic Team at the 1992 Olympics at Albertville, France. He currently provides expert commentary for television hockey games.

Face to Face

Throughout his career in the National Hockey League, Terry Crisp had been a winner, with two championships as a player with the Philadelphia Flyers in the 1970s, and a Stanley Cup win as the coach of the Calgary Flames in 1989. When he agreed to guide the expansion Tampa Bay Lightning in the summer of 1992, he knew there likely wasn't going to be another Cup ring in his immediate future. Still, he had no idea what he was getting himself into.

Terry Crisp

"None," Crisp says now, laughing. "I didn't know anybody in the ownership—the only person I knew was Phil Esposito. From start to finish I never did know who owned the darned thing."

The first year the Lightning played in an almost carnival-like atmosphere. "Our training table was outside the arena, under a palm tree," Crisp recalled. "But we had a good group of guys, people like [Rob] Ramage and [Joe] Reekie, a good bunch of veterans who knew they were there because nobody wanted them. We had a lot of castoffs that still wanted to stay in the game and show they belonged, and the fans loved them, because they didn't know any better."

Those fans were crammed into the Expo Hall, an arena with a capacity of 10,300. Although not as hockey literate as most, they warmed to the team quickly, and the players genuinely enjoyed that first year. "It was like a happening every night," Crisp remembered. "It was a fun year, nobody bitched, and nobody complained."

Through their first four years in the NHL, the Lightning had their share of ups and downs, and they had their share of char-

- June 27, 1998: Tampa Bay uses the first pick in the NHL entry draft to select future superstar Vincent Lecavalier.

- November 29, 1997: Lightning forward Rob Zamuner is selected to represent Canada at the Olympic Games in Nagano, Japan.

- September 23, 1992: Manon Rheaume becomes the first women to play in an NHL game, starting for the Lightning in an exhibition game.

acters. Veterans like Dino Ciccarelli were rubbing shoulders with Europeans like Petr Klima and Alexander Selivanov. Selivanov later married Phil Esposito's daughter, earning him the dubious nickname "son-in-law-of."

"It was a real mixed bag," Crisp said. "I wasn't used to dealing with Europeans, but one day Klima came up to me and gave me some great advice. 'Don't yell at us, we'll just tune you out.' He was right."

Another player who gave the Lightning fits was Roman Hamrlik, picked first overall in Tampa's first draft in 1992. A gifted but inconsistent player, Hamrlik relied heavily on his father for advice, something the father didn't shy away from providing. The two could often be heard yelling at each other in Czech outside the dressing room, and one night, Hamrlik's father tried to force his way into the room between periods of a game.

"Phil caught him coming down the hall and headed him off at the pass. Thank goodness, because who knows what I would have done," Crisp said with a chuckle. "That guy was a piece of work."

By their fourth season in the league, the Lightning were an intriguing work in progress themselves. As they battled for a playoff spot down the stretch, Crisp could see the makings of a good team in the future. "Our goaltending was excellent with Daren Puppa, the young kids were starting to come along, and guys like Ciccarelli and [Brian] Bellows set an excellent example. It was the perfect mix."

When they made the playoffs in the spring of 1996, few expected them to do much against the vaunted Flyers, but Bellows scored the overtime winner in Game 2 of the series, and when Selivanov scored the overtime winner in Game 3, Tampa had hockey fever. "My ears are still ringing from those nights at the Thunderdome," Crisp says today. "It was like nothing you've ever heard in a hockey arena."

The Lightning bowed out in six tough games, and after four years of steady improvement, the future looked bright. But like lightning itself, the brilliance was short lived. "We didn't stay on the game plan that we'd all agreed on," Crisp says now. "We started going for the quick fix, thinking we were ready to make the next move, and we weren't."

What happened over the next two years still saddens him. "The part that irritates me the most is that we knew we were on the right path, and then suddenly, for whatever reason, we were stupid and just let it all slip away."

Rob Zamuner surveys the ice from behind the Tampa Bay net.

A year after their brush with greatness against the Flyers, the Lightning missed the playoffs. Forced to reduce the payroll, Esposito began getting rid of veterans like Ciccarelli and Bellows, who had been a key part of the team's initial success. When the team stumbled out of the gate to start the 1997–98 season, Crisp was fired, six seasons after accepting Esposito's offer to coach the team.

"I'm proud of what we did there," Crisp said. "I just wish we had stuck with the program."

As it turned out, the Lightning descended into chaos, the ownership troubles finally catching up to them and throwing the team into turmoil. Today, when Crisp watches Tampa, he does so with mixed feelings, sad about the way things are, but proud of what they once were. Mostly, when he thinks about his time with the Lightning, he thinks back to April 27, 1996, the night they were beaten in Game 6 of the series against the Flyers and eliminated from the post-season.

"The night we got beat out, I'm walking across the ice, and we've got more than 27,000 fans at the Thunderdome, nobody had left. We'd just been beaten out, and they're giving us a standing ovation. So I stood there at center ice and took it all in—a crowd of 27,000 people cheering for a team that just got beat out. I figured I probably wouldn't see anything like it again," Crisp said.

"You know what? I was right."

The Franchise

There are two ways to look at the Tampa Bay Lightning during their short time in the National Hockey League: They're either a laughingstock with comically inept management, or they're so strong that they've survived what appear to be repeated and deliberate attempts to kill them. Either way, one thing is clear: The Lightning stand as a shining example of how a professional sports franchise should not be run.

The Bolts began as a bad idea, an expansion franchise given life because the ownership group was one of the few willing to pay a then exorbitant $50-million entry fee. Along with their expansion cousins, the Ottawa Senators, the Lightning began life on very shaky financial ground. Hall of Fame player Phil Esposito was the front man for the Tampa franchise, but the exact nature of the ownership group was a mystery.

It was made up primarily of Japanese businesses, recruited when Esposito's North American partners backed out. One of the major investors was a company called Kokusai Green, which wound up taking majority control when the team was unable to make its first expansion payment. That was the first of many ominous signs for the franchise.

The Lightning began play in the fall of 1992, with Esposito as general manager, his brother Tony as chief scout, and Terry Crisp behind the bench. A Stanley Cup winner as a player in Philadelphia, Crisp had coached the Calgary Flames to a Cup win just three years earlier, and his early work in Tampa would stand as one of the few bright spots for the franchise. With former Flame Brian Bradley leading the team in scoring, the Lightning were actually respectable by expansion standards, and they were light years ahead of their counterparts in Ottawa.

In that first season, the Lightning played on the Florida State Fairgrounds, in a building known as the Expo Hall. Dubbed the "Espo Hall" in honor of the Espositos, it was run down and seated fewer than 11,000 people. For the second season, the Lightning moved to an even more bizarre location, the Suncoast Dome, a building designed to house football and baseball, which was renovated to accommodate hockey.

The atmosphere in the newly christened "Thunderdome" was

nothing short of surreal. It could be loud on occasion, but it was also deathly quiet when the team was playing poorly, which was most of the time. The so-called arena seated 28,000 fans, but most nights, the crowds hovered around the 10,000 mark, and many of those people had not paid to get in.

As early as the team's second season, rumors were rampant that the Lightning were on the brink of bankruptcy. There was constant speculation that the team was barely making its payroll, and there were published reports that the franchise was being used as a money-laundering scheme for Japanese organized crime. If it was, a lot of money was lost in the wash.

Surprisingly, the team was showing dramatic improvement, and in the 1995–96 season, the Lightning entered the late stages of the season in contention for a playoff spot. With Daren Puppa providing All-Star caliber goaltending, and young defenseman Roman Hamrlik emerging as a potential superstar, Crisp's team put together a seven-game unbeaten streak, while the defending Stanley Cup champion New Jersey Devils collapsed down the stretch. On April 13, 1996, New Jersey lost to Ottawa, clinching a playoff spot for the Lightning in their fourth season.

Now, the Lightning's bizarre home would work to the team's advantage. When Tampa stunned the Flyers by winning Game 2 in overtime in Philadelphia, the team returned home to play in front of huge, enthusiastic crowds. On April 21, 1996, the Lightning shocked the Flyers again, winning 5–4 in overtime to take a 2–1 series lead. Two days later, 28,183 fans went to Game 4, the largest crowd ever to witness an NHL playoff game. It was the greatest moment in franchise history, but it was fleeting.

The Lightning lost that game, the series, and in the coming years, any hint of respectability. Within two years Gratton and Hamrlik were gone, Gratton lost to free agency, and Hamrlik dealt away in one of Phil Esposito's many dubious trades. Gratton was later reacquired but by then the damage was done.

Despite moving into the newly constructed Ice Palace in the fall of 1996, the team was now awash in red ink. The Lightning missed the playoffs in 1996–97, by which time the team's ownership was looking to sell. Now the problem of who exactly the owners were became a problem. One of the groups that checked out the franchise suggested that Takashi Okubu, listed as one of the major partners, did not even exist.

In the fall of 1997, the Lightning had won only two of their

Vincent Lecavalier is surrounded by New York Rangers as he battles for the puck. The future of the Tampa Bay franchise, Vincent Lecavalier had performed well in his first two NHL seasons, scoring 67 points to lead the team in the 1999–2000 season.

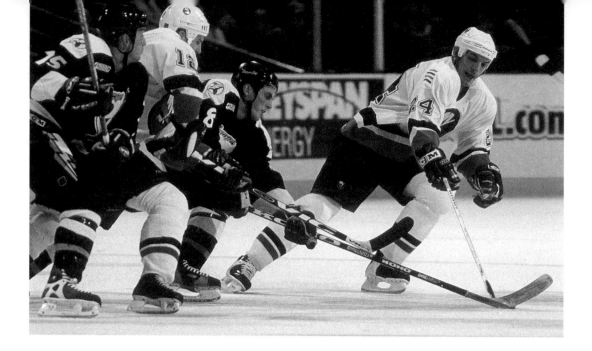

first 11 games. Crisp was fired and ultimately replaced by Jacques Demers. But there was no saving the team now. With limited financial resources, and management spinning its wheels, the Lightning posted the worst record in franchise history in 1997–98, losing an astonishing 55 games. Worse yet, the team was beset with a host of serious medical problems. John Cullen, one of Tampa's most popular players, battled cancer, while goaltender Daren Puppa, the hero of that playoff series with Philadelphia, had recurring back problems and rarely played.

By the summer of 1998, the team was a mess, on and off the ice. The Japanese owners, having lost more than $100 million, were desperate to sell—to anyone, anywhere. They finally found a buyer in Art Williams, a retired insurance tycoon who, unlike the Japanese, was visible and outspoken. Too much so, as it turned out.

Williams's first misstep occurred at the draft in 1998, when the team selected Vincent Lecavalier first overall. Beaming beside his new franchise player, Williams proclaimed that Lecavalier would be "the Michael Jordan of hockey," a comment that stunned league observers. But that was Art Williams, a man who had made his living making the hard sell. Deeply religious, Williams did not smoke or drink and did not use profanity, instead using terms like "goldangit" and "dadgummit."

He was an easy target for his NHL colleagues, who viciously called him "Jed Clampett" behind his back, a reference to the Beverly Hillbillies, and to Williams's southern twang. Sadly, his actions did little to dissuade the notion that he was out of his depth. After taking over as owner, he assured Phil and Tony Esposito publicly that their jobs were safe. Eight games into the season, he fired them, ending what was known as the reign of error.

At one early point that season, with the team hovering at .500, Williams decided to address the troops prior to a home game against the New York Rangers. Filling his speech with college football references, and using his bizarre euphemisms, Williams urged his boys to put on a good show against Wayne Gretzky and the Rangers. They didn't, losing 10–2, the first of nine straight losses that would sweep them out of playoff contention. By the end of the season, the Lightning had lost 50 games for the second straight year.

By this time, Williams had seen enough. Several million dollars poorer, he sold the team to Bill Davidson, owner of the NBA's Detroit Pistons and the IHL's Detroit Vipers. Davidson's first move was to clean house, firing Demers who was now coach and general manager, and replacing him with Ottawa GM Rick Dudley, who had previously run the Vipers. He quickly hired Detroit's coach, Steve Ludzik, reuniting the duo that had won a Turner Cup championship for Davidson.

But while the Lightning often played like an IHL team, running them would be a new experience for Dudley and Ludzik, or "Duds and Luds," as they were soon known. Aside from Lecavalier, there was little to build around, and the team was badly tarnished by the previous regimes. In 1999–2000, the Lightning ushered in the new era by becoming the first team in NHL history to post three straight 50-loss seasons. It became clear that if there was to be a turnaround, it would be a slow, painful one.

Can the Lightning become respectable, as they were for that brief moment in 1996? Can the new ownership heal the wounds inflicted by those who came before them?

Team Records

	Career	Season
Goals	Brian Bradley, 111	Brian Bradley, 42 (1992–93)
Assists	Brian Bradley, 189	Brian Bradley, 56 (1995–96)
Points	Brian Bradley, 300	Brian Bradley, 86 (1992–93)
Goals-Against Average	Darren Puppa, 2.68	Darren Puppa, 2.46 (1995–96)
Games Played	Rob Zamuner, 475	

Toronto Maple Leafs

Founded 1927

Formerly the Toronto Arenas, 1917-19; Toronto St. Pats, 1919-26

Arenas

Air Canada Centre
  1999–present
Maple Leaf Gardens
  1931–1999
Mutual St. Arena
  1927–1931
Toronto Arena, 1917–19

Stanley Cup Wins

1966–67, 1963–64,
  1962–63, 1961–62,
  1950–51, 1948–49,
  1947–48, 1946–47,
  1944–45, 1941–42,
  1931–32, 1921–22,
  1917–18,

Award Winners

see page 253

The cornerstone of the Maple Leafs franchise, Curtis Joseph is one of the few goalies in the league that can dominate the course of a game.

Profile
Red Kelly's hockey career was unique. He was a member of eight Stanley Cup teams in two different cities at two different positions, coached three National Hockey League teams, and sat in the House of Commons for three years during his hockey-playing career. Red was an All-Star for eight consecutive years, won the Lady Byng Trophy in 1951, 1953, 1954, and 1961, and was the first winner of the James Norris Trophy as the NHL's top defenseman in 1954. Apart from that he didn't do much.

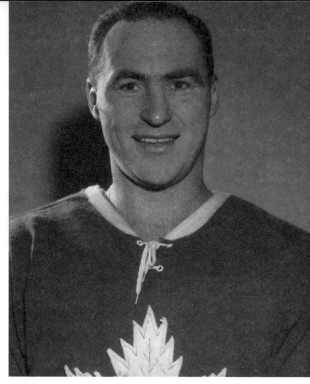

Red Kelly

Face to Face
In a bizarre swap, the testy Jack Adams, Detroit's general manager, traded Kelly at a high point in Red's career. The earnest, big-boned defenseman went to the Toronto Maple Leafs for unsung Marc Reaume, and he jumped from there into seven seasons as a center for the Leafs and four more Stanley Cup wins.

How did florid-faced Adams take temporary leave of his marbles? It all began on a cold, windswept January morning in 1959 when Adams asked Kelly if he'd mind going to Chicago where the Red Wings had a date with the Blackhawks the following night.

Nothing wrong with that; Adams was the boss, Kelly a serf. But this time Kelly was wearing a plaster cast over an ankle he'd broken only six *days* before. Even so, he said he'd give it a try. A doctor removed the cast and taped the ankle and Kelly played, though he could stand little pressure on the ankle and had no power in his stride. The team kept the injury quiet; they didn't want rivals thumping Red's wounded leg. Then he went ahead and finished the schedule for a team going nowhere that spring.

One night 13 months later Detroit had a date with Toronto. The team was back in form and so was Red. A lonely scribe visited him in his Royal York Hotel room and happened to ask how come he had been far below form last season.

"Don't know," Red said.

Then he apparently decided he'd been silent long enough.

"Might have been the ankle," he said.

The ankle? The ankle? What ankle?

- April 8, 2000: The Maple Leafs defeat the Tampa Bay Lightning to complete their first 100-point season in franchise history.

- February 7, 1976: Darryl Sittler sets an NHL record with 10 points in a game, in an 11–4 victory over the Boston Bruins.

- April 18, 1942: The Leafs defeat the Detroit Red Wings to win their second Stanley Cup title.

Whereupon the story emerged and was published.

A Detroit reporter picked up the Toronto paper's account and his paper gave it tall treatment. Predictably, when Adams read the headlines, he flared. He hotly denied Kelly's account, threatened to sue the Toronto paper, and then made the move that changed Kelly's life: He announced that Red was through in Detroit. He traded him to the New York Rangers.

But Kelly refused to report. An earnest, non-swearing, determined man, Red said he'd retire from hockey before he'd agree to accommodate Adams

Whereupon George (Punch) Imlach, Toronto's coach and general manager, jumped into the controversy, contacting first Adams, then Kelly. Adams, still furious, agreed to trade Kelly to Toronto. Next, Imlach persuaded the 32-year-old defenseman to abandon thoughts of retirement and join the Leafs. Punch said he foresaw nothing less than the Stanley Cup in Toronto's near future, even though the Montreal Canadiens were steamrolling the NHL on a string of five straight Cup titles.

Then wily Punch presented a surprise. "The road to the Stanley Cup goes through Montreal; it goes through Jean Beliveau," he told Kelly, pinpointing Montreal's nonpareil captain and center star. "I want you up against him. I want you to become my center."

Presented so intriguing a challenge, Kelly became unretired faster than he could say "By hang!"

In truth, Red may have been ready to join the Leafs without the challenge of harnessing Beliveau. As a youngster growing up on a farm near Simcoe in southwestern Ontario, he had spent Saturday nights avidly absorbing Foster Hewitt's magnetic hockey broadcasts from Maple Leaf Gardens. Knee-high to a shin-pad, he had made Red Horner, the body-thumping defenseman, his hero.

In later years Kelly confessed that Horner's principal attraction was that he had red hair and played defense, just like Red. Little Leonard Patrick had the fiery thatch and in his early teens he banged into approaching forwards as enthusiastically as Horner ever had as the NHL's celebrated bad man and penalty leader.

But that changed when Kelly became a junior play for St. Michael's College in Toronto and came under the spell of the St. Mike's coach, Joe Primeau. Here was the gentlemanly former Lady Byng Trophy winner and center for Charlie Conacher and Busher Jackson, the renowned Kid Line of the Maple Leafs, a trio extolled by Hewitt on those bath-night broadcasts.

Primeau, as a player and a coach, was no advocate of mindless thumping. "You don't help us, sitting in the penalty box," Primeau preached. Kelly listened. Like most people who knew Primeau, he was strongly attracted to him. Kelly, of course, remembered him from those Saturday-night broadcasts of the 1930s, perhaps the most popular program in radio history.

Curiously, however, the Leafs overlooked the quiet redhead in Maple Leaf Gardens, playing defense on the same ice floe as the pros upstairs.

While they slept, a scout for Detroit, Carson Cooper, locked up Red for the Wings and in his first season, 20 years old, Kelly jumped right into the Detroit lineup, playing the full 60-game schedule. The team was second that spring, then rushed off to a record seven straight first-place finishes and four Stanley Cup wins with Red a kingpin back of the renowned Production Line of Gordie Howe, Ted Lindsay, and Sid Abel.

Thirteen years after his Detroit debut, Kelly got back to Maple Leaf Gardens to stay, and for seven seasons he fed passes to a long-striding left winger, Frank Mahovlich, helping the Big M set a team record 48 goals in 1960–61.

Kelly was introduced to federal politics by a well-regarded Liberal Party backroom adviser, Keith Davey, later a senator. He decided to run, he said later, because he admired the prime minister, Lester B. Pearson. Kelly was elected and served for three years, rushing from hockey practices in the Gardens to a back bench in the House of Commons.

In the Gardens he filled Punch Imlach's need for a strong, durable center to take on Jean Beliveau and such other high-scoring centers as Beliveau's darting teammate, Henri Richard,

One of the most talented players to ever play the game, Frank Mahovlich, "The Big M," scored 533 career goals and led the Leafs in goals from 1960-61 to 1966-67. He also won the Stanley Cup four times with the Leafs. Mahovlich is currently a member of the Canadian Senate.

Chicago's scoring champion Stan Mikita, and Detroit's elusive stick-handler Norm Ullman.

In the spring of 1967 Kelly was nudging his 40th birthday and involved in Toronto's fourth Cup triumph of the 1960s. So he terminated his 20-year playing career and became the first coach for Jack Kent Cooke's expansion team, the Los Angeles Kings, for two seasons. Then he took on the Pittsburgh Penguins for four years, and in 1973 he returned to Maple Leaf Gardens to coach the Leafs for the next four. They made the playoffs each spring, but when they failed to advance past the quarter-finals Leonard Patrick Kelly concluded 30 consecutive seasons at ice level in the NHL.

The Franchise

Conn Smythe was a gambling man who believed in playing hunches and believed in luck, and as it turned out that's how he became the owner of the Toronto Maple Leafs and why they became Canada's team in hundreds of thousands of homes on Saturday nights in winter.

Smythe used betting money to help purchase the old Toronto St. Patrick's franchise for $165,000 in 1927, and he changed the team's name to the Maple Leafs. In 1930, with the team needing a spark, he bet on his own two-year-old filly, Rare Jewel, to win a thoroughbred race at outlandish odds, 100 to 1. When she won, Rare Jewel returned $214 on each $2 bet, and ecstatic Smythe was heard to exclaim, "Now I can buy King Clancy." He did, too. He bought the fiery little Irishman from the Ottawa Senators for $35,000 and two players.

Clancy ignited the required spark, helping transform the Maple Leafs into a colorful, aggressive team featuring the pile-driving red-haired defenseman Red Horner and a nicely meshed trio of Toronto-born or -raised youngsters: Charlie Conacher with a thundering shot, Harvey (Busher) Jackson with the grace of a Nureyev, and Joe Primeau, the centerman feeding pucks to the voracious pair.

But even with Clancy's added verve, the Maple Leafs needed something, and once again that something was supplied by the man with the hunch, C. Smythe. What he wanted was Foster Hewitt's broadcasts.

He remembered Hewitt as a young reporter from the *Toronto Star*, broadcasting hockey from the old Mutual Street Arena, and wanted to hire him for Leaf games. But the directors of Smythe's new rink, Maple Leaf Gardens, were opposed; they felt if fans could get the games free on radio they'd not buy tickets to watch them.

But Smythe persisted and at length prevailed and, of course, he was right again. For generations of fans, the Saturday night hockey broadcasts from Hewitt's famous gondola turned the Maple Leafs into Canada's team for decades to come.

Not everything was hearts and flowers, however. The team won the Stanley Cup in 1932, the season the Gardens opened,

Darryl Sittler possesses the NHL record for points in a game with 10. He set the record in a February 1976 game against the Boston Bruins.

but they didn't win it again for a decade. They won five more titles in the next decade, but then there was a long blank period until the 1960s, when Punch Imlach arrived at the helm to produce four championships. But by 1968 the well had run dry.

Enter the feisty Harold Ballard, who through the 1970s, 1980s, and 1990s watched seats fill with excessively patient bottoms but produced no Stanley Cups and no individual award winners. As the new millennium dawned, the most recent Stanley Cup success was in 1967.

There were, however, pockets of mirth. In the spring of 1978, a Leaf lineup featuring Lanny McDonald and Darryl Sittler surprisingly closed down the polished New York Islanders in a hectic seven-game quarter-final. Word of the win delighted the former Leaf defenseman, light-hearted Babe Pratt, who was across the sea in Prague scouting the annual world championship tournament on behalf of the Vancouver Canucks.

"Wow," enthused this amiable fellow, apprised of Toronto's triumph. "Who do they play next?"

"The Canadiens," he was told.

"The Canadiens!" Babe exclaimed of the team that had won a mere four Stanley Cups in the previous seven springs. "Jeez, that's like bustin' your ass to get on the *Titanic*."

The Leafs could have used Pratt and his one-liners in the dark days that followed the 1960s when individual achievements were as scarce as Stanley Cups. Entering the 21st century, no Leaf player since Ted Kennedy in 1955 had won the most valuable player award, the Hart Trophy; none the top rookie trophy, the Calder, since Brit Selby in 1966; none the trophy for the most skillful and sportsmanlike player, the Lady Byng, since Dave Keon in 1963; and none the goaltending Vezina Trophy since Johnny Bower and Terry Sawchuk shared it in 1965.

The rollicking H. Ballard was the principal owner through these dark years until he died in April of 1990. He'd got his foot in the door when Conn Smythe stepped aside in 1961, selling his 50,000 shares of Maple Leaf stock for $2 million to his son

Stafford, to Ballard, and to the newspaper publisher John Bassett.

They were frolicsome owners but in the summer of 1969 Ballard and the younger Smythe faced federal charges of tax evasion, and in 1971 Clay Powell, a prosecutor in the Ontario Attorney General's office, brought fraud and theft charges against them both. Clearing out, Bassett made a run at gaining control of the Gardens but, instead, his two partners bought him out, borrowing $6 million, most of it from the Toronto-Dominion Bank.

The first European captain of the Toronto Maple Leafs, Mats Sundin is the team's undisputed leader both on and off the ice.

Dave Keon, one of the best to ever don the blue and white, tries to slide the puck by former Canadiens goalie and current Leafs president, Ken Dryden.

A few months later Stafford died following surgery for a bleeding ulcer, and Ballard quickly steamed back to the bank for another loan, this one $7.5 million, to scoop up Stafford's stock.

Thus Harold became the Lord High Llama at the Gardens. That is, once he got out of jail. For in the August 1972 trial following Stafford's death, Ballard was found guilty of 47 counts of fraud and sentenced to three years in prison. He spent one year of his sentence behind bars and was paroled.

What followed his release were 17 years of the dreariest

hockey in the history of the Maple Leafs. They achieved nothing close to a Stanley Cup final and often missed the playoffs altogether. One year followed another in what Jack Batten's terrific 1994 book, *The Leafs*, called "a purely Ballardian tradition of bungling, cheapness, ego-gratification and losing."

More legal infighting succeeded Ballard's death, a sea of lawsuits and threats of lawsuits in the struggle for ownership. From this, a reclusive supermarket strongman, Steve Stavro, who hated the limelight and shied away from it whenever possible, emerged as principal stockholder, and with general manager Cliff Fletcher and coach Pat Burns in charge, the Leafs began to emerge into the long lost sunlight.

When they stalled, Ken Dryden, the intellectual who played goal for the Canadiens in the 1970s, was hired as the Leafs president. A burly former Toronto defenseman, cigar-puffing Pat Quinn, came in as coach, and after what seemed an exhaustive search, Dryden found the sort of man he wanted as this team's general manager: Ken Dryden.

Then the team abandoned the Gardens, its historic home, and moved into a glittering new area called the Air Canada Centre. Thus began the next millennium.

Team Lowlights

- August 26, 1951: Shortly after scoring the overtime goal on April 21, 1951 to win the Stanley Cup for the Maple Leafs, Leafs forward Bill Barilko's plane disappears on a fishing trip in northern Ontario. His body is undiscovered for 11 years and the Leafs do not win another Cup until that year.

Team Records

	Career	Season
Goals	Darryl Sittler, 389	Rick Vaive, 54 (1981–82)
Assists	Borje Salming, 620	Doug Gilmour, 95 (1992–93)
Points	Darryl Sittler, 916	Doug Gilmour, 127 (1992–93)
Goals-Against Average	Al Rollins, 2.06	Lorne Chabot, 1.61 (1928–29)
Games Played	George Armstrong, 1,187	

Vancouver Canucks

Founded 1970

Arenas
*General Motors Place
  1995–present
Pacific Coliseum 1970–95*

Stanley Cup Wins
0

Award Winners

Jack Adams Award
Pat Quinn, 1991–92

Calder Trophy
Pavel Bure, 1991–92

King Clancy Trophy
Trevor Linden, 1996–97

*Stan Smyl spent his
entire 13-year career
as a member of the
Vancouver Canucks.*

Profile

The playing days of rugged defenseman Pat Quinn are best remembered for a devastating hit he applied to Boston superstar Bobby Orr. He has held head coaching jobs in Philadelphia, Los Angeles, Vancouver, and Toronto. He also held the general manager title in Vancouver and Toronto and the title of president with the Canucks, at one time holding the titles of coach, general manager, and president simultaneously for the Canucks. Quinn has twice been to the Stanley Cup finals as a coach, first with the Flyers and later with the Canucks.

Face to Face

No NHL sweater has gone through more mind-boggling logo and color changes than the Vancouver Canucks'.

But Pat Quinn was always there to defend it, as a player, coach, general manager, and team president.

Take that game in Calgary when coach Quinn spotted Flames mascot Harvey the Hound wiping his bottom with a Canucks jersey and driving a RV over top of it during an intermission. Suddenly the costumed canine saw his dog years flash before his eyes at the sight of the big angry Irishman slipping and sliding towards him in dress shoes.

Pat Quinn

"I got about halfway out there and wondered 'What the hell am I doing here,'" Quinn recalled. "But you just don't do that to someone's team symbol."

An imposing presence made the 6-foot-3, 215-pound Maple Leafs defenseman a worthy choice for the Canucks in the 1970 expansion draft. The year before, Quinn's wicked body check had knocked Bobby Orr cold and almost caused a riot at Boston Garden.

While Barry Wilkins scored the first goal in team history at the Pacific Coliseum on October 9, 1970, Quinn's contribution in the 3–1 loss to the Kings was the club's first ever misconduct. Two nights later, before the first sellout in the new building's history, the Canucks won their first game, beating Quinn's old Leafs team 5–3.

Team Highlights

- July 28, 1997: Looking for veteran leadership, the Canucks sign their former nemesis, Mark Messier, to a free-agent contract.

- June 14, 1994: Led by Parel Bure, the Canucks make the Stanley Cup finals again lose to Mark Messier and the New York Rangers in seven games.

- May 6, 1982: The Canucks reach the Stanley Cup finals for the first time but are defeated by the powerhouse New York Islanders.

Rugged defenseman Ed Jovanovski (right) is a promising young player who was one of the key elements in the trade that sent Pavel Bure to the Florida Panthers. On the left is teammate Darby Hendrickson.

"When we first started, we didn't have real Vancouver Canuck fans, we had people who had cheered most of their lives for the Canadiens or the Leafs," Quinn said. "They were quiet, but over time, we built quite a following."

The newborn Canucks had a few handicaps, not the least of which was placement in the far-off Eastern Division with expansion brethren Buffalo. Half of the 12-team NHL had been created only three years earlier, so there was little to choose from on draft day. The 18 position players chosen racked up just 37 goals in 1969–70.

"They drafted a lot of good, solid guys," Quinn countered. "Orland Kurtenbach was a real leader for us. We weren't that far off in our first year."

In those days, the Canucks sported blue, green, and white jerseys, featuring a hockey stick jutting into a rink. The rudimentary design was mocked by some around the league.

"It did tell a story," Quinn argued, still defensive about the criticism 30 years later. "Green for the forest, blue for the water, white for the ice. It just had to be explained. But the next change a few years later was a real departure."

To usher in the 1980s, the team chose a shocking combination of gold, black, and red recommended by a sports psychologist. For one season, it worked, as coaches Harry Neale and Roger Neilson brought the 1981–82 team within shouting distance of .500 and a Stanley Cup win.

Neilson was best remembered for his protest in a playoff game against Chicago, waving a white "surrender" towel at referee Bob Myers. His players followed suit and towel waving took the west coast by storm that spring. But despite the spadework of checkers and a big playoff from goalie Richard Brodeur, Vancouver eventually lost the Stanley Cup finals in four straight to the New York Islanders.

Five seasons in the wilderness followed the team's brush with greatness, during which time they never made it past the first round. Attendance fell off, and some ill-advised trades—such as power winger Cam Neely for Barry Pederson and a first-round draft pick (Glen Wesley)—were haunting the team.

Pavel Bure twice scored 60 goals in a season as a member of the Canucks.

On January 9, 1987, the Canucks hired Quinn away from his position as head coach of the Kings, to take over as president and general manager. Though he had played just two years in the organization before joining the new Atlanta Flames in 1972, Quinn still had an excellent reputation in Vancouver, after retiring in 1977.

He drifted into coaching during the Fred Shero regime in Philadelphia, led the Flyers to a record 35-game unbeaten streak in 1979–80, won the Jack Adams Trophy, studied law for two years in Delaware, and spent three years coaching the Kings. Because the league ruled the Canucks tampered with him while he was under contract in L.A., it cost them $10,000 in fines and Quinn had to wait until season's end to move into his executive office.

The situation was bleak, with 11 consecutive losing seasons staring him in the face.

"They had just 4,000 season tickets and crowds between 7,000 and 9,000," Quinn said. "There was talk that the owners [the Griffiths family] might be ready to sell.

"Fortunately for Vancouver, that was a down time for the league and with some other teams in trouble, it wasn't an attractive buy."

Quinn went right to work on patching up the team's confidence.

"It was my feeling there was a caste system in place on the team at that time, four or five guys who ran the dressing room and treated the other 15 like lackeys. Their focus was only to save yourself. There was no team atmosphere and they were coming off of that disastrous [Neely] trade."

Quinn installed Bob McCammon as coach and Brian Burke as director of hockey operations. The Canucks gradually changed from plodding, unimaginative defense and small forwards, to a defense that could blend skill, toughness, and Quinn's favorite ingredient, size.

A godsend in that regard was Trevor Linden. With the highest pick in team history since expansion, the Canucks selected Linden second overall in 1988. A strapping 6-foot-4, 220-pounder, Linden was the talk of the town. He became the team captain within two years, while Quinn surrounded him with some quality help via trades. Greg (Gus) Adams, Gerald Diduck, and Jyrki Lumme were among the first arrivals, followed by Cliff Ronning, Sergio Momesso, Geoff Courtnall, and Robert Dirk.

Quinn was anxious to get in on the European invasion, bringing in two-thirds of the Soviets' big line, Igor Larionov and Vladimir Krutov. Quinn was also there to catch Pavel Bure when he jumped the Iron Curtain. The Canucks were clearly on the rise.

"Suddenly, we looked up and we won our division," Quinn said of 1991–92, the year after he added bench duties to his portfolio. "We started to learn about how to win."

Quinn, who said his courtroom training gave him an excel-

Although signing legendary leader Mark Messier was a major coup for the Canucks organization, the relationship would not last. Messier will rejoin Glen Sather and the New York Rangers for the 2000–01 season.

lent handle on both reading people and problem-solving, gave the franchise three consecutive 40-win seasons as coach. Players didn't abuse the extra rope he gave them off the ice.

There was one practice, however, when an angry Quinn sensed the team had tuned him out. As he illustrated a drill on a whiteboard, he suddenly took his beefy fist and pounded the sturdy plastic dead center, jerking the players to attention and bending the board. A couple of players later tried to match Quinn's powerful dent by swinging their sticks at the board and hardly made a mark.

By the spring of 1994, the Canucks were ready for a Cup

push. The Oilers and Flames, Vancouver's long-time rivals in the West, were in decline and no clear leader emerged in the East. Quinn picked up Craig Janney that March and, a week later, flipped him to the Blues for three more key additions: Jeff Brown, Bret Hedican, and Nathan Lafayette.

With Bure on a 60-goal clip, and a physical team that knocked off Calgary, Dallas, and Toronto, the Canucks drew Mark Messier and the Rangers in the final.

"Without sounding too cocky, it was no surprise to us we'd made it that far," Quinn said. "We had lost in the second round the previous two years. We knew the pain of being knocked out."

Vancouver had already played 101 regular-season and play-off games. The Canucks and Rangers battled then through a seven-game series, crossing the continent five times.

"It was just a valiant effort on our team's part," Quinn said. "We didn't have a big budget, but the players we had and the players we brought in gave us a sense of credibility.

"The strange thing in that '94 series was that each team was winning games they should have lost."

Down 3–1 in the series, the Canucks rallied for a 6–3 win in Madison Square Garden and then 4–1 at home. The Rangers squeezed out a 3–2 victory in the last Cup final that's ever gone the distance.

"There was a mysterious high-sticking call on Bure [a Game 3 ejection], when Messier did the same thing twice and wasn't called," Quinn recalled bitterly.

"But I had a lot of pride being involved in building something such as that and being a steadying influence on players such as Kirk. It was rewarding to see Bure score in overtime [to eliminate Calgary in Game 7 in 1994] and to watch Linden upgrade his play.

"I thought if there hadn't been a shortened schedule the next season [due to the labor dispute], we might have got back there and won the Cup."

The Franchise: Vancouver hopes to open the 21st century as a hockey power the same way it kicked off the 20th.

The Vancouver Millionaires were a famous team and won the Stanley Cup in 1915, two years before the formation of the NHL.

With explosive forwards such as skating wizard Cyclone Taylor, the team built by Frank and Lester Patrick was runner-

The Canucks' all-time leader in total points, goals, and assists, Stan Smyl played in Vancouver from 1978–1991 and led the Canucks to the Stanley cup Cup finals in 1982.

up on several occasions during the early 1920s. But the demise of the Western Hockey League, which sold all its players to the NHL, would obscure Vancouver as a hockey power for decades.

Politics got in the way of constructing a new arena and prevented Vancouver from joining the first wave of expansion teams admitted in 1967–68. A few years later, however, a Minneapolis-based group got the go-ahead for the 1970–71 season.

On June 10, 1970, in Montreal, general manager Bud Poile made Bruins defenseman Gary Doak the first pick in the expansion draft, followed by names such as Orland Kurtenbach, Ray Cullen, Pat Quinn, and Rosaire Paiement. The next day was the entry draft, in which Vancouver and expansion cousin Buffalo spun a wheel for the No. 1 pick. Buffalo won and selected Gilbert Perreault, while Vancouver took defenseman Dale Tallon.

Taylor, by then 87, helped with the Pacific Coliseum's opening ceremonies on October 9 against the Los Angeles Kings. Kurtenbach, Paiement, and Andre Boudrias were among the most accomplished Canucks in the early years, but in the ill-suited East Division, the Canucks rarely escaped the basement. They were relocated to the Smythe Division in 1974–75.

The Canucks underwent a number of coaching, general manager, and sweater changes, never getting past the first round of the playoffs, until a dramatic upswing in the spring of 1982.

Coach Harry Neale was assessed a 10-game suspension late in the season for an altercation with fans in Quebec City and Roger Neilson took over as coach. By the time the Canucks had made the playoffs and eliminated Calgary, Los Angeles, and Chicago, Neilson was the full-time coach and Vancouver went to the finals, losing to the Islanders.

By then, ownership of the team had been transferred to the Griffiths family, who operated a local broadcasting company. They chose Quinn to be architect of a new-look team in 1987. As president and GM, Quinn hung on to his top pick in the 1988 draft, impact forward Trevor Linden, while building an exciting lineup that included Igor Larionov, Petr Nedved, Pavel Bure, and Kirk McLean.

Quinn eventually replaced coach Bob McCammon in 1991 with himself, heralding three consecutive 40-win seasons and the Jack Adams Trophy. By 1994, the Canucks had the blend of speed and power Quinn deemed necessary to challenge for the Cup. Bure was a 60-goal man, Linden was a respected captain, and some shrewd trade deadline trades bolstered their chances against the New York Rangers.

Greg Adams' Game 1 overtime winner was a highlight, but Vancouver lost the next three, before succumbing in Game 7 of a spirited comeback.

The team's momentum was stopped by the NHL labor dispute the following season, and the Canucks were sold to Seattle businessman John E. McCaw in the spring of 1995. The move to the brand new General Motors Place followed a few months later, complete with new uniforms that depicted a killer whale, though Quinn was not successful working with the new owners and was relieved early in the 1997–98 season.

Brian Burke, his one-time assistant, came back from an executive position with the league to take control. One of his boldest moves was the drafting of Swedish super twins Daniel and Henrik Sedin in 1999.

Markus Naslund is part of a talented group of young Swedish players in Vancouver including the highly touted Sedin twins.

Team Records

	Career	Season
Goals	Stan Smyl, 262	Pavel Bure, 60 (1992–93 and 1993–94)
Assists	Stan Smyl, 411	Andre Boudrias, 62 (1974–75)
Points	Stan Smyl, 673	Pavel Bure, 110 (1992–93)
Goals-Against Average	Felix Potvin, 2.59	Felix Potvin, 2.59 (1999–2000)
Games Played	Stan Smyl, 896	

Washington Capitals

Founded 1974

Arenas
MCI Center 1997–present
Capital Center 1974–1997

Stanley Cup Wins
0

Award Winners

Jack Adams Award
Bryan Murray, 1983-84

Jennings Trophy
*Al Jensen and Pat Riggin,
1983-84*

Norris Trophy
*Rod Langway, 1982-83,
1983-84*

Frank J. Selke Trophy
Doug Jarvis, 1983-84

Vezina Trophy
*Olaf Kolzig, 1999–2000
Jim Carey, 1995-96*

*Olaf Kolzig's
outstanding
1999–2000 season was
good enough to win
him the Vezina trophy
as the league's best
goalie.*

Profile

Dale Hunter is the only player in NHL history to collect over 1,000 points and 3,000 penalty minutes. One of the grittiest players in the history of the game, Hunter entered the NHL and played seven seasons for the Quebec Nordiques before being traded to the Washington Capitals. With the exception of a brief stint with the Colorado Avalanche, Hunter played the remainder of his career with the Capitals and retired the second most penalized player in NHL history..

Face to Face

In June of 1987, Dale Hunter, a seven-year veteran with the Quebec Nordiques, decided to make the drive from his home in southwest Ontario to Detroit to watch the NHL draft. "It was a rainy day, there was no work to do on the farm," Hunter recalled. "We figured, what the heck." Along with his dad, his brothers, and childhood friend Bob Gould of the Washington Capitals, Hunter settled into the seats at the Joe Louis Arena.

Dale Hunter

The NHL draft is where the dreams of young hockey players come true, and Hunter had a front-row seat as a career did change firsthand—his.

"I was sitting there, and I saw that Washington had traded its first-round pick to Quebec," Hunter remembered, "and I thought, 'What's going on here?' At the same time, I saw one of the Quebec public relations guys coming up the stairs towards me, and he said, 'You'd better come with me, Dale, the general manager wants to see you.' I was shocked."

Hunter had been traded, along with goaltender Clint Malarchuk, for Alan Haworth, Gaetan Duchesne, and that first-round pick (which Quebec used to select Joe Sakic). On the drive back to his hometown of Petrolia, Hunter suddenly realized that he and traveling companion Bob Gould were now teammates.

The Capitals were coming off an agonizing first-round play-off loss to the Islanders, one in which they had taken a 3–1 series

Jim Carey eyes the puck through a mass of players in front of his goalmouth.

lead, only to lose the next three games. The loss in the seventh game came in quadruple overtime on a goal by New York's Pat LaFontaine.

"[Washington general manager] David Poile told me they wanted more success in the playoffs, and in Quebec I'd had big years in the playoffs," Hunter said. "It was as simple as that."

During his seven years in Quebec, Hunter had earned a reputation as a gritty but skilled player, one who was more than willing to do the dirty work. Along with two brothers who also enjoyed long NHL careers, the Hunters were often compared to Alberta's famous Sutter clan, which sent six of its hard-working sons to the NHL.

"We were the smaller version," Hunter deadpanned.

David Poile could not have imagined how quickly Hunter would play a role in turning the Capitals post-season fortunes around. In Washington's first-round series against Philadelphia, the Capitals and Flyers went to a seventh game, but this time the Caps came out the winner, with Hunter scoring the overtime goal. It remains one of the biggest goals in franchise history.

"Ironic, isn't it?" he said with a laugh. "It couldn't have played out any better. We were down 3–1 in the series, and then we were down 3–0 in the seventh game and we battled back. It stopped all that talk that we couldn't win in the playoffs."

Sadly, most of Hunter's time in Washington was marked by playoff failure, and although he did not win the Stanley Cup as a player, he came very close—twice. In 1990, the Caps advanced to the final four for the first time.

"We beat the Devils and the Rangers in the first two rounds, but then we played the Bruins," Hunter said, a tinge of sadness still audible in his voice. "During the Rangers series, we had lost Dino Ciccarelli and Kevin Hatcher to knee injuries that ended their season. Imagine if Boston had lost both Ray Bourque and Cam Neely." The Capitals, minus their leading scorer and top defenseman, were no match for Boston, which swept the series.

What followed was nearly a decade of frustration in the post-season, for the Caps as a team, and Hunter as a player. In 1993, Washington faced the Islanders. Although Hunter scored seven goals in the six-game series, the lasting memory is from the final game, when he shoved Pierre Turgeon from behind after the Islanders center had scored the clinching goal. Turgeon fell awkwardly into the boards and appeared to suffer a serious shoulder injury.

Even now, it's a sensitive subject for Hunter. "You have to play

with emotion in the playoffs," he said. "I went over the top, over the edge."

His timing couldn't have been worse. New NHL commissioner Gary Bettman was in his first year on the job and was determined to take a tough stance on violence. Even though it turned out that Turgeon was not seriously injured, Hunter was slapped with a 21-game ban, one of the stiffest suspensions in NHL history.

"I didn't think it would be 21 games, but they said they wanted to set a new precedent," Hunter says now. "Did it? You tell me."

There was a public outcry at the time, and it was likely justified. Bettman overreacted, and perhaps to atone for his mistake, he stunned Hunter again in 1997, naming him as a commissioner's pick to play in the NHL All-Star game. Hunter wept with joy when he got the news.

"It sure was nice to go there," he said, still beaming years later. "My boys were old enough to appreciate it, and I even got to play a few shifts on a line with Mario Lemieux and Wayne Gretzky." The following year, the Capitals went to their first Stanley Cup final, but as it had in 1990, the dream ended in a sweep, this time at the hands of Detroit.

The following year, with his team out of contention, Washington GM George McPhee did what he could to get Hunter that elusive Stanley Cup ring, dealing him to the powerhouse Colorado Avalanche at the trade deadline. The Avalanche came close, losing to the eventual Stanley Cup champion Dallas Stars in a seven-game series in the third round. That summer, after a 19-year career in the NHL, Hunter announced his retirement and immediately returned to the Capitals, taking a job in the front office as the team's director of player development.

Hunter ended his playing career with a unique distinction: the only man in NHL history to score 300 goals and accumulate 3,000 penalty minutes, testament to a career that uniquely combined toughness with skill.

"I was a small guy, and I didn't want people to think I could be intimidated," Hunter said. "I went out to prove myself every night."

Mission accomplished.

The Franchise
For more than a quarter of a century in the NHL, the Washington Capitals have been known primarily for one thing: failure. And this isn't ordinary disappointment

we're talking about, it's failure on a sweeping scale, the kind seldom seen in any sport.

The Caps failed before they ever played a game in the NHL. Awarded an expansion franchise prior to the 1974–75 season, they went to the draft armed with the first pick overall and selected defenseman Greg Joly from the Regina Pats of the Western Hockey League. General manager Milt Schmidt, a Hall of Fame player for Boston, compared his first-round pick to the Bruins' Bobby Orr, but Joly would go on to be one of the least productive first overall picks in NHL history, spending only two seasons in Washington before being traded to Detroit.

It got worse from there. The talent pool made available to the Caps and their expansion cousins, the Kansas City Scouts, was severely diminished. In seven years, the NHL had added 12 teams, and it was facing stiff competition from the World Hockey Association. The first year Caps included leading scorer Tommy Williams, a former U.S. Olympian who had been playing in the WHA, and goaltender Ron Low, who had spent the previous season with Tulsa of the Central Hockey League.

The first-year Caps weren't just bad, they were one of the worst teams in NHL history, setting league records for most losses in a season (67), most consecutive losses (17), most road losses (39), and most consecutive road losses (37). The Capitals won only one of their 40 road games that season, and the team posted a total of only eight victories, the fewest ever by a team that had played at least 70 games.

The franchise did boast a state of the art arena, the Cap Center in suburban Landover, one of the first sporting venues to feature luxury boxes. It was the Capitals' home for 23 seasons, until they moved to downtown Washington in the fall of 1997.

Sadly, the team was nowhere near state of the art. In their second season, with Schmidt holding the dual role of general manager and coach, the Caps set another league record, going 25 straight games without a win. Mercifully, their expansion

Peter Bondra and the Capitals have always struggled against the New York Islanders.

One of the best players to never be on a team that won the Stanley Cup, Mike Gartner scored 397 goals with the Capitals and holds the team records for both goals and total points.

cousins in Kansas City broke the mark later that season.

Fourteen games into the skid, owner Abe Pollin fired Schmidt, replacing him as general manager with Max McNab, who in turn hired another veteran minor leaguer, Tom McVie, to coach the team. McVie presided over the final 11 games of the winless streak and a mere five seasons later was behind the bench for the Winnipeg Jets when they began a record-shattering 30 game winless streak.

While the Scouts bolted from Kansas City for Colorado after their second season, the Caps remained in Washington, with little to show for it. Thanks to the arrival of players like Guy Charron and 50-goal-scorer Dennis Maruk, the team showed gradual improvement, but not enough to make the playoffs. Largely because he played in both Kansas City and Washington, Charron earned the bizarre distinction of playing in the most NHL regular-season games (734) without ever appearing in the playoffs.

It's not like the Capitals didn't have their chances—they were beaten out of a playoff spot on the final day of the regular season in both 1980 and 1981.

By the end of that 1980–81 season, the Caps had been in the NHL for seven seasons and were working on their sixth coach. After two and a half seasons on the job, McVie was replaced by Dan Belisle, who in turn lasted a year and a half before being replaced in 1979 by Gary Green. At the age of 26, Green became the youngest man ever to coach in the NHL and, to his credit, had a winning record after one season.

But the 1981–82 season would see the team's fortunes change dramatically. After the Caps won just one of their first 13 games, McNab and Green were fired. New coach Bryan Murray found stability behind the bench, handling the team for the next nine seasons. In the summer of 1982, David Poile was hired as the new general manager, a job he held for the next 15 years.

When he had been on the job for just over a week, Poile went to his first Board of Governors meeting and found himself seated next to Montreal's Irving Grundman. By the end of the day, the two were putting the finishing touches on a blockbuster deal, with Washington sending Ryan Walter and Rick Green to the Canadiens for Rod Langway, Doug Jarvis, Brian Engblom, and Craig Laughlin.

When told of the deal, Pollin was furious, and Poile had doubts of his own. Sticking his head out of the window of his Toronto hotel, he shouted at no one in particular, "Are you sure you know what you're doing?"

The deal was a masterstroke. The new players, combined with emerging stars like Gartner, Bobby Carpenter, and Scott Stevens, brought energy and enthusiasm to a once moribund team. In the first year of the Poile/Murray regime, the Capitals made the play-offs, falling to the New York Islanders, who went on to win their fourth straight Stanley Cup championship that year.

Thus began a new era in Washington, one of regular-season success and playoff failure. The Caps won a series for the first time in 1984, beating the Flyers, but in the second round they again fell to the Islanders, who ended Washington's season four times in five years. The fifth series was the cruellest blow of all. Up three games to one, the Capitals dropped the next two games, and then in Game 7 suffered one of the most agonizing losses in playoff history.

The seventh game was played on April 18, 1987, a contest that dragged from Saturday night into Easter Sunday. The Caps and Islanders went four overtimes, in what was at the time the fifth-longest game in NHL playoff history. The game remained tied at 2 until 1:56 a.m., when Pat LaFontaine spun and shot from the Washington blue line, beating a startled Bob Mason. Washington had outshot the Islanders 75–52 and had dominated most of the game, but the final score read 3–2 New York. Even today, David Poile has a hard time discussing it. "Heartbreaking isn't the word for it," he said.

That game, and that series, came to symbolize the Caps' fortunes. Through 1999, only 15 teams in NHL history had taken a 3–1 series lead and gone on to lose it, but Washington had done it three times, more than any other NHL team. The real problem for the Caps in that 1987 series, and many others, was goaltending. In their first seven playoff series, the Capitals started six different netminders, unable to find one they could trust. Bryan Murray's summary of that time is succinct: "Our

Olag Kolzig emerged as a star during the 1998 playoffs when he outbattled Buffalo's Dominik Hasek in the Eastern Conference Championships and lead the Capitals to the Stanley Cup finals for the first time in franchise history. One of the NHL's most international players, Kolzig was born to German parents living in South Africa. He grew up in different parts of Canada and now lives in the United States. Still a German citizen, Kolzig was the starting goalie for the German Olympic team at the Nagano games in 1998. Kolzig had a stellar 1999-2000 season and, despite a disappointing finish by the Capitals, he narrowly defeated Toronto's Curtis Joseph to win the Vezina Trophy, awarded to the league's best goaltender.

Joe Juneau wrestles with a New Jersey defender in an effort to reach the front of the Devils net.

goaltending just wasn't good enough."

The Caps were more than good enough in the regular season, Murray was named coach of the year in 1984 after guiding the team to 48 wins, and Langway won back-to-back Norris trophies as the league's top defenseman in 1983 and 1984. Poile's acquisition of Dale Hunter from Quebec in the summer of 1987 gave the Caps some much-needed grit, and he responded by scoring one of the biggest goals in franchise history. In Game 7 of the Caps' opening-round meeting with the Flyers, Hunter scored the overtime winner as Washington came back from 3–1 down in the series to knock off Philadelphia.

But the success was short-lived, and when the Caps bowed out in the first round of the playoffs to the Flyers in 1989, it was clear that patience was running thin. Bryan Murray was given a one-year contract, but lasted only until January when he was fired and replaced by his brother Terry, who had been coaching the team's minor league affiliate.

With the younger Murray behind the bench, the Caps again soared to new heights, reaching the third round of the playoffs for the first time, and the following year, Washington reached the second round with a new generation of stars like Petr Bondra and Kevin Hatcher. But in 1992, the Caps again coughed up a 3–1 series lead, losing to Pittsburgh in the first round, which began another era of playoff nightmares for the franchise.

In 1993, the Caps were ousted in the first round by their old nemesis, the New York Islanders. Terry Murray was fired midway through the next season, and new coach Jim Schoenfeld promptly got them to the second round of the playoffs. But in 1995, the Caps again lost a series after leading it 3–1, falling to Pittsburgh. And in 1996, the Penguins knocked them out in the first round again, in a series that featured the third-longest playoff game in NHL history at that time, which the Capitals of course lost, at home.

After all the years of frustration, the franchise underwent its biggest change in 15 years when David Poile and Jim Schoenfeld were let go in the summer of 1987. Hired to get the Caps to the playoffs, Poile did, 14 times in 15 years, but his team's lack of success in the post-season finally did him in.

He was replaced by George McPhee, a rambunctious former player for the Rangers and Devils who had gone on to be the assistant GM in Vancouver. McPhee quickly hired former Anaheim coach Ron Wilson to replace Schoenfeld, and they oversaw a major housecleaning that produced immediate results.

As they quite often did after major changes, the Caps responded right away. In the first year of the McPhee/Wilson leadership, the Capitals reached the Stanley Cup finals, before being swept by the defending champion Detroit Red Wings. It was a new high for the franchise, but even then, McPhee could see the challenge he was facing. After the loss in Game 4 of the finals, he and Wilson went to a Washington nightspot to celebrate their season. Inside, the televisions were tuned to the NBA playoffs, and despite the two-month playoff run, the presence of the Capitals brain trust went largely unnoticed.

But things were different in Washington. The Caps had moved to their new downtown arena that season, and the following year, Abe Pollin sold his controlling interest in the company to a group of investors headed by America Online executive Ted Leonsis, a group that would later include NBA superstar Michael Jordan.

In the 1999–2000 season, the Caps were the NHL's hottest team in the second half, but in the first round of the playoffs, they were beaten by Pittsburgh in five games, the fifth time in nine years that the Penguins had ended Washington's season.

Some things don't change.

Team Records

	Career	Season
Goals	Mike Gartner, 397	Dennis Maruk, 60 (1981–82)
Assists	Michal Pivonka, 412	Dennis Maruk, 76 (1981–82)
Points	Mike Gartner, 789	Dennis Maruk, 136 (1981–82)
Goals-Against Average	Jim Carey, 2.37	Jim Carey, 2.13 (1994–95)
Games Played	Kelly Miller, 878	

Columbus Blue Jackets

Founded 2000

Arenas

National Arena

Doug MacLean

Profile Doug MacLean played college hockey for the University of Prince Edward Island and began his coaching career as an assistant with the London Knights while earning a Master's degree in educational psychology from the University of Western Ontario. Until joining the Columbus Blue Jackets as their first president and general manager, MacLean moved back and forth between the coaching and managerial worlds in four different NHL organizations: the St. Louis Blues, Washington Capitals, Detroit Red Wings, and Florida Panthers.

Face to Face Much of Doug MacLean's early notoriety came during the 1995–96 season when, as the first-year coach of the Florida Panthers, he led the third-year NHL expansion team to the Stanley Cup finals. It was the Year of the Rat in south Florida, but even before MacLean's team became synonymous with plastic rats raining down from the stands whenever the Panthers scored, he had compiled a lengthy and impressive résumé in both coaching and administration.

In an industry that sometimes typecasts people as either a manager or a coach, MacLean happily found a chance to do both during his formative years. He worked as an assistant for two years on Jacques Martin's staff in St. Louis and then spent two more years in the Washington Capitals' organization, first as an assistant to Bryan Murray, then as coach and GM of their minor league affiliate in Baltimore. MacLean followed Murray to Detroit, where he worked his way up from assistant coach to associate coach and then to assistant GM. When Murray left to replace Bobby Clarke as general manager in Florida, he brought MacLean along with him again.

MacLean became the Panthers' director of player development in October 1994, and when Murray decided to fire Roger Neilson as coach following the 1994–95 season, he turned to his protégé as head coach. Of the seven expansion teams added to the NHL in the 1990s, the Panthers were by far the most successful right out of the gate. Bill Torrey, as president, had helped build the New York Islanders dynasty in the 1970s. Clarke, as GM, made astute choices in the expansion draft. In Florida, a non-traditional hockey market, MacLean learned about the importance of promoting the team. Nothing succeeds like on-ice success, especially if you have a cute gimmick—and the rat craze represented that for a short time.

"When you're the coach of a team like Florida, which was

different from a traditional team, you're conscious also of selling hockey in the community," said MacLean. "That's what I really valued from the Florida experience. I had so many great experiences in Florida, it's hard to pick one in three years.

The Panthers fired MacLean in 1997–98 season after a poor start to their fifth year, but he landed on his feet almost immediately. Columbus was granted a franchise as part of a four-team expansion that same year. MacLean was recruited quickly, giving him a 24-month run-up to the time when they actually stocked the team with players.

"I walked in here a year and a half ago, and the secretary was the only other person on staff and I had a blank notepad and a pencil on the desk," said MacLean. "I'm carrying around my organizational chart on a piece of scrap paper in my wallet.

"The owner says to me, 'You're going to be general manager, but you're also going to be president.' I had structured it so there would be a VP and GM and a VP business, two separate situations. He said, 'If you want to hire the business guy, that's fine, but you're the only one who reports to me.' That really changed the whole thing for me.

"All of a sudden, I'm involved in negotiating the lease on our building, the concessions, building a practice facility, the ticket operation, the corporate sales. So it was a quick education. It's really been a tremendous experience to start from scratch. People in the hockey business laugh. They say, 'What have you been doing for two years?' I've never been so busy in my life."

Columbus is known primarily as a college town, home to Ohio State and its well-supported football and basketball programs. MacLean is quick to point out that Columbus, as the largest city in Ohio and the 15th largest city in the United States, is bigger than Cleveland or Cincinnati.

"From that perspective, it's a great sports town. It has potential. It's a white-collar town. There's zero unemployment. It is one of the boom cities in the U.S. right now. It's a test market for a lot of products. It's blown me away, the type of city it is.

"I tell the story when I was in Plymouth, Michigan, watching a junior game and a guy says to me, 'What are you doing now?' I said, 'I'm in Columbus.' He said: 'Don't worry, you'll fight your way back to the NHL.' Then another guy in Toronto, after I told him I'm in Columbus, says, 'Aren't you going to miss the NHL?' So I came back and told our marketing department, 'We've got some work to do.'"

With regard to his philosophy in building a team, MacLean says he admires the way the Ottawa Senators have slowly evolved into a contender after an inauspicious beginning.

"In terms of the type of team you want to build, I get excited when I watch Ottawa play," said MacLean. "They've got speed, skills, character. If you look back at their development, they were dreadful at first. When I go back and analyze what they did in the expansion draft, they picked some pretty good characters, but the only problem they had versus a Florida or an Anaheim was they didn't get the great goaltending that Florida got. It's not a knock, but Craig Billington to John Vanbiesbrouck, at that time, they were not comparable. Now, if you look at Ottawa's drafts and how they're playing, they've really done a nice job. They did a great job of European scouting, which we're all envious of, with the [Magnus] Arvedssons and the [Andreas] Dackells."

Considering how picked over the player pool is after there's been expansion drafts in three consecutive years, MacLean lists his biggest worries as injuries and a lack of depth.

"Those two things can really bury an expansion team," he said. "Another thing that's hard on expansion teams is the second half of the season. Last year, we saw so many good playoff races from the first of February on, that teams were desperate to win games and that makes it tougher for expansion teams to win games.

"To have a philosophy of how to build a team, it's not going to be really evident from the expansion draft. You go into the expansion draft, looking for speed and for character as much as you can. But you can't go into the expansion draft, looking to put together the type of team you'll have in the future.

"Nashville has five guys left from the [1998] expansion draft and Atlanta probably has 12 left from 1999]. Florida—Bobby Clarke—did an unbelievable job of putting together a team. When we went to the Stanley Cup finals in year three, they had nine guys left from the expansion draft. That's unheard of.

"What you hope to do is find the odd young guy that can have some longevity. You try to find some character. You're really in a quandary. Maybe they have a young player with upside and a good veteran sitting there. What's going to be more critical? That young guy who is 24 or 23 that's available? Or the Kelly Buchberger type? Maybe you say, 'I'll have to sacrifice a bit of character to get a little talent.'

"I dropped down to my marketing VP the other day and said, 'Atlanta, three wins at home in their last 36 games, how are we going to handle that?' It's going to be tough, I have no doubt it's going to be tough."

Minnesota Wild

Founded 2000

Arenas
New Saint Paul Arena

Doug Risebrough

Profile

Doug Risebrough won four Stanley Cup championships playing for the Montreal Canadiens between 1976 and 1979 and then helped the Calgary Flames qualify for the 1986 finals. He moved into the Flames' front office upon his retirement and was an assistant coach on their 1989 championship team. Promoted to general manager in 1991, he held the position for four years before moving on to the Edmonton Oilers to serve as their vice president of hockey operations. Risebrough was named the Wild's first-ever executive vice president and general manager in September 1999.

Face to Face

Doug Risebrough knows something about winning championships. He also knows the challenges that his Minnesota Wild will face just to become competitive in the near future. The National Hockey League returned to the state of Minnesota for the 2000–01 season after a seven-year absence. For 26 years, between 1967 and 1993, the North Stars were a fixture on the NHL map, twice qualifying for the Stanley Cup finals but failing to win the series. Faced with dwindling attendance and what he considered an outdated building, owner Norman Green shifted the franchise to Dallas for the start of the 1993–94 season. Green subsequently sold the team to Tom Hicks, who then saw the Stars capture the final Stanley Cup of the millennium.

Meanwhile, back in Minnesota, Robert O. Naegele Jr. was in the process of winning an expansion franchise on behalf of Minnesota Hockey Ventures Group. Following a lengthy search, they settled on Risebrough as their first GM. In his 30-plus years of NHL involvement—in playing, coaching, and managing—Risebrough has learned something from Sam Pollock and something from Cliff Fletcher and something from Glen Sather, three of the brightest managerial minds in league history.

"Fortunately, for me, I've only been involved with three organizations," said Risebrough, "and I've been involved in winning Stanley Cups with two of them [Montreal and Calgary]. Basically, the people I was involved with in Edmonton were responsible for winning the Stanley Cups there, so I've been fortunate to see the parallels in how all three became winners.

"The parallels are that they're all development organizations. They create an identity for themselves that comes through the drafting of young players and the accumulation of young talent. Some of the rules and some of the player pools may have changed—the draft is bigger now than when Sam Pollock was drafting—but the basic philosophy remains the same. In my experience, you have to create an identity and that identity has to come from the young players that will ultimately become first-team players for you."

In Pollock's heyday with the Canadiens, the NHL was a tight, 12-going-on-18-team league, with more than 95 per cent of its player pool drawn from Canada. Now, it is a 30-team league, filled with players from all over the world. The sheer size of today's NHL significantly reduces the odds that you will eventually win a Stanley Cup championship in any given season.

"It's harder to be patient than it was in those days," said Risebrough. "Fortunately, we've seen enough examples of impatience, and the toll it takes in terms of being a distraction from this identity, and the economic toll its taken for teams. Teams have bucked up and changed the plan, put more pedal to the accelerator, and not necessarily have received the benefits from it."

One thing that's different in Risebrough's situation as opposed to, say, David Poile's in Nashville or Doug MacLean's in Columbus is that he will operate in a traditional hockey market. There is a history of hockey in the Minneapolis-St. Paul area—not just NHL hockey, but the World Hockey Association, the University of Minnesota, even the popular and well-attended Minnesota high school hockey programs.

Accordingly, there is no educational component to Risebrough's job, something that can be both a good and a bad thing. It's a good thing because people understand the game and thus can appreciate its nuances right from the beginning. It can be a bad thing, however, because people know mediocrity when they see it. That, in turn, can create extra pressure that perhaps other expansion GMs do not face.

"This is a traditional hockey market, with a tradition in hockey," said Risebrough. "They're two different things. Hockey has its own tradition here. I knew that coming here, but I have to say, I didn't know how strong that tradition was until I got here. It goes back to teams in the 1920s. It goes back to walking into the University of Minnesota and seeing pictures of teams from the 1930s and 1940s. Those are the same pictures that you used to see in the Montreal Forum and Maple Leaf Gardens.

"Some of the most well-known hockey people here were not

connected to the North Stars, they were connected to the University of Minnesota or the U.S. Olympic teams or the Eveleth Miners. In some ways, I find that really refreshing. I can go to a Gopher game and hook up with people who'll tell some great stories. They talk hockey. They're excited about the team coming back. They wish you luck. That's a real strength we have.

"So this has its unique challenges, but you've got to look at the strengths."

And those strengths are?

"People will understand the process better here," continued Risebrough. "They have seen a first-round pick like Mike Modano, who turned out to be a great player. They've also seen a first-round pick like Brian Lawton, who—not nurtured in the right way, pushed in the wrong direction, maybe not given the proper support—didn't succeed. So they understand the total process here.

"What does that mean? I think it means people will grade us on a broader scale, in terms of how we're doing. Now, they're not going to give us seven years for the draft to pan out, but they're also going to understand if the team is drafting well. They'll understand the mechanics.

"There is a hockey network here that can talk about hockey and knows what's going on in the hockey world. That's a positive. I was in line to fly to Dallas the other day and the two people in line ahead of me were talking about their kids in hockey. That doesn't happen in too many other airports in the U.S.— where you line up and people are talking about hockey.

"I look at my own personal situation. I'm more built to do that than to sit there and explain offsides. Not that one is bad and the other isn't. It's just for me, I'm better equipped to deal with the big issues of hockey, rather than get into the selling market."

There's also an advantage to having a fan base that boasts a body of knowledge.

"People say that [fans] will be less patient here. I don't know if they're going to be very patient in a market where there's no knowledge of the game and things aren't going real well."

The Original Six

Boston Bruins

Award Winners:

Jack Adams Award
Pat Burns, 1997–98
Don Cherry, 1975–76

Lady Byng Trophy
Rick Middleton, 1981–82
Jean Ratelle, 1975–76
Johnny Bucyk, 1973–74, 1970–71
Don McKenney, 1959–60
Bobby Bauer, 1946–47, 1940–41, 1939–40

Calder Trophy
Sergel Samsonov, 1997–98
Ray Bourque, 1979–80
Derek Sanderson, 1967–68
Bobby Orr, 1966–67
Larry Regan, 1956–57
Jack Gelineau, 1949–50
Frank Brimsek, 1938–39

Hart Trophy
Phil Esposito, 1973–74, 1968–69
Bobby Orr, 1971–72, 1970–71, 1969–70
Milt Schmidt, 1950–51
Bill Cowley, 1942–43, 1940–41
Eddie Shore, 1937–38, 1935–36, 1934–35, 1932–33

Jennings Trophy
Andy Moog and Rejean Lemelin, 1989–90

Bill Masterton Trophy
Cam Neely, 1993–94
Gord Kluzak, 1989–90
Charlie Simmer, 1985–86

Norris Trophy
Ray Bourque, 1993–94, 1990–91, 1989–90, 1987–88, 1986–87
Bobby Orr, 1974–75, 1973–74, 1972–73, 1971–72, 1970–71, 1969–70, 1968–69, 1967–68

Art Ross Trophy
Bobby Orr, 1974–75, 1969–70
Phil Esposito, 1973–74, 1972–73, 1971–72, 1970–71, 1968–69
Herbie Cain, 1943–44
Bill Cowley, 1940–41
Milt Schmidt, 1939–40
Cooney Welland, 1929–30

Frank J. Selke Trophy
Steve Kasper, 1981–82

Conn Smythe Trophy
Bobby Orr, 1971–72, 1969–70

Vezina Trophy
Pete Peeters, 1982–83
Frank Brimsek, 1941–42, 1938–39
Tiny Thompson, 1937–38, 1935–36, 1932–33, 1929–30

King Clancy Trophy
Dave Poulin, 1992–93
Ray Borque, 1991–92

Chicago Blackhawks

Award Winners:

Jack Adams Award
Orval Tessier, 1982–83

Lady Byng Trophy
Stan Mikita, 1967–68, 1966–67
Bobby Hull, 1964–65
Ken Wharram, 1963–64
Bill Mosienko, 1944–45
Clint Smith, 1943–44
Max Bentley, 1942–43
Doc Romnes, 1935–36

Calder Trophy
Ed Belfour, 1990–91
Steve Larmer, 1982–83
Tony Esposito, 1969–70
Bill Hay, 1959–60
Ed Litzenberger, 1954–55
Cully Dahlstrom, 1937–38
Mike Karakas, 1935–36

Hart Trophy
Stan Mikita, 1967–68, 1966–67
Bobby Hull, 1965–66, 1964–65
Al Rollins, 1953–54
Max Bentley, 1945–46

Jennings Trophy
Ed Belfour, 1994–95, 1992–93, 1990–91

Bill Masterton Trophy
Pit Martin, 1969–70

Norris Trophy
Chris Chelios, 1995–96, 1992–93
Doug Wilson, 1981–82
Pierre Pilote, 1964–65, 1963–64, 1962–63

Art Ross Trophy
Stan Mikita, 1967–68, 1966–67, 1964–65, 1963–64
Bobby Hull, 1965–66, 1961–62, 1959–60
Roy Conacher, 1948–49
Max Bentley, 1946–47, 1945–46
Doug Bentley, 1942–43

Frank J. Selke Trophy
Dirk Graham, 1990–91
Troy Murray, 1985–86

Vezina Trophy
Ed Belfour, 1992–93, 1990–91
Tony Esposito, 1973–74, 1969–70
Tony Esposito and Gary Smith, 1971–72
Glenn Hall and Denis Dejordy, 1966–67
Glenn Hall, 1962–63

Charlie Gardiner, 1933–34, 1931–32
Lorne Chabot, 1934–35

Detroit Red Wings

Award Winners:

Jack Adams Award
Scotty Bowman, 1995–96
Jacques Demers, 1987–88, 1986–87
Bobby Kromm, 1977–78

Lady Byng Trophy
Marcel Dionne, 1974–75
Alex Delvecchio, 1968–69, 1965–66, 1958–59
Earl Reibel, 1955–56
Red Kelly, 1953–54, 1952–53, 1950–51
Bill Quackenbush, 1948–49
Marty Barry, 1936–37

Calder Trophy
Roger Crozier, 1964–65
Glenn Hall, 1955–56
Terry Sawchuk, 1950–51
Jim McFadden, 1947–48
Carl Voss, 1932–33

Hart Trophy
Sergei Fedorov, 1993–94
Gordie Howe, 1962–63, 1959–60, 1957–58, 1956–57, 1952–53, 1951–52
Sid Abel, 1948–49
Ebbie Goodfellow, 1939–40

Jennings Trophy
Chris Osgood and Mike Vernon, 1995–96

Bill Masterton Trophy
Brad Park, 1983–84

Norris Trophy
Paul Coffey, 1994–95
Red Kelly, 1953–54

Art Ross Trophy
Gordie Howe, 1962–63, 1956–57, 1953–54, 1952–53, 1951–52, 1950–51
Ted Lindsay, 1949–50

Selke Trophy
Steve Yzerman, 1999–2000
Sergei Fedorov, 1995–96, 1993–94

Conn Smythe Trophy
Steve Yzerman, 1997–98
Mike Vernon, 1996–97
Roger Crozier, 1965–66

Vezina Trophy
Terry Sawchuk, 1954–55, 1952–53, 1951–52
Johnny Mowers, 1942–43
Normie Smith, 1936–37

Montreal Canadiens

Award Winners:

Jack Adams Award
Pat Burns, 1988–89
Scotty Bowman, 1976–77

Calder Trophy
Ken Dryden, 1971–72
Jacques Laperriere, 1963–64
Bobby Rousseau, 1961, 62
Ralph Backstrom, 1958–59
Bernie Geoffrion, 1951–52
Johnny Quilty, 1940–41

Hart Trophy
Guy Lafleur, 1977–78, 1976–77
Jean Beliveau, 1963–64, 1955–56
Jacques Plante, 1961–62
Bernie Geoffrion, 1960–61
Maurice Richard, 1946–47
Elmer Lach, 1944–45
Toe Blake, 1938–39
Babe Siebert, 1936–37
Aurel Joliat, 1933–34
Howie Morenz, 1931–32, 1930–31, 1927–28
Herb Gardiner, 1926–27

Jennings Trophy
Patrick Roy, 1991–92
Patrick Roy and Brian Hayward, 1988–89, 1987–88, 1986–87
Denis Herron and Rick Wamsley, 1981–82

Bill Masterton Trophy
Serge Savard, 1978–79
Henri Richard, 1973–74
Claude Provost, 1967–68

Norris Trophy
Chris Chelios, 1988–89
Larry Robinson, 1979–80, 1976–77
Jacques Laperriere, 1965–66
Doug Harvey, 1960–61, 1959–60, 1957–58, 1956–57, 1955–56, 1954–55
Tom Johnson, 1958–59

Art Ross Trophy
Guy Lafleur, 1977–78, 1976–77, 1975–76
Bernie Geoffrion, 1960–61
Dickie Moore, 1958–59, 1957–58
Jean Beliveau, 1955–56
Bernie Geoffrion, 1954–55
Elmer Lach, 1947–48, 1944–45
Toe Blake, 1938–39
Howie Morenz, 1930–31, 1927–28
Newsy Lalonde, 1920–21, 1918–19
Joe Malone, 1917–18

Frank J. Selke Trophy
Bob Gainey, 1980–81, 1979–80, 1978–79, 1977–78

Conn Smythe Trophy
Patrick Roy, 1992–93, 1985–86
Bob Gainey, 1978–79

Larry Robinson, 1977–78
Guy Lafleur, 1976–77
Yvan Cournoyer, 1972–73
Ken Dryden, 1970–71
Serge Savard, 1968–69
Jean Beliveau, 1964–65

Vezina Trophy
Patrick Roy, 1991–92, 1989–90, 1988–89
Richard Sevigny, Denis Herron, and Michel Laroque, 1980–81
Ken Dryden and Michel Laroque, 1978–79, 1977–78, 1976–77
Ken Dryden, 1975–76, 1972–73
Gump Worsley and Rogie Vachon, 1967–68
Gump Worsley and Charlie Hodge, 1965–66
Charlie Hodge, 1963–64
Jacques Plante, 1961–62, 1959–60, 1958–59, 1957–58, 1956–57, 1955–56
Bill Durnan, 1949–50, 1948–49, 1946–47, 1945–46, 1944–45, 1943–44
George Hainsworth, 1928–29, 1927–28, 1926–27

New York Rangers

Award Winners:

Lady Byng Trophy
Wayne Gretzky, 1998–99
Jean Ratelle, 1971–72
Camille Henry, 1957–58
Andy Hebenton, 1956–57
Edgar Laprade, 1949–50
Buddy O'Connor, 1947–48
Clint Smith, 1938–39
Frank Boucher, 1934–35, 1933–34, 1932–33, 1930–31, 1929–30, 1928–29, 1927–28

Calder Trophy
Brian Leetch, 1988–89
Steve Vickers, 1972–73
Camille Henry, 1953–54
Gump Worsley, 1952–53
Pentti Lund, 1948–49
Edgar Laprade, 1945–46
Kilby MacDonald, 1939–40

King Clancy Trophy
Adam Graves, 1993–94

Hart Trophy
Mark Messier, 1991–92
Andy Bathgate, 1958–59
Chuck Rayner, 1949–50
Buddy O'Connor, 1947–48

Norris Trophy
Brian Leetch, 1996–97, 1991–92
Harry Howell, 1966–67
Doug Harvey, 1961–62

Art Ross Trophy
Bryan Hextall, 1941–42
Bill Cook, 1932–33, 1926–27

Conn Smythe Trophy
Brian Leetch, 1993–94

Vezina Trophy
John Vanbiesbrouck, 1985–86
Ed Glacomin and Gilles Villemure, 1970–71
Davey Kerr, 1939–40

Toronto Maple Leafs

Award Winners:

Jack Adams Award
Pat Burns, 1992–93

Lady Byng Trophy
Dave Keon, 1962–63, 1961–62
Red Kelly, 1960–61
Sid Smith, 1954–55, 1951–52
Syl Apps, 1941–42
Gordie Drillon, 1937–38
Joe Primeau, 1931–32

Calder Trophy
Brit Selby, 1965–66
Kent Douglas, 1962–63
Dave Keon, 1960–61
Frank Mahovlich, 1957–58
Howie Meeker, 1946–47
Frank McCool, 1944–45
Gus Bodnar, 1943–44
Gaye Stewart, 1942–43
Syl Apps, 1936–37

Hart Trophy
Ied Kennedy, 1954–55
Babe Pratt, 1943–44

Art Ross Trophy
Gordie Drillon, 1937–38
Charlie Conacher, 1934–35, 1933–34
Harvey Jackson, 1931–32
Ace Bailey, 1928–29
Babe Dye, 1924–25, 1922–23

Frank J. Selke Trophy
Doug Gilmour, 1992–93

Vezina Trophy
Terry Sawchuk and Johnny Bower, 1964–65
Johnny Bower, 1960–61
Harry Lumley, 1953–54
Al Rollins, 1950–51
Turk Broda, 1947–48, 1940–41

Stanley Cup Winners 1917-2000

Year	W-L IN Finals	Winner	Coach	Finalist	Coach
2000	4-2	New Jersey	Larry Robinson	Dallas	Ken Hitchcock
1999	4-2	Dallas	Ken Hitchcock	Buffalo	Lindy Ruff
1998	4-0	Detroit	Scotty Bowman	Washington	Ron Wilson
1997	4-0	Detroit	Scotty Bowman	Philadelphia	Terry Murray
1996	4-0	Colorado	Marc Crawford	Florida	Doug MacLean
1995	4-0	New Jersey	Jacques Lemaire	Detroit	Scotty Bowman
1994	4-3	NY Rangers	Mike Keenan	Vancouver	Pat Quinn
1993	4-1	Montreal	Jacques Demers	Los Angeles	Barry Melrose
1992	4-0	Pittsburgh	Scotty Bowman	Chicago	Mike Keenan
1991	4-2	Pittsburgh	Bob Johnson	Minnesota	Bob Gainey
1990	4-1	Edmonton	John Muckler	Boston	Mike Milbury
1989	4-2	Calgary	Terry Crisp	Montreal	Pat Burns
1988	4-0	Edmonton	Glen Sather	Boston	Terry OíReilly
1987	4-3	Edmonton	Glen Sather	Philadelphia	Mike Keenan
1986	4-1	Montreal	Jean Perron	Calgary	Bob Johnson
1985	4-1	Edmonton	Glen Sather	Philadelphia	Mike Keenan
1984	4-1	Edmonton	Glen Sather	NY Islanders	Al Arbour
1983	4-0	NY Islanders	Al Arbour	Edmonton	Glen Sather
1982	4-0	NY Islanders	Al Arbour	Vancouver	Roger Neilson
1981	4-1	NY Islanders	Al Arbour	Minnesota	Glen Sonmor
1980	4-2	NY Islanders	Al Arbour	Philadelphia	Pat Quinn
1979	4-1	Montreal	Scotty Bowman	NY Rangers	Fred Shero
1978	4-2	Montreal	Scotty Bowman	Boston	Don Cherry
1977	4-0	Montreal	Scotty Bowman	Boston	Don Cherry
1976	4-0	Montreal	Scotty Bowman	Philadelphia	Fred Shero
1975	4-2	Philadelphia	Fred Shero	Buffalo	Floyd Smith
1974	4-2	Philadelphia	Fred Shero	Boston	Bep Guidolin
1973	4-2	Montreal	Scotty Bowman	Chicago	Billy Reay
1972	4-2	Boston	Tom Johnson	NY Rangers	Emile Francis
1971	4-3	Montreal	Al MacNeil	Chicago	Billy Reay
1970	4-0	Boston	Harry Sinden	St. Louis	Scotty Bowman
1969	4-0	Montreal	Claude Ruel	St. Louis	Scotty Bowman
1968	4-0	Montreal	Toe Blake	St. Louis	Scotty Bowman
1967	4-2	Toronto	Punch Imlach	Montreal	Toe Blake
1966	4-2	Montreal	Toe Blake	Detroit	Sid Abel
1965	4-3	Montreal	Toe Blake	Chicago	Billy Reay
1964	4-3	Toronto	Punch Imlach	Detroit	Sid Abel
1963	4-1	Toronto	Punch Imlach	Detroit	Sid Abel
1962	4-2	Toronto	Punch Imlach	Chicago	Rudy Pilous
1961	4-2	Chicago	Rudy Pilous	Detroit	Sid Abel
1960	4-3	Montreal	Toe Blake	Toronto	Punch Imlach
1959	4-1	Montreal	Toe Blake	Toronto	Punch Imlach
1958	4-2	Montreal	Toe Blake	Boston	Milt Schmidt
1957	4-1	Montreal	Toe Blake	Boston	Milt Schmidt
1956	4-1	Montreal	Toe Blake	Detroit	Jimmy Skinner

Year	W-L IN Finals	Winner	Coach	Finalist	Coach
1955	4-3	Detroit	Jimmy Skinner	Montreal	Dick Irvin
1954	4-3	Detroit	Tommy Ivan	Montreal	Dick Irvin
1953	4-1	Montreal	Dick Irvin	Boston	Lynn Patrick
1952	4-0	Detroit	Tommy Ivan	Montreal	Dick Irvin
1951	4-1	Toronto	Joe Primeau	Montreal	Dick Irvin
1950	4-3	Detroit	Tommy Ivan	NY Rangers	Lynn Patrick
1949	4-0	Toronto	Hap Day	Detroit	Tommy Ivan
1948	4-0	Toronto	Hap Day	Detroit	Tommy Ivan
1947	4-2	Toronto	Hap Day	Montreal	Dick Irvin
1946	4-1	Montreal	Dick Irvin	Boston	Dit Clapper
1945	4-3	Toronto	Hap Day	Detroit	Jack Adams
1944	4-0	Montreal	Dick Irvin	Chicago	Paul Thompson
1943	4-0	Detroit	Jack Adams	Boston	Art Ross
1942	4-3	Toronto	Hap Day	Detroit	Jack Adams
1941	4-0	Boston	Cooney Weiland	Detroit	Ebbie Goodfellow
1940	4-2	NY Rangers	Frank Boucher	Toronto	Dick Irvin
1939	4-1	Boston	Art Ross	Toronto	Dick Irvin
1938	3-1	Chicago	Bill Stewart	Toronto	Dick Irvin
1937	3-2	Detroit	Jack Adams	NY Rangers	Lester Patrick
1936	3-1	Detroit	Jack Adams	Toronto	Dick Irvin
1935	3-0	Mtl. Maroons	Tommy Gorman	Toronto	Dick Irvin
1934	3-1	Chicago	Tommy Gorman	Detroit	Herbie Lewis
1933	3-1	NY Rangers	Lester Patrick	Toronto	Dick Irvin
1932	3-0	Toronto	Dick Irvin	NY Rangers	Lester Patrick
1931	3-2	Montreal	Cecil Hart	Chicago	Dick Irvin
1930	2-0	Montreal	Cecil Hart	Boston	Art Ross
1929	2-0	Boston	Cy Denneny	NY Rangers	Lester Patrick
1928	3-2	NY Rangers	Lester Patrick	Mtl. Maroons	Eddie Gerard
1927	2-0-2	Ottawa	Dave Gill	Boston	Art Ross

The National Hockey League assumed control of Stanley Cup competition after 1926

Year	W-L IN Finals	Winner	Coach	Finalist
1926	3-1	Mtl. Maroons	Eddie Gerard	Victoria
1925	3-1	Victoria	Lester Patrick	Montreal
1924	2-0	Montreal	Leo Dandurand	Cgy. Tigers
	2-0			Van. Maroons
1923	2-0	Ottawa	Pete Green	Edm. Eskimos
	3-1			Van. Maroons
1922	3-2	Tor. St. Pats	Eddie Powers	Van. Millionaires
1921	3-2	Ottawa	Pete Green	Van. Millionaires
1920	3-2	Ottawa	Pete Green	Seattle
1919	2-2-1	No decision – series between Montreal and Seattle cancelled due to influenza epidemic		
1918	3-2	Tor. Arenas	Dick Carroll	Van. Millionaires